"Ms. Atwell writes with c   gh the triumphs and tragedies of   needs. At times funny and always (every woman should enjoy readin   where they fall on its relationship spectrum."

—KATHLEEN CREMONESI, author of *Love in the Elephant Tent: How Running Away with the Circus Brought me Home* and 2016 Gold Medal Independent Publisher Awards for Coming of Age/Family Legacy

"Told with astonishing honesty and candor, this is a story about the courage and bravery of daily life in a family bringing a 'forever child' into adulthood. It's a story about real love in real life."

—CORINNE TIPPETT, author of *Just a Couple of Chickens* and *When No One Else Would Fly*

"Linda Atwell is a master storyteller, and does a phenomenal job of sharing the love and grievances that come with raising her daughter. The moments and years of joy and frustration every family feels are especially touching as she navigates life with her sweet, defiant girl. *Loving Lindsey* is an exquisitely told account of a mother's protection, pride, frustration, and is, ultimately, a story about never giving up. I highly recommend *Loving Lindsey* to every parent."

—KRISTI RIEGER CAMPBELL, speaker, author, advocate, and Finding Ninee creator

"Atwell shines a light on the complicated issues involved in loving and living with someone with special needs. Whether you are a family member of someone with intellectual disabilities or just looking in from the outside, you will be moved."

—TERESA SULLIVAN, author of *Mikey and Me: Life with My Exceptional Sister*

"The reader gets to see this family in a world we don't usually get to share—raising a teenage daughter compounded by the difficulties of developmental disability. Told with clear-eyed empathy for her daughter and the other members of her family, Atwell's memoir is unflinchingly honest, allowing us to drop midstream into this remarkable family's life."

—DIANA Y. PAUL, author of *Things Unsaid*

"This harrowing journey—a page-turner that's every parent's nightmare—will stay with you long after you have put down the book. Highly recommended."

—BARBARA DONSKY, award-winning author of *Veronica's Grave: A Daughter's Memoir* (Canadian version: *Missing Mother*)

"Linda Atwell is a beacon of light in her book about the richness of raising a daughter with special needs. Lindsey's stories are woven into the midst of Atwell's own very full life, and she truly tells it like it is. She shares her experiences through the lenses of love, humor, and the human condition."

—DIANA DOLAN MATTICK, special education teacher and learning specialist

"As the parent of a child with disabilities, I often wonder and worry about what the future holds for my son. Atwell's tender, funny, real, and at times heart-wrenching memoir about her daughter—who as an adult woman still sleeps with a Cabbage Patch doll yet holds a job, gets a place of her own and falls in love, as doomed as it may be—portrays the self-sufficiency and experiences that I want my son to someday enjoy. *Loving Lindsey* shows that it is entirely possible to have intellectual disability and also have a good life."

—ELLEN SEIDMAN, author of the award-winning blog Love That Max

"Atwell's strong relationship with Lindsey, her special needs adult daughter, carries her (and us) through heartbreaking times that include fear, frustration, and disappointment that are always tempered by unwavering love and a determination to equip her daughter with skills for an independent life. A riveting narrative of mother-daughter struggles and rewards."

—Matilda Butler, memoir coach
and award-winning author of *Rosie's Daughters:
The "First Woman To" Generation Tells Its Story*

"*Loving Lindsey* is a mom's heartbreakingly honest account of letting go of her daughter, Lindsey. The heroes of this book are Atwell's fierce and imperfect love for her daughter and Lindsey's determination to be as independent as possible. *Loving Lindsey* offers parents of children with special needs a glimpse of the challenges their children will face in adulthood and food for thought about how to prepare and navigate them."

—Jolene Philo, author of *A Different Dream for
My Child* and *Does My Child Have PTSD?*

"Atwell's evocative descriptions provide added depth to the characters, particularly Lindsey, whose voice emanates from the pages. A brutally honest, affecting memoir of family resilience."

—Kirkus Reviews

LOVING
LINDSEY

LOVING
LINDSEY

Raising a Daughter
with Special Needs

A Memoir

LINDA ATWELL

She Writes Press, a BookSparks imprint
A Division of SparkPointStudio, LLC.

Published 2017

Printed in the United States of America

Print ISBN: 978-1-63152-280-2
E-ISBN: 978-1-63152-281-9
Library of Congress Control Number: 2017936433

For information, address:
She Writes Press
1563 Solano Ave #546
Berkeley, CA 94707

Cover design © Julie Metz, Ltd./metzdesign.com
Cover photo © James Annen
Interior design and typesetting by Katherine Lloyd/theDESKonline.com

She Writes Press is a division of SparkPoint Studio, LLC.

Names and identifying characteristics have been changed to protect the privacy of certain individuals.

Segments of Chapter 1, titled, Swing, Drive, Sex, first appeared in *Perceptions Literary Magazine of the Arts* in 2012.

A version of Chapter 26, titled "A Window in my Heart", first appeared in *Perceptions Literary Magazine of the Arts* in 2016.

For John,
I am a better person because of you.
Thanks for believing in me, especially during the
moments I found it difficult to believe in myself.

❧

And for all the strong women in my world,
but particularly Betty, Nora, and Lindsey.

When my kids were growing up, I didn't know there was a manuscript in our future. I didn't walk around with a recorder, taping every conversation or logging every outfit worn. I've re-created stories to the best of my memory. Although all incidents in this manuscript are real and did occur, some may have taken place in a different order. For various reasons, some names have been changed.

1

~⁂~

t was 113 degrees on the last day of June 1999. My husband and I strolled the five blocks toward the Hard Rock Café, holding hands sticky from the heat. We passed a Vegas nightclub. "Billie Jean" blasted into the street as a Michael Jackson impersonator moonwalked on the concrete, enticing us to come in, have a drink, relax. I paused for a moment to watch.

"Let's go. I'm hungry," John said, pulling me through an intersection with a green light. Late the night before, under the sheets at the Rio, he and I had both admitted that the music, the flashing lights, even the shrieks on Las Vegas Boulevard—everything in this city—although exciting, temporary diversions from our small-town life, paled in comparison with raising our two kids. Especially our nineteen-year-old daughter, Lindsey.

Technically, she was John's stepdaughter. When I was eighteen, my sister introduced me to her eighth-grade teacher. As soon as I met John, I knew I wanted to marry him. But, as many love stories go, we were too young to get too serious. At least, that's what John said when he broke off our relationship. Yet my heart refused to forget that middle-school teacher.

The next guy I dated wasn't right for me. I knew this long before I walked down the aisle, but I married Marty anyway. Two years later, Lindsey was born, and we divorced soon after her first birthday.

John and I started going out again. My belief that he was the man I should've been with all along was quickly reconfirmed. We wed and had a son we named Michael. I was pleased to see my new husband treat the kids as if they were both biologically his—despite Lindsey's being a challenging toddler, child, and eventually teen, because of her essential tremors and developmental delays. For years we tried to figure out why. Heck, we were still trying to figure out our daughter, but one of the first clues that something more might be amiss was her inability to relate to kids her own age. And they didn't relate to her, either. Although it was hard to admit this, it was more difficult to deny when the incident occurred right in front of me.

On the morning Lindsey started fourth grade, a neighbor girl volunteered to walk to school with my daughter. The moment I opened the door, I could see Carla had agreed to do this only because her mother had insisted on it. Carla's eyes surveyed my girl from head to toe, widening when she spied my ten-year-old shoving a tremoring arm through the strap of her pink backpack with a Hello Kitty decal. Carla wore a brown leather backpack, similar to one I'd pointed out at Mervyn's that Lindsey had rejected without hesitation. The neighbor girl's lips scarcely moved when she asked me if her classmate was ready. A few seconds later, the girls walked out onto our driveway and down Eureka Avenue. Carla walked faster and faster, pulling several strides ahead of my girl. *She doesn't want to be seen with her!* Tears stung my eyes. *Why is it so hard for Lindsey to make friends?* I closed the door so I wouldn't have to see.

For Lindsey, relationships outside our extended family were few. Yet she craved attention. Lots of attention. And although we tried to give her as much as she needed, it was never enough. At times her demands were draining. Over the years, we sought counseling to learn better ways of dealing with her special needs.

"You can't be good parents if you aren't good partners," the counselor told us. "You need to plan 'couple time' so you can reconnect. You'll come home stronger, be better prepared to deal with Lindsey's next challenge."

His advice seemed wise. And well timed. Three weeks earlier, Lindsey had graduated from Silverton High, an achievement we hadn't been sure would ever happen. When she was a grade-schooler, my husband and I both dreamed she would someday receive her high school diploma with the rest of her classmates. As she aged, it was obvious her delays were greater than we originally wanted to believe. When graduation day finally arrived, instead of a diploma, Lindsey received a certificate of attendance. She'd worked so hard for that victory, and her face radiated nothing but pride. The moment my daughter's feet touched the stage, tears flooded my eyes. Our family cheered and screamed and shouted until Lindsey had completely crossed the platform and exited the end staircase.

Ever since John and I had arrived in Vegas, we'd felt like newlyweds. We stayed up late, slept in, and ate whenever we wanted. In the back of our minds, we understood that as soon as we returned home, our world would change. For ten years I'd owned Country Neighbors, a home-decor business that I'd recently sold. I'd taken time off but was now ready to go back to work. A few days after we'd get back into town, I'd start a new job as a claims adjustor for Farmers Insurance. But that June night, as we strolled down Las Vegas Boulevard toward the restaurant, John and I were feeling the mental high of Lindsey's graduation day and my final hours of unemployed bliss.

As we stepped through the doors and into the Hard Rock's air-conditioned lobby, goose bumps appeared on my bare arms. I squeezed John's hand and said, "I want to call home. Check in. There shouldn't be any drama to report."

"You sure?" he asked.

I nodded, fumbling through my purse for my cell phone. *What could possibly go wrong in only a few days?* The smirk on John's face caused me to hesitate. Our sixteen-year-old son was staying at a friend's house, so we didn't have to worry about him, but Lindsey was always a different case. During her senior year, we had spent every extra minute, along with every extra dollar we could spare, converting a barn-shaped building behind our house into the cutest little two-story cottage any kid could ever want.

Twenty-two steps from our back deck was a French door that opened into a sitting area, dining room, and kitchen. I visualized the blue-and-yellow Tweety Bird cookie jar sitting on Lindsey's kitchen counter and the denim futon and white wicker chair in her living area. Up the stairs was a loft with a dainty floral design I'd stenciled in pastels on the walls of her bedroom and en suite bathroom. Lindsey had handpicked all the furnishings. We wanted our daughter to try living independently from us and figured there was no better place to attempt this feat than steps away from our back door.

The day after graduation, Lindsey had moved into the cottage. Things had gone remarkably well so far. Still, we had asked my mom to sleep in our guest room and keep tabs on our daughter while we were out of town. Just in case.

A blond Hard Rock hostess approached us.

"You go and get a seat," I said, shooing my husband in her direction. "I'll catch up in a minute."

John followed the hostess to a nearby booth, leaving me in the lobby to dial Lindsey's number. The phone rang. I turned away from the other girls at the hostess stand.

"Hello." *Gasp.* "Mom? Isthatyou?" Lindsey yelled into the phone. She gasped again. Sometimes when my daughter talked too fast she couldn't breathe in air quickly enough, and for a moment she sounded as if she were choking. "I-don't-wanna-ruin-your-vacation." *Gasp.* "But-you're-gonna-be-mad-at-me."

Oh, dear. Now what? My shoulders tensed. I reminded myself that everything is a crisis to Lindsey. She often used similar lines when she called to tell me she'd forgotten her school lunch, that she couldn't find an overdue library book, or that she hadn't turned in her homework as promised. None of these issues irritated me nearly as much as Lindsey's saying, "You're gonna be mad at me."

I sighed, picturing my daughter standing in the cottage, wearing bright pink shorts and a pink Hello Kitty T-shirt, her thick, dark hair pushed away from her face by a hot-pink headband. *She's probably making something out of nothing. Like always.*

"Now, why would I be mad, Linds?" I said, keeping my tone even and cool. I didn't want the conversation escalating, and if I stayed calm, Lindsey often followed my lead.

Her voice changed to light and airy. "I went to the park today."

"You're allowed to go there," I said, recalling the many times I'd watched Lindsey amble along the sidewalks of our small Oregon town. She walked everywhere in Silverton, and Coolidge-McClaine Park was safe. I took a deep breath, hoping Lindsey would hurry her explanation. I wanted to get back to my husband and order dinner.

"Gabe was there," she said, sounding smug. "And we were swinging on the swings."

"You've seen Gabe at the park before." I glanced at the clock. Gabe and Lindsey had met years before, when they had both played on the Challengers softball team for developmentally disabled youth. We'd talked with his parents at the games. Later, Gabe and Lindsey had attended special education classes together at Silverton High. Gabe had Dubowitz syndrome, a rare genetic disorder that caused a normal-size body with a small, narrow head. His reasoning skills were better than Lindsey's, and he'd passed the Oregon driver's license test. After Lindsey saw Gabe's sienna Oldsmobile, she told us, "I've always wanted a man with wheels." But, as far as we knew, they were casual friends. We were aware that Gabe struggled with emotional issues, ones that resulted in controlling his temper, but we'd never witnessed any outbursts. "He's gettin' counseling," Lindsey had told us once. "To work on it. Just like I have to."

Lindsey gasped again, bringing me back to the moment.

"I asked Gabe if he wanted to keep swinging," she said. "But he said no." I glanced in John's direction, half listening to my daughter. "So I asked him if he wanted to go for a ride in his car. But he said no. So I asked him if he wanted to have sex. And he said yes."

Immediately, the temperature inside the Hard Rock lobby hit 120 degrees. I wiped the sweat from my forehead, squeezing my eyes tight, shaking my head, wishing her words would go away.

"What?" I gripped the phone with all my might as I stepped away from the group waiting for seats. *Did I hear correctly? She went from swinging to sex in less than sixty seconds and didn't even get dinner first?*

"You had *sex?*" I steadied my voice, wondering why I hadn't seen this coming. She'd been boy crazy ever since I could remember. There was an instance when two playground bullies spit on Lindsey and called her "retarded" and "Little Miss Shaky Hands." Scott von Weller stepped in to protect his classmate. After that day, every time my girl heard his name, she smiled widely, saying, "Scott von Weller told those girls to leave me alone" and, "Scott von Weller's really nice." When we passed by him at parent-teacher conferences, it was the first time I'd heard Lindsey use a seductive tone. "Hi, Scott von Weller," she cooed, her baby blues ogling. Scott waved, then hurried toward the exit. He looked so uncomfortable with Lindsey's overt attention, I blushed. I talked to her about toning it down a bit, but she told me, "You don't know what you're talkin' 'bout, Mom!"

As Lindsey aged, she morphed from a geeky preteen into a beautiful young lady. She'd never had a boyfriend, but that didn't stop her insatiable curiosity about boy-girl relationships. Whenever she asked us a question, John or I answered honestly. In my head, Lindsey seemed innocent, but that didn't stop me from worrying that someone might try to take advantage of her. Finally, I bought Peter Mayle's illustrated book, *Where Did I Come From?*. It explained the facts of life better than I could, and we read it together. Lindsey seemed satisfied with the explanation, but for several months after, I'd occasionally come upon her looking at the pictures and giggling. It had been a couple years since I'd seen it in her room. We'd probably given the book to Goodwill.

"Yes, I did," Lindsey said. "I had sex."

"You are right. I *am* mad." *What if Gabe didn't use protection? What if she got pregnant? What if she had a baby?* I'd come across an article about children conceived by parents with mental challenges. The author said their child could be born mentally healthy, yet the child was prone to environmental disabilities due to the parents' circumstances, even more so if they tried to raise the baby without help. *Could a child of Lindsey's be born typical?*

"Did you really have sex?" I closed my eyes, wishing for a different answer, hoping this was just a ploy to get attention while we were in Vegas.

"Well, Gabe took me to his house," she said. "But either he was too big or I was too small, but it didn't work so well."

Too big . . . too small . . . didn't work so well. Maybe it didn't work at all.

"We've talked about sex, and you agreed to wait till you were married," I said, exasperated. My sister had given Lindsey a promise ring on her sixteenth birthday. "You promised Aunt Kandi and God that you'd wait. Remember?" Although our immediate family didn't practice a religion, Lindsey had decided to join a local church and had been baptized.

"You know, Mom," Lindsey said, "I don't 'member so well. Stuff you say just goes out one ear and through the other."

"Well, remember this, young lady. You. Are. In. Big. Trouble! We'll talk about this when we get home. You are never going to the park ever again. You hear me? You're grounded." I didn't give my daughter time to respond before I pressed END so hard I thought the phone might break.

I trudged through the café toward my tanned, gray-haired husband. *He's so handsome*, I thought, staring at his long, strong profile. I adored that face. And those ocean-blue eyes. The red T-shirt he'd pulled on that morning made his irises appear bluer than usual. The seat back supported John's slender frame as he studied Hard Rock's food choices. His expression was so content, I almost turned and ran out the lobby doors.

"What's wrong?" John lifted his brow and peered over the top of his menu. I turned my head side to side, avoiding my husband's gaze. Nervousness gripped my throat; my jaw tightened with tension.

"Nothing that we can deal with here," I finally said. "Besides, I don't want to spoil your weekend." The sting of tears came to my eyes.

"You have to tell me." He closed the menu and set it on the table.

John was right. I choked on a breath. "Lindsey had sex with Gabe," I said, blinking hard to keep the tears at bay.

"Shit." John's face curdled, his leg jiggled under the table. "What if she's pregnant? What are we going to do?"

"I'll call my mom later and tell her Lindsey is grounded for the rest of her life."

But we both knew Lindsey would not be grounded for the rest of her life. And neither of us had expected our daughter to stay celibate forever. But we'd hoped she would date someone for several months—or years—before she considered a sexual relationship. We'd certainly hoped she would talk with us before her first time so we could've prepared her more. Heck, so we could've prepared ourselves more.

Dinner plates and glasses and utensils clattered as a busboy cleared and wiped a table nearby. The hostess sat families all around us. They chatted; they laughed. My shoulders sagged. *That would be us*, I thought, *if I hadn't called home*.

The server took our orders. John and I sat silent for several minutes. I repeatedly twisted and untwisted a long strand of hair around a finger. John pulled at one of his gray eyebrows. His leg jiggled wildly. I placed my hand on his knee, and it stopped.

The waiter delivered my grilled chicken salad with the dressing on the side, and John's bacon burger with fries. We picked at our meals quietly. John squirted ketchup on his plate.

"Do you think it's possible she got pregnant?" my husband finally said. "Could she have contracted a sexually transmitted disease? Nine months from now, will we be raising a grandkid?"

I poked a piece of lettuce with my fork. *Wonderful dinner conversation*, I thought, instantly jealous of the other patrons in the restaurant. I wanted grandkids. Just not yet.

"Do you remember when I talked to Lindsey about starting her period?" I said, changing the subject. I set my fork on my plate and took a drink of Diet Pepsi. John nodded, a thin smile forming on his face.

Lindsey was eleven, closing in on twelve, when she paraded through our living room. Tiny breasts budded beneath her T-shirt. I whispered to John, "Do you think she's starting to develop?" Since he was a teacher in a middle school, I figured he was more of an expert than I was. I didn't want to broach the topic too soon, but I wasn't into avoidance, either.

John nodded. "You should talk to her," he said, encouraging me. "She needs to learn the facts from you, before she hears them from someone else."

Before I had "the talk," I planned to find out exactly what Lindsey already knew. I wandered into her room. She was dressing her Cabbage Patch Kid in a new outfit. The rest of her dolls and stuffed animals were lined up in a neat row on her bed. Her actions didn't indicate menstruation was around the corner. She had the appearance of a child. Yet what if she started her period and didn't understand anything? I'd feel terrible.

I inhaled deeply and let the air out slowly. In the lightest, happiest tone I could muster, I asked, "Do you know anything about having your period?"

"Yes." Lindsey grinned like a four-year-old who had just earned a gold star. "Yes, I do. I know all about periods."

This was going to be easier than I'd thought. I clapped my hands together. "That's great! Tell me."

Lindsey's eyes darted right, then left, as she searched for the exact words. "At the end of every complete sentence, you put a period."

Yikes! We definitely were not on the same page. We weren't even in the same book. Giggles rose inside me, as if sparkling fizz was fighting to escape an uncorked bottle of bubbly. I forced myself to keep them contained.

"Lindsey. You are right, there is a period at the end of every complete sentence," I said, racing from her bedroom, choking on the chuckles.

Sitting in our booth in Vegas, we laughed at her innocent answer, momentarily forgetting about the recent "I had sex" declaration.

"And we still find that funny, even after all these years," I said, feeling naive. I'd gone back a few days later and explained menstruation. I was relieved when, at thirteen, Lindsey was uncharacteristically calm on the day she started her period. She invited me into the bathroom to check her panties. We got out a Kotex pad, I showed her how to attach it, and that was that. She handled it by herself from that point forward.

John pulled a pickle slice off his burger and tossed it onto his plate. "I never expected Lindsey to say 'complete sentence,'" he said, his voice deep and husky. "She must have repeated her lesson exactly as she learned it in school." I nodded because I had thought the same thing. John's face turned deadpan. "We'll get through this, Linda," he said, reaching over and squeezing my hand.

After a bit more discussion, John and I realized our anger, our frustration, wasn't only because Lindsey had had intercourse. We also worried she might consider engaging in casual sex with multiple partners.

"Could we get Lindsey on the pill?" I said.

"Would she remember to take it every single day?" John said, scratching his chin.

She already took medication for tremors and seizures. Adding another prescription to her regimen couldn't possibly have a positive effect on our daughter. And even though it was unlikely, Lindsey could have contracted a venereal disease. But the most important question for us was, did she want a baby?

John and I wanted to go home right then, but our flight didn't leave until the next day. We contemplated changing our tickets but knew we'd get home only a few hours earlier.

"I'll call my mom." I pulled out my cell phone and headed back to the lobby. John walked to the bathroom.

"What'd she say?" he asked when I hung up.

"She feels responsible," I said. "But I reassured her this is no one's fault. We let Lindsey go to the park all the time. I told Mom this could've happened on our watch, too."

When we left the Hard Rock Café, the sky had turned dark. The strip was lit up like a Christmas tree with too much tinsel. Young girls sauntered by, dressed in skimpy leather outfits and fishnet stockings. Nirvana's "Dive" boomed from a nightclub. The bass vibrated my legs, my body. I reached up and covered my ears to prevent some of the clamor from entering my head. Someone had puked on the sidewalk. A wave of stuffy, putrid heat hit us in the face. John and I sulked back to the Rio Hotel and waited for the minutes to crawl by.

2

The next morning, we packed up hours before we were scheduled to leave, took a taxi to McCarran Airport, and waited at the gate for our Portland flight. John and I rehashed how to handle the situation once we arrived home. I wanted to call Gabe's parents. John didn't think I should.

"What would you say?" he asked.

"I don't know," I said, recognizing it would be an awkward, uncomfortable conversation, but I thought it was a discussion that needed to take place. "He has special needs, too. His parents should know they're having sex."

On the hour drive from Portland to Silverton, I told John I'd decided to call. My husband frowned. When we pulled into our carport, John grabbed the bags and put them in our bedroom, then dashed outside to mow the lawn. He didn't want any part in confronting Gabe's parents.

As soon as the back door closed, I located the Posts' number in the telephone book. When Mrs. Post picked up, I identified myself as Lindsey's mother.

"I remember you. From the Challengers team," she said. "Call me Susanna."

"Well, Susanna," I said, pausing, "I don't know any other way to say this, but Lindsey and Gabe had sex."

"Oh, dear," she said. "As far as we know, he's only had sex one

13

other time. When he told us, we talked about the importance of using condoms. I hope he used one this time."

"Us too," I said. "I think our families should meet. I think we need to discuss this together, in front of the kids. We don't want any unplanned pregnancies."

"Of course not," she said, and agreed to come over the following evening.

~❧

John and I greeted Gabe and his parents at the door. Lindsey sat on the tartan love seat in our living room and fidgeted. It had been years since the kids had played softball together, and we politely exchanged bits of superficial chitchat until Gabe lost patience with everyone. He sauntered past Lindsey, wearing loose gray sweats and a matching pullover, and called dibs on a green wingback chair. His parents followed close behind and sat on the second love seat, across the room. They held hands, looking as if this were the worst possible way to spend a summer evening.

I stared at Mrs. Post's gray hair. I didn't remember her locks being so long. Now they hung to the middle of her back and, I swear, looked like silk. My hand darted up and smoothed my frizzy brown mane, wishing it responded the same way as Susanna's.

The July evening was hot for Oregon, yet both of Gabe's parents wore jeans, and Gabe's dad had on a long-sleeved Western shirt with pearl snaps on the two front pockets. Mrs. Post's azure cotton top had cap sleeves. The blue matched her eyes. The same clear blue as Gabe's. Like the sky on a sunny day.

I offered sodas, iced tea, water. When no one accepted, I peered around the living room. Everyone sat stiffly in his or her place. Mrs. Post tossed her head again. I pulled an oak chair from the kitchen to sit near Lindsey. John sat on the love seat next to her, crossing his legs and arms, looking surprisingly more relaxed than the rest of us.

"Do we need to plan a wedding?" I asked, forcing my lips into a smile.

Lindsey's blueberry eyes widened. Gabe's face turned pasty white. He rolled his eyes. "No way! I don't want to marry her." He shook his head and crossed his arms.

"I don't wanna marry him, either," Lindsey said, brushing a piece of lint off her lime-green shorts. Her long, bronze legs were fit but not hairless. She tried shaving, but sporadic patches of dark hairs sprouted on her calves and knees and thighs.

"Then why are you doing married stuff if you don't want to get married?" *Isn't that what a mother should say in a situation like this?* Although John and I had encouraged our children to abstain from premarital sex, at least until they were older, neither he nor I had done so at Lindsey's age. I glanced around our full living room. A group discussion of my daughter's sex life was not something I'd ever anticipated.

Mrs. Post broke the silence. "Did you use a condom, son?" All eyes shifted to Gabe. His hands lay clasped together in his lap. He stared at them.

Please say yes.

Gabe's features seemed small against the strong side supports of the green wingback. "We talked about this after the last time," Mrs. Post said, tracing the gold lines in the sofa fabric. "Do you remember how to use one?" Gabe lowered his head and stared at his hands.

The teacher in John came out. He quickly stood, thrust a balled fist in the air, and enthusiastically demonstrated—as if he were teaching a history lesson in his junior high classroom—the proper position for putting on protection. He used no banana, cucumber, or any other visual aid, just an index finger that fell limp.

"In this position, Gabe, you can't put on a condom," John said. He straightened his finger. "When it's up like this, you put one on." He moved his extended digit up, down, up, down. His demonstration was meant to be serious, but his finger looked ridiculous stiffening and relaxing. I chewed on the inside of my lip to keep from laughing, then glanced at the Posts. They sat still, mouths gaping, eyes fixated on my husband's index finger. Gabe's blue irises followed the up-and-down movements, but he remained poker-faced.

"Dad, this is em-bar-ass-ing." Lindsey covered her eyes with her hands.

"Well, do you want a baby?" John said.

"No," she said.

"Gabe, do you want one?"

"No way!" Gabe raised his arms, crossed them over the front of his gray sweatshirt in a protective ninja stance.

"Then you need to be responsible," John lectured.

Gabe dropped his hands and frowned. Lindsey hid her face.

"There's no reason to bring an unwanted child into the world," Mrs. Post said.

"It's best to wait until you're married," Mr. Post added.

"But if you can't wait, you need to use birth control." I looked at Lindsey, then at Gabe. Part of me wanted to lock Lindsey in her cottage, or buy a chastity belt—the Renaissance device my dad had teasingly threatened to use on my sisters and me when we were teenagers. But neither of those notions was realistic. Besides, how could we stop these two kids? They could sneak around like typical teenagers. The Posts couldn't police Gabe every second of the day, nor could we constantly guard Lindsey.

"Do you two plan to have more sex?" John said.

Lindsey looked at Gabe. Gabe stared at Lindsey.

"Do we have to decide right now?" Gabe said, his head bent toward his lap.

"No," all the parents answered at the same time, causing uncomfortable laughter.

"Okay," Gabe said, standing. "I get it."

But did he? Did Lindsey?

Everyone else stood, too, and Gabe bolted toward the front door.

"Bye, Gabe." Lindsey's voice sounded sultry. She opened and closed her hand, waving good-bye. He ran out the door, mumbling something like "adios." His parents followed, thanking us, saying we'd speak again soon.

John disappeared into our family room and turned on the TV, giving me a chance to talk to Lindsey privately.

"Do you ever want a baby?" I asked my daughter. Ever since Vegas, I'd been thinking about this question. My heart and head knew she couldn't handle additional responsibility. It would add too much stress to her life.

My girl sat down and tilted her head.

"I dream of having a baby," she said. "But I don't think I'd wake up at night." Her eyes darted upward, searching for more words. "I could love a baby." *Gasp.* "But I don't think I could change diapers. I shake too much. I might poke the baby. What if I dropped it? That would hurt."

"Well, there are ways to permanently prevent pregnancy. One option is a tubal ligation. Do you know what that is?" Mixed emotions surged through me. I remembered having my tubes tied after Michael was born. Two kids, a boy and a girl. Exactly what I wanted. So having the procedure was an easy decision. At least I thought so initially. The doctor performed the operation the morning after our son was born. When the anesthesia wore off, I worried it had been too soon, that maybe we weren't finished having children. And the first time we made love, I wondered how John would feel, if it would be different because of the inability to conceive, and I cried afterward. John held me in his arms, assuring me nothing had changed, that he was thrilled with two kids.

As I waited for Lindsey's answer to my question, I studied my nineteen-year-old's face. She looked so young. My chest tightened, and it was hard to breathe.

"No. I don't know anything 'bout that." Lindsey squirmed, then picked at a torn cuticle.

"Do you remember talking about periods?"

Lindsey lost interest in the cuticle, nodded, leaned forward, and waited.

"How about eggs and fallopian tubes?"

"I 'member that from health class," Lindsey said. "But I can't say 'flop-on tubes.'"

"Fa-lope-e-an." I isolated each sound in the word.

"Flop-on."

"No, Lindsey, but how you say the word isn't important," I said, trying to be patient. She probably already felt bombarded with information, but there was more to cover. I reviewed eggs, sperm, and fertilization, then explained how a tubal ligation worked. "Since the egg can't be fertilized, you can't get pregnant."

"I could have sex and not get pregnant?" Lindsey's voice changed to excited.

"Well, there's no guarantee, but the chances are greatly reduced," I said.

Lindsey's eyes darted to the side. I assumed she was thinking about all the sex she could have. "You'd need to talk to the doctor, though," I said. Her head and arms tremored. "And . . ." I paused, knowing my next offer might seal this proposal. "If you decide to have the operation, we'll bring you lots of presents and flowers."

"I'd get presents and flowers?" Lindsey smiled widely. A few years earlier, she had started asking for presents and flowers for every birthday or special occasion, so I knew these were the items she desired most. Lindsey's tone and face turned serious. "I don't know if I want my flop-on tubes tied."

"You don't need to decide right now. This is an important decision. You should think about it. Dad and I love you no matter what." I slipped an arm around one of Lindsey's slim shoulders and patted her back. "There are good reasons to choose a tubal," I said. "But there are consequences, too. It's permanent. You can't change your mind. Once you have one, you shouldn't plan to have children."

Lindsey sat expressionless. "I'm going to the cottage," she said, standing. She shuffled her feet as she left the room. I watched my forever-child, the one old enough to have the desires of a young woman, walk the short path between our house and hers.

I sat in the living room for a long time, wondering, *What will she decide?*

3

n July, one week after our visit with Gabe and his parents, Lindsey appeared in our kitchen while I was rinsing a handful of spoons and forks and loading them into the diswhasher.

"If I have that flop-on operation, will you still bring me presents and flowers?"

I sucked in air, holding my breath for a moment, before releasing it more loudly than I'd planned. Lindsey probably thought her question had annoyed me, but that wasn't the case. I'd been thinking about the Clearblue pregnancy test she'd taken two days before. Based upon the description she'd given of her sexual encounter with Gabe, "Either he was too big or I was too small, but it didn't work so well," John and I didn't think she could possibly be pregnant. And we were right. When it turned negative, Lindsey clapped her hands. But what if the stick had turned blue?

I turned off the water and regarded my daughter. Khaki shorts and a pink cotton, button-down flowered shirt. The shirt needed ironing, but, other than that, Lindsey had done a good job coordinating her outfit. Her anklets were scrunched, not folded over once, like she'd been taught. Half up, half down, the right sock partially disappeared into her Nike tennis shoe. Her body wasn't trembling much, and her eyes were more focused than usual.

"Yes, we will bring you presents and flowers," I said, feeling exhausted and sad and pleased all at the same time. "Have you decided?" I asked, a bit afraid to hear the answer. Either choice was heartbreaking. I tried to keep my face blank.

"Yes," she said. "When can I do it?" Her voice sounded eager, like she'd have the operation that minute if I said, "Let's go." I wondered if her bags were already packed, but there was no suitcase in sight.

I wanted Lindsey to have the operation for the right reasons. Not because of presents and flowers or because she thought it would make her dad or me happy. When I asked her why, she repeated all her previous reasons.

"Babies are a lot of work," she said with conviction.

My worry relaxed some.

"Besides, I'm already a mom," Lindsey said. "I don't need a baby of my own."

What?

"I 'dopted Kayla, from Children International," she clarified, after seeing my confused expression. "'Member?"

I had forgotten. Lindsey had just turned sixteen when she saw a commercial on television about children in faraway lands who needed sponsorships. I wasn't keen on the idea at first, thinking she'd commit to the program for a while, then lose interest. And I wasn't sure if the majority of money went to the children or toward hefty program-director salaries, but Lindsey wouldn't give up.

For several weeks she begged, "Mom, I wanna sponsor a child. I wrote their toll-free number on this." Lindsey dug a crumpled piece of paper from her jeans pocket and showed me. "I've carried it around so I won't lose it." The handwriting was poor. I sometimes struggled to read my daughter's words, but Lindsey had no trouble deciphering the cryptic message. I asked how she planned to pay for this child.

"I'll use part of my allowance," she said. "It only costs twelve dollars a month." It surprised me that my teenager would want to devote a portion of her pocket money to a youngster in the Philippines. My heart melted.

During the first week of every month, Lindsey walked to Safeway and purchased a money order, mailing it to the Children International Headquarters. In exchange for twelve dollars, she received a school photo of a smiling seven-year-old girl with straight black hair, intense, dark brown eyes, and skin the color of light brown sugar. Two times a year, Lindsey also received a letter and a more recent photo in the mail. The little girl's handwriting was childlike but precise—nothing like Lindsey's trembling scrawls. I peered over my daughter's shoulder as Lindsey read Kayla's words aloud. Her sponsor child lived with her sister and mother and dad in a small village. Math, reading, and geography were her favorite subjects.

My mouth turned into a smile. *I guess Lindsey does already have a daughter.*

"Mom. Are you listening to me?" Lindsey waved both arms in the air, trying to get my attention.

"Yes. Now I remember." I closed the dishwasher door, recalling the day Lindsey asked to frame all of Kayla's photos so she could display them in her cottage. "You've been very responsible. I'm proud of you." I studied my daughter's pure blueberry eyes, admiring her dark, thick lashes. "Are you sure? About the tubal?"

"Yes, I am." Her voice didn't falter.

"Then you'll need to talk to Dr. Sanford. You can make the appointment yourself."

"I get to go by myself?"

Lindsey had never scheduled her own doctor's appointments before. I wondered if I should call and decided no. She was making an important decision, and she needed to be responsible for it. And since she lived alone in the cottage, now was the time for her to start doing more things on her own.

I wrote Dr. Sanford's number on a Post-it and handed her the yellow paper, explaining he'd ask her questions and discuss the pros and cons of this decision.

"Like we did," I said. "If he agrees, he can call and schedule a time." I examined Lindsey's face for any indication she felt pressured to go through with this. "I want to make sure there are no other conflicts. Dad and I want to be at the hospital."

"Really? I can do everything myself?"

"You're nineteen. If you're old enough to decide to have a tubal, you're old enough to visit Dr. Sanford on your own." My voiced cracked. My mind said this was right. My heart wasn't so sure. I cleared my throat and explained she needed to give him permission to talk with me. "You're an adult," I said, wondering exactly what that meant in Lindsey's situation. "So he'll want to make sure you understand this is permanent." I reached over and gently brushed a wayward curl out of my daughter's face. "And that this is truly your decision."

Lindsey crossed her arms. "It's my idea. You can't make me do it."

When she dialed the Silverton Family Clinic's number, I hovered, listening.

"This is Lindsey Atwell. I want to make an appointment with Dr. Sanford. I want my flop-on tubes tied."

"Fallopian," I whispered. "It's called a tubal ligation."

Lindsey's eyes darted in my direction, irritation all over her face. "I mean tubal li-ga-shon." She turned her body away from me, bent over the kitchen counter, and wrote something on a piece of paper.

Four days later, I watched the back of my daughter's brunette head, curls bobbing, as she marched, arms swinging with purpose, out our driveway and down Eureka Avenue. The doctor's office was eight blocks away, an easy trek for Lindsey.

"I love you," I yelled.

She turned and waved. "Love you, too, Mom."

Waiting at home was torture. I sat in the wingback chair, staring out the living room window at nothing. This tubal meant my daughter would never feel a baby grow inside her; she'd never hold a child of her own in her arms, nor would she pass on those slender legs, her movie-star eyelashes. I hugged my chest and rocked back and forth. My gut ached. But she also wouldn't pass on any of her disabilities to a child, either.

John arrived home from teaching and walked in the back door. I jumped up. "If she goes through with this, she'll never be able to have kids." I peered into his steady blue eyes.

"Linda. We've gone over this. A million times. You know Lindsey can't handle having a kid. We'd have to raise it. Is that what you want?" He set his red grade book and a stack of student papers on the kitchen counter.

I shook my head. Raising a grandchild would change our lives dramatically, and Lindsey's challenges had already changed our lives dramatically. John and I were looking forward to a little freedom in the future decades of our married life. As much as I longed to have grandchildren someday—way off in the future—I didn't want the responsibility of raising them. I didn't want to make such a sacrifice if we could prevent it.

"No," I finally said. "But do you think she's too young to make such a drastic decision?"

"No, I don't. Lindsey's boy crazy. I think it's better now, before she gets pregnant and we have to deal with a bigger issue."

"But what if she regrets it?"

"We'll deal with that then."

"But what if she meets someone who wants kids?"

"Linda. She still couldn't handle it. Lindsey can take care

of herself, but she doesn't have the ability to care for another human being. Especially a baby."

I nodded. "But what if we don't ever get grandkids?"

"Michael might want kids. He might give us grandchildren. You shouldn't rule that out. But if we don't, we don't. It won't be the end of the world." John leaned down and kissed my lips.

Dr. Sanford called before Lindsey returned home.

"She says you're comfortable with this decision," he said. "Is that correct?"

"Well, I wish she could handle a baby, but that's not likely," I said. My legs felt as if they might collapse under the weight of my body. "So, well, yes. John and I have talked about this, and"—my voice quavered—"we think it's best."

"I know she has disabilities, but she also gave valid reasons for not wanting kids. In Oregon, the pendulum has swung toward extreme liberal thinking in this area. Some special-interest groups do not like doctors performing sterilizations on mentally challenged individuals—"

"What?" I interrupted. "Are you saying someone might try to stop Lindsey?"

"Like I said, the pendulum swings both ways. Right now, the current opinion is that every person has the right to procreate. I'm just saying, if this got out, someone might oppose the operation."

I was speechless. Was a special-interest group willing to take on the responsibility of raising her child when Lindsey couldn't? I was incredulous that someone who had not walked in our daughter's shoes could meddle with her decision.

"Based upon my conversation with Lindsey, I'm comfortable performing the procedure," Dr. Sanford said. "She asked me to work out a time with you." Papers shuffled in the background. I grabbed a calendar. "Silverton Hospital has availability a week from Friday."

On the morning my daughter's tubes were tied, John and I sat in the Silverton Hospital waiting room and waited. My emotions teeter-tottered. I felt enormous sorrow for my daughter. The joy of carrying, delivering, and raising a child of her own would never happen for her. Yet I also felt raw and selfish. My heart grieved the loss of all the potential grandbabies who would never be a part of our lives. I didn't know their perfect little names, but I already missed their perfect baby powder–smelling bodies.

In the end, realism won out. Lindsey had made a wise decision, and when the operation was over, I was relieved. My daughter was okay, and pregnancy was one less thing we'd have to worry about.

When the grogginess from the general anesthesia wore off, Lindsey sat in a metal hospital bed, her head supported by pillows and a soft mattress angled at forty-five degrees.

"Look, Mom. The bed moves!" Lindsey held a remote control in her hand and pressed a button. Her legs lifted toward the ceiling and stopped. She pressed another button, and her legs slowly returned to their prone position. "Can I get a bed like this at home?"

"No," John said, walking through the door. He carried a bouquet of three helium-filled, Hello Kitty balloons attached to a vase filled with pink, white, and purple flowers. "So enjoy it while you can." He grinned and handed Lindsey an envelope.

She opened the card with her shaking hands. "I love Hello Kitty! Thanks, Dad! Thanks, Mom!"

"I'll put these over here on the shelf," John said, setting the bouquet next to a card from Aunt Kandi.

Grandma, Grandpa, and Michael walked into Lindsey's room, carrying more flowers, more helium balloons, and a stuffed Hello Kitty doll. "There's our girl," Grandpa's voice boomed.

"Grandpa!" Lindsey's arms reached out to give him a hug.

"How are you feeling?" Grandma stroked one of my daughter's blanket-covered legs, then leaned in for a kiss.

"Great! I love all my presents and flowers," she said.

Michael slapped his sister a high five. *Smack!*

"That was a good one!" Lindsey's eyes sparkled. For a moment, I thought I saw a young girl who might be able to mother a child someday. My hand went to my chest; I turned toward the shelf and pretended to rearrange one of the impeccably placed roses in the vase.

"You did the right thing, Lindsey," Grandpa said.

"You're very brave," Grandma said.

I turned around and faced my daughter. "Yes. You are very brave. We're all proud of you."

The next morning, John packed the flowers and gifts and Lindsey's pink Barbie suitcase into the car. I walked by my daughter's side as the nurse wheeled her down the hall. As the hospital doors opened automatically, Lindsey turned to me and said, "It didn't even hurt that much, Mom."

I reached over to squeeze her hand, truly hoping this decision wouldn't hurt my girl in any other way, either.

4

he weeks after Lindsey's tubal ligation ticked off the calendar without any new drama. We assumed she would continue seeing Gabe, but he never got around to asking her out on a "real" date. By the time she turned twenty, Lindsey quit talking about him. As far as we knew, there weren't any arguments between them, probably because they had never been in an actual relationship. We hoped Lindsey had given up on men for a while, but even though Gabe had turned into ancient history for our daughter, we soon learned men in general were not. A month after her birthday, Lindsey came home from her Goodwill job in a whirl of excitement.

"I got a new job!" she said, slamming the back door and racing toward the kitchen. I stopped wrapping newsprint around a canister lid and reached out to brush a damp strand of hair from my girl's sweaty face. She swatted at my hand. "I can do it after Goodwill!"

Although she was standing right in front of me, Lindsey used a voice that could be heard down the hall and into our family room.

"Inside voice, please," I said, putting my finger to my mouth.

Lindsey shook her head and scowled, but her voice quieted.

"You already have a great job, Linds. Won't two be too much?" I studied the kitchen clock and the five freshly labeled cardboard boxes sitting in front of me: KITCHEN MISC., KITCHEN LINENS, DINNERWARE, DOWNSTAIRS BATH, MASTER BEDROOM. The scent of Sharpie ink lingered in the air.

Our life was changing again. Seven days prior, John and I had returned home from a Caribbean cruise to accept an offer on our house. Now that Lindsey had made huge strides in her independence by living alone in the cottage for the past year, and Michael would be leaving for college in another year, my husband and I had decided to build a house. I wrapped a pottery canister in newsprint and placed the item in the KITCHEN MISC. box.

I eyed the perpetual mess. I hadn't been sure how the kids would feel about being uprooted from the only home they had ever known. When John and I told them we were moving, Michael said, "As long as I have my own room, I don't care where we live." Lindsey clapped her hands spastically, jumping up and down, saying, "Now, I can move into a *real* 'partment."

For several months, Lindsey had begged to move downtown. I couldn't understand her eagerness to live elsewhere. The cottage was so cute, even Michael talked about living there someday. "Maybe after I graduate from college," he had suggested. We told Lindsey she could move when the house sold, thinking that would be months away, but the quick sale accelerated our plans.

Now I worried about whether my daughter was ready for such a major change. John and I could live to be one hundred, or we might die tomorrow and Lindsey would need to fend for herself. More likely, we'd live to an average old age, but if something dire happened, I wanted to be certain she could take care of herself. With our supervision and guidance, Lindsey took her medications as scheduled, bathed daily, and came into our house every week to do her laundry. If she no longer lived twenty-two steps from our back door and had to take her dirty clothes to a Laundromat, would she continue to wear clean outfits? Would she spend her entire food budget within days of receiving it, run out of food, and go hungry until her next payday? Would she walk to the pharmacy and refill her prescriptions and take her medications on time? Because our house had sold so quickly, we were going to find out the answers to those questions sooner, rather than later.

"No, Mom, two jobs won't be too much," Lindsey said, bringing me back to the moment. "I really want to do this." I studied my daughter's bright eyes as she struggled to use her inside voice. "Emmett's so nice. He says Goodwill's my first pri-or-i-ty." I tilted my head, listening, pleased my girl had used this word correctly, even if it took breaking it into syllables. Lindsey stood in the kitchen, waiting.

"Where *is* this place?"

"The take 'n' bake company, Mom—Sophia's Pizza-ree-a. Emmett owns it. He says I can work a few hours a night." She gasped. "After I get off at Goodwill."

I vaguely recalled the business, a minor space in an old strip mall. The place had changed hands in recent months, but it didn't matter. For our pizza purchases, we were loyal Home Place fans. John and I had been going there ever since our first date, back when Lindsey was a toddler. We'd never tried Sophia's, nor did I know anything about this Emmett guy who owned it.

"I'm gonna help clean up and make pizzas." Lindsey's voice increased in volume; her head, shoulders, and arms shook. "I've always wanted to make pizzas." Lindsey had mentioned nursing, child care, and playing professional basketball as potential careers, but pizza making had never made any list she had ever shared with us. She gasped again. Her hands moved fast, keeping pace with her mouth. "He has game machines, too. People play vid-os. Emmett said I can get them drinks." Lindsey tittered as her eyes darted around. "It's part-time. I can still do Goodwill."

"Is he busy enough?"

"Yes, very busy. Ever since he added the vid-o machines."

This wasn't the first time a Silverton business owner had been kind to my daughter. More than once, Lindsey had purchased my favorite springtime blooms—pink, yellow, or red tulips—from Norma Jean at Silverton Flower Shop. Unable to wait until Mother's Day, Lindsey would hand me the bouquet several days early. "These only cost three dollars," she'd tell me. "Norma Jean gave me a bargain." Her broad smile would light up her entire face. On Oak Street, Allison and Israel Jewelers charged far less than retail to put a new battery in her watch; the five bucks Lindsey paid to the woman who cut her hair sure seemed like a deal compared with the amount I spent; and when Lindsey had an extra set of holes pierced in her ears, the technician said, "I want to do this for you. No charge." Sometimes Lindsey walked through the door, words already spilling from her mouth. "Mom, somebody bought me lunch today." She talked about dining at O'Brien's and how she'd ordered a cheeseburger and chocolate shake, then asked for her bill, "but the waitress said someone had already paid. Wasn't that nice?" she said. "They left before I could thank them." The kindness strangers showed my daughter touched me greatly.

"Where are the video games?" I asked, wrapping newspaper around a set of coffee mugs that we used only when company came over.

"They're on the side. The other side of the pizza parlor." Lindsey talked with her hands, pointing to an imaginary corner, as if she thought I visualized in my head the same images that she did in hers.

"Come see," she said, gasping. "Emmett wants to meet you and make sure you're okay with me working there." My daughter giggled again.

"You can't be tired or show up late for Goodwill. You need

to work hard when you're there," I lectured. My voice echoed off the bare kitchen walls. Her sudden enthusiasm about this businessman gave me a gnawing uneasiness, yet I was irritated that I felt that way. On occasion kids had taken advantage of Lindsey, borrowing money and never paying it back, for example, but no adult had ever crossed the inappropriate-behavior line. I made myself circle back to my tangible concern. "I don't want you jeopardizing your job at Goodwill."

"I won't, Mom. I promise. Goodwill is very im-por-tant. I won't do anything to mess it up." She hugged me, then clomped through the living room and the family room and out the sliding glass door toward her cottage.

⸽

Lindsey and I often clashed, but one thing we always agreed on was helping her develop as much independence as possible. Part of this was so John and I could have more independence, too. And I wanted to work outside the home and have my own interests, to be defined by details other than motherhood. That's why I started Country Neighbors when my kids were little. I even went back to college and completed my degree during that time. The year before, after selling my company, I had started working in the insurance industry. But much of our focus on Lindsey's independence stemmed from the fact that she thrived on it and raged when she had none, even as early as first grade.

During the first few mornings of that school year, my seven-year-old kept getting sidetracked as she readied herself, and I was afraid she would miss the bus. When I got on her case, she raised her voice. "Don't tell me what to do!" she said, stomping from room to room. Books and a backpack banged against the wall in her bedroom as she grumbled, "Why does she always tell me what to do? I hate it. I'm not a baby."

My daughter was not a morning person, and I could relate. She came by the trait naturally. All my life, I'd longed to wake "bright-eyed and bushy-tailed," the description my paternal grandmother bestowed on her morning mood. And my dad started almost every weekend morning of my childhood singing, "Oh, happy day, the sun is shining, the birds are singing, get up, sleepy heads." I'd pull the covers over my face and hold them tight around my ears, trying to block out my father's made-up-as-he-went lyrics. But Dad continued singing, drawing out the words, gaining volume with each new verse, until all four of his children were out of bed. I couldn't carry a tune, nor was my morning disposition patient enough to constantly coax my daughter.

After one difficult morning, I lost it. "I'm tired of your bad attitude!" I told my first grader. "I'm going to make you a list." I jotted her morning routine on a piece of scratch paper and shoved it in her direction. "You'll be responsible for yourself. I won't nag you in the morning, as long as you're at the bus stop on time."

Lindsey's eyes grew wide. She nodded, and, as if in slow motion, her mouth turned into a grin. "I like that idea." She snatched the paper from my hand. "I don't like to be bugged."

That afternoon, I went to Payless Drug and purchased a clock radio for her room. When John plugged it into the socket, Michael walked into the room and said he wanted his own alarm clock, too.

"When you're seven, we'll get you one," I said. Michael nodded, said okay. I watched as John began teaching his alarm clock–setting class.

"How much time do you need, Linds?" He showed her the dials, the volume, the snooze. Lindsey didn't set the alarm right on the first try, so Michael said, "No, Linds. Do it like this." His four-year-old hands twisted the dial to the exact time. John scratched his chin, surprised our preschooler had taken over instruction. Lindsey tried again and again. Her hands shook, but when she got it, I could hear John and Michael saying, "That's right. Good job."

Then John reiterated my earlier conversation. "We have one rule: you can't miss the bus."

I typed my daughter's morning tasks on a fresh sheet of paper, laminated the Get Ready for School List, and gave it to Lindsey. "You can do them in any order," I said. "Except the first and last ones."

1) Wake at 6:15
2) Eat breakfast
3) Take medicine
4) Shower
5) Brush teeth
6) Comb hair
7) Get dressed
8) Gather books and backpack
9) Be at bus stop by 7:30

The next morning, I watched Lindsey carry the laminated list to the table. In between spoonfuls of Cheerios, she recited the words aloud. After breakfast, she took the list with her into the bathroom. It was in her hand when we passed in the hall. I kept my promise and didn't nag my daughter. When she headed out the door and hollered, "Bye, Mom. I love you," I was pretty certain I saw her crack a smile. Seconds later, the big yellow school bus pulled up in front of our house. Lindsey climbed aboard, then turned around in time to see me wave and blow her a kiss.

As the days and weeks passed, Lindsey's morning mood improved. So did her independence. She was getting ready without any help. One morning when we passed in the hall, I bent over, pulled her to me, and hugged her tight.

"I'm proud of you," I said. Lindsey's face lit up. "You're doing such a great job. I sure do love you."

"I love you, too, Mom." Lindsey wrapped her arms around my neck. "And I love my list. It works good."

Since the Get Ready for School List, John and I had done whatever we could to allow Lindsey a level of independence appropriate for her development. When she started high school, we opted to keep her in special education classes, where she learned life skills instead of academics. I struggled, though, wondering if the decision to forfeit a diploma for a certificate of attendance was a good idea, at least until the afternoon she came home carrying a green three-ring binder.

"I'm building a po-fo-li-o," Lindsey said, setting the binder on the oak table and opening it.

"Portfolio."

"Mom. Don't int-rupt me."

I didn't have time to correct her mispronunciation, because she turned a page and pointed at the copies of her Oregon identification and Social Security cards. "So I can fill out job applications." She turned another page. "Tomorrow we learn to fill out this." Her slender index finger landed on a W-4, an Employee's Withholding Allowance Certificate. Next were two reference pages that included not only Lindsey's current duties as an assistant in the main office of the high school, but also her past responsibilities as my employee at Country Neighbors. There were evaluations and certificates of accomplishment scattered throughout the binder. My hand touched a copy of one for perfect attendance. I smiled, recalling her Get Ready for School List. The special education classroom was doing exactly as it had promised: preparing my daughter for a job, for real life.

"We're gonna keep adding to it, Mom. All through high school. Whenever I do something new or get another award, we're gonna make a copy and put it in my binder." Lindsey grinned, turning the pages with shaking hands. She told me how her teacher planned to help her complete a practice job application. "I think we're doing that next week," she said. Lindsey closed the green binder and shoved it in her Hello Kitty backpack. "I just wanted you to see."

Lindsey was learning valuable life skills; she was moving toward independence. My heart swelled.

"Good job, Linds," I said.

⤳

As I stood in the kitchen, packing boxes for our upcoming move, I wasn't sure if the pizzeria job was what I—or Lindsey's special education teacher—had had in mind.

The next day, after I finished handling my insurance claims, I stopped at Sophia's. Lindsey stood in the doorway, wearing a large brown work shirt I'd never seen before. It was so loose, so long, it hung all the way to her knees. She could have worn a winter coat underneath the shirt, and it still would have been huge.

The owner, Emmett, was African American, and his face was unfamiliar to me. I hadn't seen him around town. He looked about my age, in his forties, and at six feet five inches tall, he towered over Lindsey's five-foot-four frame. A baggy, flannel button-down that splayed at the bottom covered his rounded belly. When he moved, the plaid shirt shifted around his torso, reminding me of a short muumuu. He wore black sweatpants and tennis shoes with gray laces. His head was covered with a brown cap. Dingy white cursive stitching spelled out "Sophia's Pizzeria." Emmett removed the hat and scratched his round, bowling ball–smooth head.

"Your turn to be boss," he said, handing Lindsey his cap. When she put it over her wavy brunette hair and tugged the hat into place, I winced, then quickly smoothed a few wrinkles in my blouse in an attempt to hide my discomfort.

The pizzeria consisted of two rooms: a tiny kitchen with a minimal amount of pizza-making supplies and a toaster oven, and a game room crammed with three card tables and five chairs. Four video-game machines stood along the rear wall, pinging and flashing and dinging. Lindsey strode over to a table cluttered with two dirty glasses and a cardboard pizza box. She placed both hands around one glass and carried it to the counter, then repeated the process. When she picked up the box, the lid slipped open, exposing several gooey slices missing single bites. She grabbed a rag from the counter and scrubbed the tabletop with more zeal than necessary, causing the legs to wobble. If any pizza orders were pending, Emmett was in no hurry to fill them. I couldn't figure out why he needed help. I glanced at my watch. Four o'clock, and the place was deserted. *Shouldn't it be full with the after-school crowd?*

"Lindsey, aren't you going to introduce me?" I said. Lindsey stopped scrubbing and stepped in my direction. Her entire body shook, her face twitched, and she clasped her hands together and pointed them at me.

"Emmett, this is my mom, Linda." She turned her body toward Emmett. "And, Mom, this is Emmett." She gasped, then pointed both hands at him. "He's my new boss." Her grin widened as her eyes squinted into fine lines.

Emmett told me he used to live in Los Angeles. "Actually, I growed up in Watts," he said. "I used to preach. Now I'm a businessman." His huge grin exposed crooked, discolored teeth. "Your daughter sure is nice. She likes to play the video games. When she asked if I had any work, I felt real bad I couldn't give her more hours." The grin never left his face.

I thanked him for thinking of Lindsey and explained the importance of Goodwill in her life. "If you're willing to work around her hours, I guess there's no reason she can't work here, too."

I left Sophia's Pizzeria confused. Emmett certainly seemed amiable. But the way he spoke made me wonder if he could have some sort of disability, too. He paid Lindsey a lot of attention, and my daughter obviously liked that, but his attention felt excessive for a boss. On the other hand, I hadn't seen him do anything inappropriate. *Would I be concerned if this man were white?* I questioned myself. *Asian? Any other race? Yes,* I decided. *Yes, I would.* But still, I didn't have any tangible evidence to keep Lindsey from working there. Besides, maybe Emmett was just a nice, older, retired preacher who was kind to everyone who came in to his business. Maybe everything was really okay.

5

indsey worked for Goodwill Monday through Friday and then at Sophia's Pizzeria two nights a week. Normally she came home in the afternoon, watched a movie in her cottage, made a Lean Cuisine dinner, and went to bed by eleven. But in her third week of working both jobs, John and I saw no afternoon activity in our backyard, no lights turned on in the cottage at dusk.

"I like hanging out at Sophia's Pizza-ree-a when I'm not working," Lindsey said when I questioned her. "I play the vid-o games. Emmett gives me free quarters. I just help out, and then he doesn't have to pay me." Her tone turned agitated when I frowned. "It's like volunteering, Mom!"

John picked at his gray eyebrows. "You shouldn't work for free."

I twisted a strand of hair around and around my index finger, keenly aware of the nervous habits John and I had developed in our constant worrying about our daughter. "You need to come home after your shift," I said, feeling the locks thread tightly around the first joint on my finger.

"You never listen to me, Mom." Lindsey stomped out our back door and marched the twenty-two steps to her cottage. John and I looked at each other.

"Should we be worried?" I twisted the strand tighter, faster.

"I don't know." John jiggled his leg.

Most Silverton businesses closed by ten. We learned Sophia's stayed open late, catering to a younger clientele and moles, people who came out only after dark. Lindsey set her alarm for 7:00 a.m. so she could get to her Goodwill job on time—but she wasn't calling us to come and pick her up until late at night: ten thirty, eleven, even eleven thirty. Then, one evening, Emmett brought her home and walked her to the cottage. They stood in the shadows. From our upstairs bedroom window, I spied Lindsey's hands shaking as she tried to stick the key in the French door's lock. She flipped on the light switch, and the interior of the cottage lit up like a theater stage. Our backyard was so private, we had never hung any window coverings in her place. It had never occurred to me that I would need to spy on my daughter someday, but now I was glad nothing hindered my view.

Emmett lumbered into the living room. His large frame stood two man-size steps away from my daughter; his stiff arms hung at each side. He shook his head, gave a formal wave, and left. Lindsey walked to the phone, lifted the handset, and pressed some buttons. When our phone rang, I picked up the receiver.

"I'm home," Lindsey said. Before our daughter had moved into the cottage, we'd agreed on a few rules. Despite our many conversations about what she'd done with Gabe, we still weren't convinced she'd use good judgment when it came to boys, so they weren't allowed to stay overnight. And although we hadn't had to worry about these behaviors, we told her no smoking, no drinking, no drugs, and that if she stayed out late, she had to call and let us know.

I watched Lindsey walk into the kitchen, lift the lid off the Tweety Bird cookie jar, and set it on the white counter.

"You should've called us. We want to pick you up," I said. Her hand disappeared into the bird's belly, before reappearing with an Oreo. "Your boss shouldn't give you a ride." I used a voice that reminded me of the one my dad had used when he'd lectured me.

John grabbed the phone. "An older man driving you home late at night and hanging out in your apartment doesn't look right. We'll pick you up."

The next day, I stopped by the pizzeria after work. I sat in the car and watched Emmett and Lindsey through the plate-glass window. They weren't making any pizzas. They were just sitting and talking at a table in the dining area. *What is this guy up to?* I sucked in a puff of air, stepped out of the car, and marched through the glass door.

"Hi, Emmett. Hi, Linds," I said, nodding at them. They looked up and smiled. "John and I were talking, and if it's still light out, Lindsey should walk home. She needs the exercise. Otherwise, John or I will come and get her."

"I don't mind bringing her home," Emmett said. "It's no problem. Really." His voice sounded polite. "Besides, she can play the vid-o games for free until I close up." When Emmett used Lindsey's pronunciation, he grinned and scratched the back of his bald head. "I don't mind."

My daughter laughed, and her eyes filled with glitter.

"In California, people were prejudice," Emmett said, changing the subject. "People aren't so prejudice here."

My thoughts cycled through all the businesspeople who kept an eye on my daughter. *How can you be so distrustful, Linda?* I chastised myself. *Is it because he's older? Or because he's paying way too much attention to my daughter? Because he's black?* I shuddered, not believing I'd be concerned about a person of any race appearing in either of my children's lives, but something about this situation made me uncomfortable. Yet, after what Emmett had just shared, I didn't want him to think we were prejudiced, too.

I left Sophia's wondering if I was overreacting. *I'll handle it after our move—when I have more time*, I thought, driving away. A list of need-to-do's hijacked my mind, and I spent the next few days packing, separating necessary items from unnecessary ones. At the end of the week, John donated the good stuff to charity and took the junk to the dump while I helped Lindsey pack her possessions.

In the middle of all the moving activities, Lindsey grinned, giggled, told me Emmett thought she was pretty. "He thinks you're pretty, too, Mom." An electric shock surged down my spine, and I felt as if I'd backed into a hot wire. My girl loved compliments, especially from men.

"Can Emmett come for dinner?" Lindsey said, in the middle of an explanation about her boss having no family in the area. "He's all alone."

My eyes scanned the kitchen and living room. We had put the love seats and wingback chairs in storage. Other than the dining room table and chairs, there were only two places left to sit. Boxes were stacked against the wall, five feet high and three feet deep. We had packed most of the cookware. To eat, we used paper plates and plastic silverware.

"Yes, Linds," I said. "Invite Emmett. That's a good idea." In fact, I thought dinner was the best idea she'd had in a long time. Our earlier chat, plus the fact that Lindsey had continued to ignore our requests to give her a ride home, made me realize Emmett wasn't somebody to be put on hold. My gut said he'd never show, and if that happened, my belief that he was up to no good would be confirmed. If he did come, we'd have an opportunity to get to know him better.

꒱

Fifty-some hours later, I made a simple green salad and homemade calzone, a family favorite, prepared with extra mozzarella cheese for John and gobs of sauce for Lindsey. The aroma of baking bread filled the air as Emmett shared stories about Watts.

"My mom still lives there," he said, his voice smooth as Barry White's. "I call her every Sunday." Lindsey beamed. I served up the calzone and salad as Emmett changed subjects and talked about his new business idea. "I'm thinking about selling pizzas on the intranet."

In 2000, I couldn't imagine how this tactic might work. My face puzzled, I leaned in. "If you get an order in New York and you're in Oregon, how will you deliver?"

"I don't know," he said, scratching the hairless skin behind his ear. The remaining dinner conversation revolved around how Emmett might improve his pizza sales.

John got the vanilla ice cream out of the freezer. I cut the wacky cake into squares and slid a piece onto each plate. John placed a scoop of vanilla on top, then delivered a dessert to each person.

"I'm concerned Lindsey's getting home too late, Emmett," I said, when we were all back at the table. I loaded my fork with chocolate cake.

"Close to midnight many evenings," John said, frowning. "That's way too late."

"She hasn't overslept yet," I said, trying to keep my tone even. "But she can burn the candle at both ends for only so long."

Emmett agreed. Wholeheartedly. He nodded and smiled and nodded some more. "I tell her she can go home." He picked up his milk glass and drank. "But she doesn't want to leave," he said. I remembered when Lindsey shared Emmett's "pretty" statements. My belly turned queasy, and I realized he spoke the truth: Lindsey probably *didn't* want to leave.

I surveyed my girl: her long, fit legs; her slender build; her full breasts; her shoulder-length chestnut hair; her creamy complexion; her round blueberry eyes. *And those movie-star eyelashes.* She'd had those ever since she was born. When I held her for the first time, I counted her fingers and toes, four times, to make sure she had them all. I didn't notice her long, dark eyelashes at first. My daughter screeched with such force, her nose wrinkled and her eyes scrunched together tightly enough for the lashes to disappear. I recalled Lindsey's white, greasy head as she latched onto a nipple and gagged. An unladylike grunt erupted from her seven-pound, eight-ounce form, and, just like that, I fell in love.

She'd been born with the umbilical cord wrapped twice around her neck. A few minutes after her birth, a nurse whisked her away. "For the Apgar tests," she explained. "The first one evaluates how your baby handled the birthing process. The second lets us see how she's progressing in her new environment." I was relieved to hear Lindsey scored eight and nine. Out of ten. *My daughter is a superstar!* I thought, realizing the umbilical cord must not have harmed her.

I continued to believe this through Lindsey's early development. Just after she turned two, I finished reading *Toilet Training in Less Than a Day* and decided my girl was ready. I stripped Lindsey naked, planning to use the author's techniques.

"You won't be wearing diapers anymore," I said. "You're a big girl now."

We threw the cloth diaper in the garbage bucket. Lindsey waved bye-bye, repeatedly opening and closing both hands. I helped slide her chubby legs into big-girl panties, and she pulled them up. Bluebirds were screen-printed on the fabric and hung loose around her bottom for easy removal when the time was right.

The birdies on her panties infatuated Lindsey. She toddled about, pointed to the feathered fowl, and said, "See the birdie?

Pretty birdie." I wondered if I should've picked the plain white panties instead. I grabbed a doll I'd bought with a hole between the legs, filled the cavity with water, and told Lindsey the baby needed to go potty. My daughter's eyes grew wide. I showed her how to squeeze the dolly's belly so the plastic dish filled with pretend pee.

"Good baby," Lindsey said.

"Good baby," I said.

We clapped our hands, then pretended to give the doll some apple juice and an M&M. As the teacher, Lindsey got to drink and eat whatever the dolly couldn't, and she loved this game. She showed the dolly how to sit and earned an M&M. We raised the requirements: the potty chair must have traces of urine. Lindsey sat several times before any pee wet the plastic bowl. Then we clapped our hands, shrieked, and jumped up and down.

"Good job, Lindsey!" I said

"Good job, Lindsey!" John said.

Lindsey drank apple juice and ate M&M's and a sandwich. By the end of the day, she was potty-trained. She had one accident the following week, but that was it. We called Grandma and Grandpa and both my sisters to tell them the good news, and then we clapped some more. Many of my friends shuddered when they shared toilet-training stories. "The worst experience ever!" they said. I believed potty training in one day proved my daughter was an exceptional, possibly even brilliant child. Well, that is, if I didn't take Lindsey's tremors into consideration. And I wasn't focusing much attention on them, or on the event that seemed to ultimately change our lives.

Eight months before she was potty trained, when Lindsey was sixteen months old, we had just arrived home after a wonderful weekend with John. She was running a slight fever. I gave her half a baby aspirin and continued unloading the car. Juggling an armload of toys and clothes, I tottered through the sliding glass door to find Lindsey on her side, body jerking, limbs and torso rigid.

"Lindsey!" I threw everything on the floor and scrambled over to her. "You'll be okay. Mommy's here." I cradled her toddler body. "Hold on, baby. Hold on." Vacant eyes rolled upward and disappeared. "Please don't die!"

I grabbed the phone and dialed 911. *Breathe. Stay calm. You must stay calm.* Violent shakes racked my girl's body. An alarming gurgle escaped her mouth. *Is she choking?*

"Nine one one. What's your emergency?"

"My baby is convulsing. I . . . I . . . I don't know why."

"What's your address?"

I froze, unable to remember our new address. *I need to get help!* I dropped the phone and drove like a maniac, running red lights to get to the hospital. When we arrived at the ER, a woman in scrubs ran toward me. She scooped up my toddler and motioned with her head toward an exam room. Lindsey wheezed, her breathing erratic.

Another nurse hurried into the space and stripped Lindsey's overalls and pink T-shirt from her body. They pulled shoes and socks from her feet, then the transparent plastic pants and her cloth diaper. Lindsey didn't flinch. Her eyes remained closed, her body sweaty and sticky. A reddish, bumpy rash covered her face, her belly, her buttocks. One nurse placed my baby on a stainless-steel table covered in paper-thin white sheets. She produced a thermometer, shook it several times, and slid it into Lindsey's rectum.

"One hundred and four," she said.

My hands covered my mouth. "One hundred and four? It was only one hundred when I took it."

A doctor wearing blue scrubs rushed in. A mask hung loose around his collar. In one long breath, I told him about Lindsey's fever, about the aspirin I'd given her, how she'd jerked, the stiff-ness in her limbs, the convulsing, maybe even choking, that she'd gone limp. "Did she have a reaction to the aspirin?" I asked. A nurse scribbled notes.

"I don't think so," the ER doctor said, directing another nurse to administer an aspirin suppository. She inserted a gel tab into my daughter's rectum, then flipped her over, laying Lindsey on her back. The doctor opened my baby's eyelids, shining a pen-light into each pupil. Lindsey lay still. His stethoscope rested on her naked chest.

"Strong heartbeat," he said, repositioning the scope in several places. "Appears to be a seizure. Kids are more susceptible because their fevers escalate rapidly." The doctor shifted Lindsey's body on the table, lifting her arms and legs one at a time. "It turned into a grand mal." Before I could comprehend what he was say-ing, the ER doctor continued, sounding far more textbook than compassionate, "A grand mal is a combination of convulsions, muscle spasms, and lost consciousness." He picked up Lindsey's chart. "She's stabilizing. Go ahead and schedule a follow-up appointment with her general practitioner in the morning."

My mind raced with possible causes. *Epilepsy? Diabetes?* I rocked back and forth, wringing my hands more and more quickly. I wanted answers. Reassurance. Something. Anything.

Lindsey opened her eyes and squinted. In this strange, bright room, I knew nothing would look familiar.

"Mama." Lindsey's eyes met mine as her arms reached for me.

Relief rushed through my body. My eyes welled up. "Thank you, God," I said under my breath, hugging my daughter tight as the tears flowed toward my chin.

After that, Lindsey had several more fever-related seizures and developed almost constant tremors that increased when she tried to do anything related to fine motor skills: eating with a spoon, holding a crayon, or nudging simple puzzle pieces into wooden slots. We visited a variety of doctors and specialists, tried different medication combinations, and attempted to obtain a diagnosis. The closest we ever got was when Lindsey was six years old and a team of specialists at Oregon Health & Science University (OHSU) completed an extensive assessment.

"She's mildly mentally retarded," one young doctor said.

My body recoiled. I wanted to cover my ears and run away from that room as fast as I could.

"From an unidentified syndrome," added another.

"She has a short in her neurological system," the first doctor clarified. The team said that Lindsey's condition was most likely from a birth defect they could not pinpoint.

My voice shook when I asked about the fact that the umbilical cord had been wrapped around my daughter's neck two times. "Did that cause the damage?"

"We'll probably never know," one said.

Feeling as if I'd been shocked by a stun gun, I stared at the medical team's faces and asked about the role childhood vaccinations could have played in their evaluation. I'd watched a *20/20* exposé on the damage pertussis vaccines could cause.

"Vaccinations may have exacerbated her situation, but they didn't cause Lindsey's condition," the head physician assured me. But his words didn't sound reassuring at all. Instead, they sounded mechanical, rehearsed.

I left OHSU feeling sucker-punched. *The doctors are wrong!* They had to be, and for years, I fiercely held on to the belief that my daughter was a superstar. Sure, there were differences between Lindsey and the other six-year-olds, but I believed she'd get past this—if only we could figure out the right tools to unlock the neurological short in her brain, and if she tried really, really hard.

Even before Lindsey started school, John or I read to her

every night. We sang songs, and she learned her ABCs. We enrolled her in preschool, then kindergarten at Eugene Field with the other five-year-olds, and at the end of the school year, she was promoted to first grade. The next year, whenever Lindsey brought home reading, writing, or arithmetic, John or I helped her with it. But it wasn't long before my patience wore thin because she struggled to retain many of the lessons. Since John taught middle-school kids, I thought he should take over the responsibility of homework, and, for the most part, he did.

Still, her final grade-school progress report of the year said, "Lindsey demands a lot of teacher time but makes more advancements when given individual attention." And although we regularly coached our daughter on acceptable behaviors with other children, the teacher had written, "She is often impatient and needs improvement in the areas of working and playing with others." Her final recommendation: "Lindsey should repeat first grade."

Despite the developmental issues that became more and more apparent as Lindsey grew older, she always had an innocence, a vulnerability, that enhanced her childlike features. Now that she was twenty, that innocence seemed even more prominent somehow. Almost every day I told her, "You're so beautiful, Linds." A lot of other people commented on my daughter's good looks, too, so, normally, compliments like Emmett's wouldn't have concerned me. But I quickly learned that Emmett told Lindsey and me exactly what we wanted to hear.

After our dinner of calzones, salad, and chocolate cake, Emmett drove away from our house, waving. John and I put the leftovers in the fridge, then loaded the dishwasher, chatting about the evening. When we headed to bed, we both agreed Emmett was a nice guy. *For a boss.*

6

～⤳ ⤳～

By mid-June, I'd orchestrated two moves, a huge coordination nightmare. John, Michael, and I stacked our remaining nonessentials in a storage unit and moved our necessities into a townhouse, the place we'd rent until our new home was fully constructed. Later the same day, we trucked Lindsey's furnishings to her new one-bedroom apartment.

While John and Michael returned the U-Haul and started unpacking things at the townhouse, Lindsey and I unpacked her belongings. During a break, I pointed out her front window in the direction of the grocery store. "Roth's is right across the street, Linds. And you're a half mile closer to work. Remember? We practiced walking both routes." Lindsey nodded.

After we made her bed, she pulled her favorite doll, a Cabbage Patch Kid, from a cardboard box and laid her on the bed, making sure Darby's head was centered on top of the pillow.

"This is our new home, Darby," Lindsey said, pulling four more dolls from the box and putting two on either side of the Cabbage Patch Kid. "You're gonna love it here." She placed a doll-size quilt over the babies and tucked the ends under their malleable bodies. "Time to go to sleep."

Lindsey helped me arrange her living room furniture and put her clothes in drawers and closets, her towels in the linen cabinet, her personal-hygiene articles in the bathroom, and her few kitchen gadgets, cups, dishes, and utensils in the kitchen.

"I love it, Mom!" Lindsey clapped her hands and jumped up and down.

I straightened a framed family photograph from Lindsey's high school graduation party and stood back to admire our work. "Your place looks so homey."

"Finally, I have my very own 'partment downtown." Lindsey smiled so widely, she exposed both rows of perfect white teeth, with an adorable little gap between the top front ones. I knew my girl didn't understand how much an apartment would cost, or that her Social Security disability payments wouldn't cover all the expenses associated with living there. So I had applied for subsidized housing on Lindsey's behalf and completed pages of paperwork, wondering how other intellectually disabled individuals did this on their own. When Marion County granted her a one-year, renewable lease, it was a huge relief. The grin my daughter now displayed certainly made all my recent efforts worthwhile.

As I stood in Lindsey's new little living room, I reflected on the day OHSU doctors had diagnosed her as mildly mentally retarded, using terminology I still hated. But that wasn't what I wanted to remember right now. Those doctors had also advised me that Lindsey would eventually live in a group home. I tilted my head and reached for a strand of hair. I still could not understand how those medical professionals could have made such a prediction when she was just six years old. The strand found its way around my finger. I'd resisted group-home living. I knew my daughter could develop the necessary skills to live independently. *She sure has proven them wrong!*

Lindsey interrupted my thoughts when she handed me two

small pewter frames containing snapshots of a girl with coal-black hair. "They're of Kayla," she said. "My daughter from the Philippines."

Four years had passed since Lindsey had adopted this little girl. "She's beautiful," I said.

"And I've never missed a payment," Lindsey said matter-of-factly. "Can you find a place for these, too?"

I nodded, positioning the two pewter frames on the end table near her graduation picture. "Since Kayla is your daughter, she should be right here, next to the rest of your family." My voice cracked on the last statement, and my mind spiraled back to the day Lindsey had her tubal ligation.

Wow. A quiet sigh escaped my lips. *Time sure flies. That happened almost a year ago.* As I stood in my daughter's new living room, looking around, I realized that even amid the passage of time, my heart still hoped Lindsey would never regret her decision. Since there was little chance she'd ever get pregnant, Kayla was the closest thing to having a child Lindsey might ever get. I brushed a dark curl from my twenty-year-old's face. "You've done good, Linds," I said.

On the drive from Lindsey's new downtown apartment to our townhouse, I realized she had fulfilled, even exceeded, my vision for her independence. Not only was she responsible, she also displayed compassion for others. She was an adult, her own legal guardian, and I couldn't have been prouder.

My glee was short-lived.

A few days before the next month's rent was due, Lindsey called and told me, "Emmett and I are boyfriend and girlfriend." Her voice egged me on, daring me to challenge her announcement. I stood in the kitchen of our townhouse and glared out the window. I recognized the tone in my daughter's voice. It was a tone I'd heard countless times before: "I wanna be a pirate, not a fairy!" at Halloween when she was seven; "Why did you divorce my bi-logical father?" when she was nine; "You're never here," "Why won't you let me have a horse?" and "You're mean!" when she was eleven. Counseling had helped us both learn better communication tools, but the power struggles between us continued. The year before, my nineteen-year-old daughter had stomped like a five-year-old when she'd seen the decorations for her high school graduation party. "You didn't do it right!" she'd screamed. "There are too many pictures!"

As I gripped the phone more tightly, I braced for a major showdown with Lindsey. My brain coached me, *Stay calm, be logical, use reason*, but my hand wanted to reach through the damn phone and force my daughter to change her mind.

"How old is he?" My voice sounded shrill. I knew it did.

"Thirty-five."

"Are you sure?" My sharpness escalated with every word. "He looks older than thirty-five. What do you know about him?" I couldn't breathe. I felt as if someone had torn open my chest and smashed my lungs. "Has he ever been married?"

"He's divorced."

Every muscle in my body stiffened. "He's your boss. This isn't appropriate."

"I love him, and he loves me."

My mouth opened and closed, but nothing came out. How could a man of typical intelligence choose a partner with special needs? That smacked of taking advantage. *Could he be unstable? A registered sex offender?*

As soon as I slammed the phone into its base, I told John. The veins around my husband's temples looked like they might explode. He clenched both fists, and his face turned dark red. Never before had I seen him look like he could punch something. But he did now.

"I'm going down there," he said, pulling the car keys from a pocket in his shorts. "Emmett has no business getting involved with a girl Lindsey's age."

Like a shadow, I trailed after my husband, saying hurriedly, "We'll make her quit the pizza job. We'll get her more counseling."

A ringing phone interrupted my rants.

"Lindsey quit today," said a frustrated voice on the other end.

It took me a moment to realize I was speaking to the manager of Goodwill.

"And she didn't give two weeks' notice," she said, exhaling loudly. "So she can't be rehired."

I was still processing the manager's words when a call-waiting beep interrupted. I asked her to hold on and clicked over.

"Lindsey's moving," her apartment manager told me. "The truck's loaded. They've taken all her stuff. She didn't even give notice."

I dropped the phone on the counter. Incredible dread filled me as John drove our Camry over the twenty-five-mile-per-hour speed limit to Lindsey's new apartment. My eyes zeroed in on a large, white rental truck, its oversize bed loaded down with all our daughter's possessions. Emmett wore his signature long-sleeved flannel shirt and the dirty brown Sophia's Pizzeria cap. Two huge hands gripped the steering wheel. John parked in the first spot he found.

"Get out of the truck, Linds." John said, in his deep teacher's voice—the one he reserved for regaining control of his classroom on a rare, chaotic day.

The truck's engine revved. "We need to talk," I yelled, as a mixture of dryer exhaust, hot asphalt, and rotting fruit smacked my nostrils.

"I'm not getting out." Lindsey's voice was loud, piercing. "I'm moving in with Emmett." She turned and smiled at him. "That's what I want."

"Why did you quit Goodwill?" I said, crossing my arms to steady my trembling body. The July afternoon sun burned my skin. Lindsey sat on the bench seat next to Emmett. She looked fifteen: slender, innocent, wearing a short-sleeved light blue top. Her eyes seemed bigger and bluer than the sky. He looked fifty as sweat trickled under his hat and down his round face. He swiped a plaid sleeve across his brow, wiping away the perspiration.

Lindsey leaned out the truck window. "I'm gonna work for Emmett! Full-time!"

I wanted to cry, scream, kick the truck. I wanted to beat something with my fists.

"You can't stop me, Mom." Lindsey sounded so damn stubborn, so damn coached. "I'm twenty years old. I can move wherever I want."

That was partially true. She was twenty; she'd had a birthday two months ago. *But she's barely twenty*, I justified. And, under the circumstances, shouldn't we still have control over where she lived and what she did? Yes, we'd always worked for her to be independent, but I thought there was an understanding that we'd meant *independent to a certain extent*.

My husband walked to the driver's side window.

"She's too young," John yelled, trying to make his voice louder than the revving engine. "We need to talk. Man to man."

Emmett leaned his head out the window. "This is what she wants," he said, putting the rig in gear and driving away.

Stunned, we stood there and watched.

"I'm going to the police station." I grabbed the keys out of John's hand. We both jumped into the Camry. My arms and body shook harder as I maneuvered through the narrow side streets, gunning the gas after each of the three rolling stops along the route. On Water Street, a diesel truck backfired in front of us. Its fumes sucked through the Camry's air-conditioning vents. I held my breath and gunned the car again, passing illegally in front of the Silverton Police Department.

Within seconds, I was inside the precinct and standing in front of a glass window. I bent my body in two and spoke into the half-moon opening, giving Emmett's full name to the officer on the other side.

"He's run off with our daughter," I said, demanding they complete a report and arrest the Sophia's Pizzeria owner this very minute. "He must be a registered sex offender." My mouth was tight as a hyphen; my body shuddered. I felt cold, like I'd been locked in a walk-in freezer.

"If she's twenty years old," the officer said, "she's of legal age." He studied the computer screen. "No warrants for Emmett Hockett." He typed a couple more keystrokes, then shook his head. "If she's gone willingly, there's nothing we can do."

"I'll go to his house and physically take her back," I told the officer.

"You can do that, ma'am." He shuffled a stack of papers on his desk. "But if she doesn't want to leave, you could be arrested for kidnapping."

"Kidnapping my own daughter?" My brow furrowed. I wrapped my arms around my torso and rubbed, trying to warm myself.

"Again, ma'am, in the state of Oregon, after she turns eighteen, she can do what she wants." He slipped the pen behind an ear and left it there. "If she wants to be with him, we can't interfere."

"She has intellectual challenges," I said, more loudly than I'd intended. John patted my shoulder; I jerked away.

"She has special needs," John's deep voice interrupted. "Doesn't that mean anything?"

"The developmentally disabled are allowed to make the same mistakes typical individuals make," the officer said. "She may have bad taste in men, but that's not a crime. Unless you're her legal guardians, officially, there's nothing we can do."

I stood in the lobby, glaring at the officer. My gut hurt, as if someone had kicked me. My mind raced as it tried to figure out a way to correct this wrong. But I had nothing. I could not think of one damn thing.

7

❧ ❧

When John and I left the Silverton Police Department, my fists and jaw were clenched. With every step, the muscles in my neck, back, and shoulders tightened. In the car, I gripped the steering wheel until my knuckles turned white, then sat there, thinking. John pulled at his eyebrow and jiggled his leg, staring at nothing.

How could it be that the police weren't able to help us? Wasn't it their job to protect and serve? After all, they'd helped us with Lindsey once before, the summer after she finished fifth grade. Lindsey had begged to go to Girl Scout camp, and we'd thought the experience might help her build a few new friendships. Besides, her bickering had intensified in recent months, and most of her unexplained anger was directed at me. A weeklong camp seemed like the perfect opportunity for me to reset my patience threshold. As a bonus, John and I could spend some one-on-one time with our son.

When the day came to drop Lindsey off at camp, I coached myself the entire way home and every day thereafter: *Listen. Be more patient. Don't overreact.* If I did these three things well, I thought, a Mother of the Year award might actually be in my future. But when the time came to pick up my girl, Lindsey greeted me with a scowl.

"You're late." She grabbed her suitcase with a tremoring hand. I steeled my psyche for more of my daughter's wrath.

Mother of the Year. Remember? I forced air in through my nose. I wasn't late; in fact, I was right on time. *Don't overreact.* I chirped questions, trying to emulate a sunny disposition and improve my daughter's mood. Michael sat in the backseat with our family dog, reading a book, ignoring his sister. Fortunately, with each reply, my twelve-year-old's voice warmed. As we got closer to home, I spotted a familiar red-and-white sign. "Do you two want Blizzards?"

"Yeah!" Michael folded the corner of his page and set *Tom Sawyer* on the seat. Lindsey nodded with fervor, echoing, "Yes!"

This brilliant plan rapidly disintegrated, though, as the puppy pawed at and jumped all over Lindsey in an attempt to get at her Blizzard. Then Lindsey refused to let me hold her cup of ice cream while she tried to put Beethoven in his kennel. It spilled, and the dog lunged to lick it up.

"*Lindsey! Give me your Blizzard!*" I snapped, trying to negotiate through heavy traffic. In an instant, my Mother of the Year award vaporized. That's when I felt something hit the back of my head. I jerked my face upward. *Drip.* My right eyeglass lens looked like a bird had shat on it. I peered in the rearview mirror and saw Lindsey's face twisted from anger and her hand coated in chocolate. A sticky mess speckled the van's cloth headliner. It took a second to register. *She's thrown her Blizzard on me!* Beethoven did his best to clean it up—licking, swallowing, licking some more, spastically following his nose.

I pulled the van over and stared Lindsey down.

"It's all your fault," my daughter said. The fury in her voice started off shaky but grew stronger with every word. "You divorced my bi-logical father." *Gasp.* "That's why I threw my Blizzard on you." For a brief second, I pondered her rationale. Marty and I had divorced when Lindsey was one, and shortly after I had married John, he'd stopped calling and visiting. Now, whenever Lindsey got upset, she blamed me for his transgressions. I let her accusations tumble around in my head. "You can't do anything to me," she said, gasping. "I'll call the police if you do."

My hands gripped the wheel so tightly they ached. I stepped on the gas, keeping my eyes focused on the road. *Fourteen miles to go.* My insides simmered, churning, boiling. My neck and shoulders knotted and burned.

"Mom," Michael said, his voice calm and matter-of-fact, "you have a blue M&M stuck in your hair."

I touched the back of my head and found the M&M. *Evidence!* When we reached Silverton, instead of turning toward home, I stopped under a shade tree in front of the single-story cream building. SILVERTON POLICE DEPARTMENT was written in block letters on the front of a full-length glass door. Lindsey's eyes darted between the police station and me. "Are you turning me in?"

Michael looked up from his book. I didn't say one word as I rolled the van windows down halfway, locked the doors, and marched into the precinct. After speaking with the dispatcher, I walked outside and met an officer who had just stepped out of his squad car. The policeman wore dark blue from neck to toe; a thick black belt cut the uniform in half. A holstered gun hung on his right hip. His shiny gold badge read OFFICER STONE. He adjusted his weapon, then stood with one hand at his side, a notepad in the other.

Out of the corner of my eye, I watched the kids as they sat in the van, staring. I detailed the events of the day, my hands waving in the air, turning around so he could see the blue M&M. Officer Stone nodded, and I slid open the side door.

"Young lady." The officer addressed my daughter with his eyes, as well as his words. "Please step out of the vehicle." Lindsey's hands shook hard. It took several attempts for her to unbuckle the safety belt. She half crawled, half stepped over the kennel, out of the van, and onto the sidewalk.

"What happened today?" Officer Stone's voice boomed. Lindsey gasped, then told him about the dog and the Blizzard.

"You threw a Blizzard on your mother?" He scribbled notes.

"Yes." Lindsey tremored, her head bent, her eyes cast toward the sidewalk.

"Was that a good thing to do?"

"No."

"If you don't mind your parents, I can take you into custody. Did you know that?"

Lindsey shook her head.

"Sometimes kids have to live in foster homes," Officer Stone said, maintaining an erect posture, a rigid manner. "Is that what you want?"

"No." Lindsey's eyes darted right and left. Her face twitched.

"Throwing anything on your mother, or anyone else, for that matter, is disrespectful. Do you understand?" Officer Stone flipped the notebook closed, his left hand resting on his weapon.

"Yes." My daughter's body trembled; her blue eyes remained alert and wide.

"Do you think you can obey your parents?" His deep voice had mastered sternness.

"Yes." *Gasp.* "Are you gonna arrest me?"

"Not this time. But it seems to me that you owe your mother an apology. And it looks like you have some cleaning up to do." He bent over and peered inside the van. I followed his gaze. Chocolate ice cream had dried on the back of the driver's seat. It looked like someone had barfed.

"Sorry, Mom," Lindsey said, staring at the sidewalk.

"You can get back in the vehicle," Officer Stone said. "And don't forget to buckle up."

Lindsey scurried into the van, pulled the belt across her body, and latched it around her waist. I rolled the side door shut, then turned and mouthed, "Thank you." Officer Stone nodded once before he swaggered into the station.

Lindsey was still argumentative after that, of course, but the officer had made an impression on her. She cleaned the van without complaint and never threw anything at me again.

Right now, sitting in the Silverton Police Department's parking lot with John, I wished for an officer to agree to talk to Lindsey and help my daughter see that well-behaved young ladies don't run off with their middle-aged bosses, quit very good jobs without notice, and suddenly decide to break their leases. And, to be honest, what I really wanted was for someone to force her to come home with us.

Desperate, I picked up the cell and dialed our friend who worked at the Marion County sheriff's office. "Maybe Doug can help," I told John as the phone rang. I figured Doug, being a commander and all, must possess greater knowledge of the law, and would possibly have more authority over a situation like this.

But the conversation didn't go the way I envisioned.

"The police can't do a thing," Doug said, sounding miserable. I knew he'd help if he could. "You might want to talk to an attorney," he offered, before hanging up the phone.

Even though we would have no law enforcement backup, I decided we should drive to Emmett's house to save our daughter. I'd happened upon his place by accident after my cousin had moved into a new, Salem neighborhood. Her directions said turn right, but I turned left and ended up in an older subdivision. I was about to make a U-turn when I saw a blue van parked in a driveway. I immediately recognized it as Emmett's because of all the religious bumper stickers covering the tailgate. Then I saw him standing on the front porch, his bulk bent over as he stuck a key into the lock on a salmon-colored door. I didn't honk and wave. I pressed down on the gas, sped past, and drove off his street as quickly as I could, hoping he hadn't seen me. Now, that accidental wrong turn would come in handy.

Ten miles west of Silverton, all the houses on Longhorn Street looked the same: one-thousand-square-foot, ranch-style tract homes lined up in an uncared-for row. Only the paint colors differed. Emmett's entire house was painted salmon, but the color had faded and the paint was chipping, especially on the eaves.

Emmett stood in the bed of the white rental truck; Lindsey waited on the concrete driveway. He handed my daughter a whitewashed wooden barstool. She grabbed its legs with both hands. Her arms and torso shook as she turned her whole body and set the stool next to two wrought-iron lamps with muslin shades and the Tweety Bird cookie jar. I wanted to yell, *Stop! You're not staying!* I parked on the opposite side of the street and scrambled out of the car, rushing to Lindsey's side. She glared at me. My eyes bore into hers. More than anything, I wanted to drag my girl across the street and stuff her into our Camry. I didn't care if she went kicking and screaming. But when I opened my mouth, my voice sounded hollow.

"I want to talk to you. Privately."

Lindsey shuffled toward our car but stopped three feet away, in the middle of the road. John stayed near the sedan, his body rigid. Emmett climbed out of the truck bed and stood ominously nearby, looking as if he might tackle us if we tried to take her away. My head bowed, and my shoulders sagged.

"Lindsey," John said, using his teacher's voice, "you shouldn't have quit your job."

"You're moving back into your apartment," I said, equally loudly, sounding braver than I felt.

"This isn't how you were raised." John took a step in Lindsey's direction and stopped. My head bobbed in agreement. This wasn't how my daughter was raised, and these actions were out of character for her. She was a worker, not a quitter. Even as early as sixth grade, we noticed that Lindsey tried to do more than her share. By that time, she'd been on an Individualized Education Program—a program requiring teachers to modify assignments to my daughter's abilities—for years. Lindsey had noticed the work she was given was different from her peers' and didn't like that one bit. Unbeknownst to her teacher or us, Lindsey pulled worksheets out of the trash, bringing them home in her backpack to work on in the evening. And she would've continued sneaking work home if we hadn't found out and put a stop to it. She was so determined. In my wildest dreams, I never could have imagined this daughter of mine would quit a perfectly good job or move from a perfectly good apartment—an apartment she'd wanted so badly. It just wasn't in her nature.

"Why did you move without telling us?" I placed both hands on my hips and sighed loudly.

"You didn't handle this like a mature twenty-year-old." John shook his head.

"You were sneaky." I wagged my finger in my daughter's face. "This was wrong. Plain wrong."

John and I bombarded Lindsey with questions and demands, never waiting for a response. I knew this wouldn't work—it was just like my repeated demands for her to hold her ice cream while she tried to put Beethoven in his kennel. But John and I kept badgering, trying to guilt our daughter into conceding and coming back to Silverton with us. We were treating her like a child, but I didn't care. I thought we could come up with an angle that would touch her heart or mind, so we'd achieve the outcome we wanted. At the same time, I knew this approach would sound like double talk to Lindsey. Her head and eyes bounced back and forth between John and me.

Finally, she focused her wide blue eyes across the hot asphalt onto Emmett's brown ones and said, "This is what I want. I love Emmett, and he loves me." They smiled at each other, exchanging sweet grins that sickened me. I looked away. A German shepherd hunched his rear end and took a dump in the brown grass behind us. I covered my mouth with my hand and gagged.

"We love you, too," I said, managing a feeble smile. *Don't say something you might regret.* When Lindsey had been involved with Gabe, I'd asked the couple if we needed to plan a wedding. This time, though, I wasn't certain the answer would be no. There was no way in hell I was going to plan a ceremony for my girl and this old pervert. Not now. Not ever. *Be careful. Choose your words carefully,* I told myself. "And I want to be joyous when you move in with a man," I finally said.

Lindsey had a blank look on her face, like she didn't understand our concern or our distress. "I love you, Mom, but we're moving in together." Her eyes darted right and left. "Why can't you be happy for me?"

"Because it's wrong. The way you handled this is all wrong." I took a step toward my daughter, begging. "Please come home with us."

"Get in the car." John's deep, firm voice didn't offer Lindsey an option.

"No. You can't make me. I'm twenty, and I'm staying." Lindsey turned her back to us and tramped toward Emmett's house. I grabbed her arm. "Let go of me!" She jerked it loose. My whole body quivered. For one long moment, I didn't move or speak. *I'm losing my daughter!* Lindsey scurried up the driveway. Like a linebacker, Emmett followed, blocking my view. I ran around the wrought-iron lamps and hopped over the Tweety Bird cookie jar, but they were already inside the salmon-colored house and closing the door when I reached the threshold. *Click.*

"I'm not done talking to you, Lindsey!" I banged my fists on the door.

"We'll call our attorney tomorrow," John said. I felt his breath on my neck, and when I turned toward my husband, his face looked bleak. "We can't do anything right now." He touched my shoulder, but I shook loose and pounded on the door some more. I cupped my hands along the side of my face and tried to peer in the two front windows. Between the drapes and the grime, not even a sliver of light made its way through the glass.

"I'm going to try the back door." I rounded the side yard. John walked toward the car, his shoulders hunched forward. A layer of fresh clippings lay on top of the grass. Four-foot-tall weeds filled the flowerbeds. The side windows were covered in tinfoil. Yellowed tape held the foil in place. A faded gray, six-foot-tall fence stopped me. No gate. A BRINKS SECURITY sign stood among the weeds, warning: THIS HOUSE IS UNDER SURVEILLANCE. I turned and ran back to the west side of the house to find the gate chained and padlocked. A rusty nail tacked a NO TRESPASSING sign at eye level.

Back at the front door, I knocked and yelled more. "Lindsey, come outside. I need to talk to you." No one answered. *"Please, come back out!"* If I'd not witnessed the pair going inside and heard the click of the lock, I'd have sworn no one was home. Except for the fresh grass clippings and a few of my girl's furnishings scattered in the driveway, the house appeared vacant.

I trudged over to the Camry, where John waited. We drove home in silence as Lindsey's words played on repeat in my mind. *You can't stop me. I'm twenty years old. I can move wherever I want.* Lindsey had never spoken to us about her legal rights. The closest she'd come had been to say, "You can't do anything to me. I'll call the police if you do," after the Blizzard incident. This new attitude scared me.

I need to get my daughter back.

I wanted to reverse time, go back to the days before Lindsey took the job at Sophia's Pizzeria, but that was impossible.

"This would never have happened if I hadn't been so distracted with the move," I finally told John.

"You don't know that," he said, frowning.

"There has to be a way to fix this." In my head, Lindsey would be back in her apartment and working at Goodwill by the end of the week. I mentally strategized, practicing the speeches I planned to give to her boss and her housing manager.

But in the end, those conversations didn't go as I'd hoped, either.

"Lindsey was manipulated by an older man," I informed the Goodwill manager the next morning. "Can't you make an exception under these circumstances?"

The manager said, "Sorry. No exceptions." Marion County Housing answered the same way.

All the work we'd done to provide Lindsey with some independence felt washed down the drain in a few irresponsible minutes. I criticized myself for not listening to my gut, for not reacting sooner, for focusing on our new house—instead of my daughter. *What kind of mother allows someone like Emmett to run off with her baby girl? A bad one*, I told myself over and over. *How did I let this happen?*

We met with our attorney, and he confirmed what we'd already learned. At twenty, Lindsey had the right to pick her own partner.

"Parents of typical kids deal with this, too," he said, reminding us that parents do not get to pick their child's mate in our country. He suggested we apply for guardianship but warned that judges weren't eager to take away someone's rights unless there was proof that she was harming herself or was mentally unstable. "And it's not so easy," he said. "Is there any evidence Emmett is hurting her?"

No, John and I admitted reluctantly.

The attorney confirmed once again, as if I needed to be hit over the head with a wooden plank, that if we forced her home against her will, we could be arrested for kidnapping.

"But would a judge agree?" A sarcastic tone laced the attorney's voice. "There's no telling. But you'd have to defend yourselves."

I already knew that even if we were successful in bringing Lindsey back to Silverton, how in the world could we keep her from running away with Emmett, or someone else, again? How would we monitor her twenty-four hours a day? Up until then, she'd been allowed to roam around town, so we couldn't take that freedom away. If Emmett came by, Lindsey might climb into his rig and drive off. We might never know where they'd gone. Although living with Emmett didn't even come close to being an ideal situation, at least we knew where to find our daughter.

And we had a trump card: I managed Lindsey's money. Because of her intellectual disabilities, when she'd qualified for Social Security, an agent had urged her to select a representative payee to help handle her finances. Surprisingly, Lindsey had selected me. Now, she didn't have access to those funds unless she went through me. I sighed, remembering a recent conversation.

"Emmett says you need to give me all my money," Lindsey had said. "Why don't you?" We'd gone over this, but I'd shared my concerns once again, reminding her that she'd given the one hundred dollar bill her grandma Fiona had gifted her for her birthday to a kid in the park because he'd asked; she continued to buy pens, papers, and pencils with any cash on hand, even though her drawers were overflowing; and she had trouble filling out a check properly. "Your writing is difficult to read," I'd said, but Lindsey had dismissed my responses and started her next few money-related statements with "Emmett said this" and "Emmett said that."

Emmett sure has a keen interest in Lindsey's financial situation, I thought. Was he attracted to Lindsey? Or to her steady income? After the appointment with our attorney, I went to Sophia's Pizzeria and told Emmett, "This is so wrong. You are way too old for our daughter. John and I do not support this relationship at all. Lindsey needs to come back home."

"But I love her and she loves me," he said, crossing his arms. "We want to be together. She wants to stay."

I shook my head. "If Lindsey stays with you, plan on having the rest of her family in your life, too. We intend to maintain a regular presence around here."

"Family is impotant." Emmett grinned. "Come by anytime." I thought his tone sounded more sinister than sincere. Emmett removed his brown Sophia's cap and scratched his bald head. He put the cap back on and tugged the bill into place.

John or I drove by Sophia's every day, sometimes twice on the same day. We'd stop in to see if Lindsey was okay, if she needed any help, if she wanted to leave. We kept hoping she'd change her mind, but Lindsey always said, "I'm fine, Mom. Emmett's good to me." Mother's intuition told me she was trying to convince herself as much as she was me. At every opportunity, I pulled her aside to say, "Call us anytime. Day or night. We'll come and get you."

Unannounced, I stopped by Emmett's house one day and knocked on the front door. When no one answered, I hollered and pounded, "Lindsey, it's Mom. Open up. I'm here to visit."

Eight minutes passed before Emmett cracked the door a couple inches. "What you doin' here?" he growled. One dark brown eye peered through the opening, drilling into my face. "You can't come in. It's not a good time," he said, shutting the door.

I clenched and unclenched my fists. For several long moments, I remained on the concrete porch, staring at veins of salmon-colored paint flakes. "There must be a way to get my daughter back," I said to no one. "There must be a way."

8

When Emmett shut the door in my face, I realized it would be impossible to monitor the goings-on at his house twenty-four-seven. With slumped shoulders, I walked toward my logo-plastered company vehicle. How could I keep an eye on my daughter when she lived fourteen miles away? My job at Farmers Insurance had me handling property claims throughout Salem and the Willamette Valley, but sometimes I had to drive to the coast, or Hillsboro, or Milwaukie. Basically, wherever they needed me, I had to go. As I reached out for the car door handle, a movement at the aqua house on the other side of the street caught my attention. A blond woman held a hose over a planter of red geraniums. I walked over to introduce myself and explain the situation.

Bonnie shut off the water and accepted my business card. "I'd be happy to keep an eye on the place," she said.

"It has all my contact numbers." I pointed to an additional phone number I'd written on the backside. "That one's my home. If you see anything unusual, please call me." We both waved as I drove away.

The bulldozers broke ground and cleared the footprint of what would be our new, two-story home. In six weeks the foundation had been poured, the subfloor was in place, and several first-floor rooms had been rough-framed. John and I walked the construction site every night, taking pictures of whatever progress had been made that day.

"We're right on schedule," our builder assured us. "Only seven more months to go."

"Seven more months?" I said to John later that evening, examining our cramped, un-air-conditioned townhouse. I pulled my sweaty T-shirt over my head and tossed it in the hamper; John did the same. "How will we ever make it that long? I hoped we'd be in by Christmas."

"I guess we shouldn't get our hopes up," John said, as the phone rang. I checked my watch: 10:52.

"Who would be calling this late?" I asked.

Our son bagged groceries at Roth's IGA, but he'd been home for over an hour and was in his bedroom doing homework.

I picked up the receiver. "Hello."

"Mom?"

I covered the receiver and mouthed, "Lindsey."

"I'm ready to come home." Her voice quivered more than usual.

"Okay, we'll be right there." I said, hanging up the phone and turning toward John. "She wants us to come and get her."

We snatched our soiled T-shirts and tugged them back on. I grabbed the car keys from my purse, and we raced to Longhorn Street in the moonless night. I sped into Emmett's driveway, stopped, and thrust the gearshift into park. Our headlights illuminated the sagging, salmon-colored garage door—and a man with balled fists batting air. It was Emmett. And he looked mad.

"Keep it running." John opened the passenger door. "I won't be long." My husband's tennis shoes squeaked when they hit the concrete. "Where's Lindsey?" John's eyes scanned the driveway, then the yard, before they landed back on Emmett.

"*You prejudice!*" Emmett shouted, boxing his fists in John's direction. Emmett's long-sleeved flannel shirt looked out of season for August. The cap that usually covered his head was missing. Sweat ran along his temple. He swiped a flannel arm across his forehead, yelling, "*You prejudice! Because I'm black! You prejudice!*" His voice was so loud, I expected the neighbors to sprint from their houses to investigate.

John planted his feet firmly on the driveway, as if they were set in cement. He raised his arms in a protective stance and balled his fists. As long as I'd known my husband, he'd always said, "I'm a lover, not a fighter." *He can't fight Emmett. Emmett's huge. It would be an unfair match.*

"No, Emmett," John said, using a voice of authority. His white hair reflected the bright light. "I'm not prejudiced. I just want my daughter."

"You prejudice!" Emmett's eyes were wild. His fists moved as if he were boxing with an imaginary opponent. "That's why you don't want Lindsey with me!"

Will he strike my husband? I worried, remembering a recent conversation I'd had with Lindsey. Emmett seemed to have an implausible power over my daughter; I'd fretted that he'd threatened her to get her to stay and asked if he owned any weapons. "That's personal. It's none of your business, Mom," she'd told me. Now I wondered if she'd been vague because he had an arsenal inside his home that she didn't want us to know about. *Could he have a pistol tucked in his sweatpants? Did his huge flannel shirt hide a knife?* He certainly seemed angry and irrational enough to stab someone.

My hands shook. I grabbed the cell phone and punched 911, but I didn't push SEND. *Hold on a minute*, I thought, remembering a time when Lindsey had told me Emmett hated the police. When I'd asked why, she'd closed her mouth and pantomimed locking her lips and throwing away the key. So I sat in the car in Emmett's driveway, holding the phone like it was a lifeline, and waited.

"We're taking Lindsey home." John's legs locked in place. "And you're right, Emmett. We don't want her to be with you. Not because of the color of your skin—but because you're taking advantage of her. She called us, and now she's coming with us!"

I held my breath, watching the argument between my husband and my daughter's lover escalate. The car lights flooded the driveway, the garage door, the men—like a spotlight floods an arena. Emmett loomed above John's slender, five-eleven frame. They each took a step closer together. I wondered if they'd bump chests. John would lose. Emmett could snap my guy in two.

Should I push SEND? *Should I?* My heart pounded in my chest, and my palms turned sweaty. I squeezed the cell phone tight, glancing down to make sure 911 still lit up the screen. My thumb hovered over the button. *Will the police even help us this time?*

I had spent much of my spare time investigating Emmett online. In 2000, the information on the Internet was limited. Still, I searched for any available public record that might expose him. My sleuthing paid off when I discovered he was forty-four—nine years older than we'd been told! I also learned he'd been married twice. Of course, that could have been a misunderstanding on my part because when Lindsey said he was divorced, I assumed he'd only been married once. There were also a couple minor traffic violations and six unpaid parking tickets—but those did not set off any internal alarms.

Lindsey stepped into the light, wearing clothes I didn't recognize: baggy khaki pants and a man-size white T-shirt with yellow stains under the arms. Her hair looked stringy and greasy. She had gained some weight, but even if the clothes she left with were a bit snug, they should still fit.

"I'm not coming home." Lindsey raised her arm to shield her

eyes from the headlights. "I don't wanna leave."

My heart pounded against my chest. I slid my phone into my pocket and scrambled from the idling car.

"Lindsey. Get in the car." I gestured toward the Camry.

"No." She shook her head. "I've changed my mind."

John reached for Lindsey's arm, tried to grab skin, but she stepped backward and stumbled.

"We're not prejudiced." I turned and faced Emmett, trying to control the anger in my voice. "We don't care if you're pink with purple polka dots, and we certainly don't care if you're black." I glared at him, my lips pressed together into a tight, thin line. "But I don't like being lied to." I wanted to shake my finger at him, but I held my hands against my sides. "You said you were thirty-five." My eyes bore into his face. "But you're forty-four—two years older than I am!" I'd been saving that information until Lindsey and I could talk in private. I wanted to show her the evidence, proving Emmett had lied to us.

In an instant, Emmett's mood morphed to calm. "Let's go in the house." He motioned his head in the direction of the pathway leading to the front door.

My heart skipped a beat. I wasn't sure we should go. Watching him turn off his anger like someone turning off a faucet frightened me. This newfound hospitality felt like a ploy: invite us inside, kill us there. If we stayed out here, we'd have a better chance of someone witnessing any crime.

Lindsey ambled up the pathway and disappeared into the open door. *No need to be so dramatic,* I told myself, shaking the violent thoughts from my head. I turned off the engine and pulled the keys from the ignition, but I couldn't shake the eerie feeling. I plodded into Emmett's house, imagining intense background music like in *All My Children* when Erica Kane did something appalling and the producer built suspense by playing a sinister tune.

The air was hotter inside the house than it was out in the yard. In an instant, my armpits were soaked. "Leave the door open, Emmett." My eyes gradually adjusted to the dimly lit living room. Emmett flipped a switch, turning on one weak bulb in a chrome floor lamp. I squinted. Lindsey sat on one end of a threadbare, avocado-colored sofa. Piles of newspapers lay on the other end. A corner fireplace occupied most of one wall. At least ten American Girl dolls in unopened packages were stacked on the hearth. Cabbage Patch Kids and Barbie dolls were also piled around the room, their boxes in pristine condition.

Lindsey's pine armoire had been moved into a corner, the doors firmly shut so I couldn't see what was stored inside. They weren't using the denim-covered futon we'd bought her. The TV, the VCR, and her stereo were stacked in a haphazard heap on top of the futon like pieces in a Jenga game. Opposite the electronics, someone had set the two wooden barstools on the futon's upholstery, the legs pushed into the soft cushions, leaving eight small marks. The wrought-iron lamps poked out in two different directions, and their parchment shades sported numerous dents. If someone sneezed, the whole mess might topple over. Around all the furnishings were more boxes, more newspapers, more magazines.

This wasn't like Lindsey. Her nature was to be neat and tidy. We'd assigned her age-appropriate chores starting when she was a toddler. She'd learned to pick up her toys, clean her room, make her bed, bathe every day, and wear clean clothes. Of course, like any typical kid, she didn't do these things as quickly as we wanted all the time, and there were times when she argued about her expected household responsibilities ad nauseam. But by the time Lindsey was a teenager, then a young adult, she preferred order in her life. Once she moved into the cottage, I couldn't ever remember walking into her home and seeing something out of place. She tidied the kitchen, living room, and bedroom every single day. "I sure got the clean gene," she'd told me numerous times.

Sometimes Lindsey struggled to get the seams on her tights straight or her shoes on the correct feet, and anytime cleaning or organization required fine motor skills, the tasks were infinitely difficult for her, but she always tried her best. Here, standing in Emmett's living room, she didn't appear to have tried at all. But where would she have put her things? There wasn't any room. *They live like pack rats*, I thought, trying not to look disgusted.

"Sit down." Emmett shoved newspapers over to make room on the sofa.

"I prefer to stand," I said.

"Me too," John said, staring at Lindsey. "She said she wanted to come home. That's why we're here."

"Go get your clothes." I crossed my arms over my chest.

John modeled my stance. "We're taking you home."

Lindsey watched Emmett; she didn't move. My imagination stayed wild. *Has he threatened to harm her—or us—if she leaves?* My daughter's face possessed no fear; in fact, her expression lacked emotion altogether. I wondered if his tirades were a regular occurrence for her.

"I'm sorry." Emmett's tone warmed, reminding me of the night he'd had dinner at our house. *He's a chameleon.* Emmett stepped over to a nearby table, picked up a large book, and hugged it to his chest. *Holy Bible* was written in gold letters on the front. "I was gettin' ready to read the Bible," he said. "I didn't know she called." He smiled, and his eyes settled on Lindsey. If that were true, why had he stood in the driveway, yelling inflammatory words into the night, just as we showed up? "I shouldn't of yelled," he added, seeming to read my mind.

We left without our girl, but that evening, all my suspicions were confirmed. Emmett had a temper. He was an angry man who didn't appear to be as godly as he'd professed.

Some friends, family members, even acquaintances told us, "Just go and get her." One relative said, "I'd shoot him."

We shook our heads. Violence wasn't the answer. First of all, we didn't own a gun, nor had we ever used one. And when you raise your children to be independent, you're not always going to agree with the decisions they make. John and I weren't willing to commit a violent crime in order to change the situation. How would we help Lindsey if we were locked in a prison cell? But when I thought about Emmett manipulating my daughter, what he might be doing to her behind closed doors, vigilante thoughts crept into my mind. I promptly pushed them out. I didn't want Emmett to use force, and when it came down to it, neither would we.

"It's easy to give advice," I told my husband. "But if a person hasn't walked in our shoes, how can he possibly know how we feel or what we're going through?"

John told me to ignore the armchair quarterbacks. "They can't possibly know." He ran a hand through his gray hair and jiggled his leg. I twisted a strand of hair around my finger. At the moment, they were the only things we could do.

～

When Lindsey first left with Emmett, I counted every day she was missing from our lives. The days turned into weeks and the weeks into months. John taught and coached kids, I handled insurance claims, and we both monitored the construction of our new home. All these responsibilities occupied a lot of our time, but as November approached, I felt certain Thanksgiving would be our greatest chance to spend time with Lindsey. Certainly she wouldn't miss out on a holiday with family.

"We'll be going to Aunt Beth's again this year," I said, standing out front of Sophia's Pizzeria, stroking my daughter's lengthening, dark locks. It was hard to touch her hair when it was so greasy, but I longed to connect with my girl in some small way. "Grandma and Grandpa and your dad and brother and all your aunts and uncles and cousins will be there!" My voice radiated much more excitement than necessary, to make it harder for her to turn me down. Lindsey stared at me as if the names no longer held any meaning for her. "And Aunt Beth will be making her delicious yeast rolls!" I added, knowing how much my daughter enjoyed my middle sister's homemade buns.

Lindsey's blue eyes brightened. "I do like Aunt Beth's rolls." She licked her lips.

"I'm making shrimp dip, and there will be turkey and dressing. All your favorite foods! And we'll play games! Everybody is coming!"

Lindsey peered over her shoulder. Behind the plate-glass windows, Emmett stood at the tiny stainless-steel counter and watched us.

"We have to work that day," she said.

"On Thanksgiving?" My voice choked. "Who'll order pizza for Thanksgiving dinner?"

"Sorry, Mom. We have to work." She turned away from me, opened the glass door, and stepped inside.

Every time Lindsey chose Emmett over us, it felt as if an iron door had been slammed in my face. Tears stung my eyes; I blinked hard and held them in. Driving home, I was certain I couldn't feel any worse than this, but on Thanksgiving, when my siblings' children were all present at the dinner table, grief overpowered me. I excused myself from the table and ran into the bathroom, where I hid until my emotions were under control. During dessert, our clan took turns announcing the one thing we were most thankful for that year, but I struggled to come up with anything substantial. My mind kept repeating, *Lindsey should be here. Lindsey should be here.* I finally mumbled something stupid about being thankful for having gotten to sleep in that morning.

When Lindsey was growing up, I got my hopes up whenever we saw an improvement in school, in the making-friends arena, in decision making. She'd progress a few steps forward, and we'd cheer and tell her how proud we were. Then she'd seem to slip twenty steps backward. Watching these gains and losses was disappointing, but much of my distress was aimed at my daughter's feelings. She struggled so hard. Yes, OHSU had offered a diagnosis, but as far as I was concerned, it was an unsatisfactory one, and I still clung to the possibility of finding a cure for her issues.

Once, when she was in first grade at Eugene Field, her teacher asked if Lindsey had been tested for food sensitivities. I shook my head, then tilted it in the teacher's direction. None of the doctors we'd visited had suggested such an idea.

"Milk can cause all sorts of negative reactions. I use this doctor in Salem," she said, handing me his address and phone number. "He practices homeopathic medicine. Give him a call."

I walked down Eugene Field's hallway and out the double doors, wondering if something as simple as allergies could be the cause of Lindsey's tremors and learning disabilities.

John and I had never discussed alternative medicine. Our insurance didn't cover it, nor did we know enough about such treatments, so I was apprehensive. In high school, my health instructor discussed doctors who used unconventional methods to try to cure patients. Some of these treatments made the patient worse.

I made an appointment anyway and drove Lindsey to West

Salem. We walked in together. I stopped abruptly inside the door, relieved at my surroundings. The office looked exactly like our doctor's office in Silverton. In fact, it looked like all the other doctors' offices we had visited over the years. I didn't know what I had expected. Weird music playing? Incense burning? Indian tapestries hanging on the wall? Instead, familiar magazines were scattered on the coffee and end tables in the waiting room. I let the air out of my chest, picked up *People*, and flipped through the pages until a nurse called Lindsey's name.

The examination room was clean and sterile. A nurse drew Lindsey's blood, swabbed her saliva, scraped skin cells from her arm, and cut snippets of hair from her head. *What will skin cells, saliva, and hair samples tell us?* An eerie, uncomfortable buzz settled in my stomach. *Could this be what my high school teacher referred to?* But since a highly regarded educator had made this referral, I dismissed these doubts.

One week later, the test results were in.

"She has too much vaccine serum in her system." The homeopath studied Lindsey's chart. I couldn't believe it. Finally, a professional physician agreed with me. Vaccines caused Lindsey's tremors. I wanted to dance a jig and shout, *I've got answers!*

He nodded. "She has too much of the measles vaccine."

I scratched the back of my head, shaking it from side to side. "What?" My brow lifted slightly as I remembered the *20/20* exposé I'd watched several years earlier. "I thought pertussis caused the problems."

"No," he said, reiterating that the measles vaccine was the culprit. "Our test results didn't indicate excess pertussis. Her body needs rebalancing." *Rebalancing?* "Once that's done, the tremors should diminish. They could completely stop. I've got pills for this."

Mounted on the wall was a locked glass cabinet. The doctor

turned a key, opened the door, and selected a bottle. He tapped two pills into the palm of his hand. The round silver balls looked like BBs or decorations bakers use on wedding and specialty cakes. They rolled around in his palm. I sat in the room, watching the silvery balls, mesmerized by their promised power and wanting more than anything to believe they would change my daughter's life.

"Place one under Lindsey's tongue in the morning and one at night." He rolled the balls in his palm. "Let the pill dissolve on its own. No chewing or crunching." He slipped the capsules back into the container. "Don't expose the bottle to excessive light or magnetic fields, such as a microwave." He twisted the cap on tightly. "Store the bottle in a dark place, like in the back of a cupboard." *There sure are a lot of weird instructions*, I thought, scrunching my face, feeling a bit more skeptical as each second passed. "You should see a noticeable difference in two weeks," he said.

I took my seven-year-old's hand in mine, squeezed it, and smiled. In my other hand, I grasped the container of twenty-eight precious, silver-colored, would-be *miracles*.

Outside, the afternoon sun burned bright. I squinted and shoved the container deep into my front jeans pocket. I didn't want to ruin the medicine.

On the way home I wrestled with the doctor's words. His instructions were odd—eccentric even. As much as my heart wanted to believe in the pills, my head still screamed: *Charlatan!* It irritated me that my wants and beliefs were so contradictory. *Why, oh why did I have to be so suspicious all the time?* I reprimanded myself as I vacillated between wishful thinking and level-headedness.

At home, four-year-old Michael perched himself on a wing-back chair, watching *Diff'rent Strokes*. Lindsey hop-skipped in disconnected, clipped movements toward her brother and the television. John sat on the sofa, correcting history papers.

"I think we just wasted our hard-earned dollars," I whispered, explaining the rules for storing and taking the pills. "I think he's a quack."

Still, at bedtime, I handed Lindsey her first pill. "Slide it under your tongue. Let it dissolve slowly. Sit here until it does." Despite my misgivings, I wanted to cure my daughter, so I stashed the silver-colored pills in the deepest, darkest part of the cupboard, far away from the microwave.

Every morning and every night for the next two weeks, Lindsey took the pills as prescribed. John and I stared at our first-grader throughout the day, scrutinizing her movements, speech, and temperament.

"Do you notice anything different?" I hoped my husband saw something I didn't.

"No. You?"

Every day we repeated the same exchange, and at the end of two weeks, there were no more pills and there was no noticeable change in Lindsey.

"I'm glad I don't have to put those slippery pills under my tongue anymore," Lindsey said. "They tasted weird."

"Silvery," I corrected, pulling Lindsey close for a hug.

"No, Mom, they were slippery. They kept sliding around."

Why did I subject my daughter to this weird treatment? I wondered. But I knew why. It was the "What if?" question." What if I hadn't checked out this possibility and it had turned out to be the solution that eliminated my daughter's tremors? I would have felt terrible. Yet I felt terrible anyway. From disappointment. I was definitely having trouble accepting things being the way they were, instead of the way I wanted. Every letdown caused the pain to intensify, and I began building a wall around my heart. One brick here, two bricks there. A thin layer of protection, so I wouldn't feel so much pain all the time.

As I sat at my sister's Thanksgiving table, I felt the sting of discontentment bite me hard. My girl was missing out on the hugs and the love of her extended family. I sucked in a lungful of air and added a dozen more bricks. I grabbed another yeast roll from the wicker basket, slathered butter on the bread, and took a big bite.

A few weeks later, Lindsey refused to come home for Christmas and Michael said, "Can't you make her?"

"No, we can't." Grief hit my gut. The wall of bricks wasn't working so well. I held on to the kitchen counter, blinking faster and faster, reliving a recent conversation with Lindsey.

"I want to be with Emmett," she told me.

"But Emmett can come, too," I said.

"He'll be uncomterble," Lindsey said, making excuses. "We don't like people."

Christmas Day dinner was rather depressing. I couldn't get used to having one of my kids missing from the festivities. Afterward, John and my dad watched a football game, Michael went to his girlfriend's house for a second holiday meal, and Mom and I drove to Lindsey's place. I'd held on to her gifts. I told Mom and Dad to hang on to theirs, too, truly believing she would change her mind and show up. It was now obvious that wasn't going to happen. Mom and I weren't sure she'd even open the door, but we had to try.

During the fall, my mother had spent hours compiling hundreds of pictures of Lindsey, meticulously arranging them in a sixty-six-page album. "A keepsake of her childhood," Mom said, looking at all the memories. "Someday Lindsey will look at these and see how happy she used to be. And she'll come back to us."

We stood on Emmett's porch and pounded on the faded salmon wood slab, hollering, "It's Mom and Grandma. Open up." Several minutes passed before Lindsey opened the door three inches. She placed her entire body in the small gap, as if she were guarding a vault. She didn't invite us in, but she did agree to come out to the Camry and sit in the backseat to open her presents. There were new tops and bottoms and underwear and socks—things John and I hoped she'd use. There were cartoon coloring books and stickers and a jewelry-making kit—things we hoped she'd enjoy.

"Thanks," she said, after she opened each gift. But when Lindsey saw the photo album, she smiled and giggled and touched each picture before turning the page.

"I'm gonna take real good care of this, Grandma. Thanks." She closed the album and hugged it to her chest. "Will you tell Grandpa I love him?"

✎

By the middle of January, Sophia's Pizzeria sat empty for three days in a row. Twelve or so to-go boxes were stacked along the back wall of the kitchen, six silver pizza pans lay on the stainless-steel counter, and the cash drawer was open. In the game room, video machines sat dead. The sign on the glass door was turned to CLOSED.

I drove to North Salem to see Lindsey and find out what the heck was going on. My daughter stood on the front porch and refused to let me in. She still wore the unfamiliar, oversized, stained clothing; her dark, long hair still looked damp, scraggly, and greasy. Blackheads and acne blotches now covered her face. When I hugged her, she smelled like dirty socks and onions. I let go of Lindsey's body quicker than I intended.

"Emmett's bathroom doesn't work so well," she said.

"Really? Then maybe you should come home. Our bathrooms work really well."

An agitated expression appeared on my daughter's face, and she shook her head.

"What's going on at Sophia's?" I asked, changing the subject.

Lindsey crossed her arms. "Emmet says that's pry-vit! It's none of your business!" A half second later, she added, "We're closing down."

"Forever?" I asked, feeling an agitated expression appear on my face, too.

Lindsey frowned. "I gotta go, Mom."

Urgency soared inside me. "Please come home with me," I begged. My daughter shook her head, stepped into the salmon-colored house, and closed the door.

⤳

The construction on our new home was completed in March—just as the contractor had predicted. Lindsey had been living with Emmett for eight months when John, Michael, and I moved into our new home. While our contact with Lindsey remained hit-or-miss, I longed to spend more time with my daughter. Wanting to do something special for her twenty-first birthday, Grandma and I offered to take her to the coast. It was the one place I thought she might agree to go.

"It's my favorite place on Earth," Lindsey said. "I'll count down the days on my calendar. I can't wait."

On the morning we arrived, Lindsey schlepped across the street to the car wearing dark blue denim jeans and a sweatshirt big enough for Emmett. She'd squeezed her oily hair into a ponytail, exposing a complexion that hadn't improved since the last time I'd seen her. Emmett followed close behind, like a shadow. When Lindsey opened the back door and climbed in, she moved as slowly as an ailing, ninety-six-year-old woman. She scooted her heavy bottom in first, pulled one foot in, rested, then pulled in the other. Her hand tugged on the seat belt, trying to strap it across her body. It took four tries before the metal end snapped into the latch.

I lowered the driver's side window. "Hello, Emmett," I said, my voice cool. He leaned into the car, and I backed away. He smelled like dirty socks and onions, too.

Emmett locked his eyes on Lindsey. "I planned to take you someplace special today," he said. "But I guess you're going with them instead."

I asked about his plans, but he was vague, stumbling over his words.

Lindsey hesitated. "I don't know if I should go. 'Specially if Emmett has something planned."

My heart sank to my toes. Grandma frowned and said she'd be disappointed if Lindsey didn't come with us. I reminded my daughter that we'd planned this outing several weeks ago and that she'd been counting down the days. "Besides, we want to spend time with you."

Her eyes darted between Emmett, Grandma, and me. "I'll go with you, Mom." She fidgeted with her fingers, her eyes focused on the hands in her lap.

As we drove away, I worried Emmett might punish my daughter for this decision, and asked, "Does he hurt you?"

"No."

"What do you do all day?"

"We read the Bible a lot. Emmett's the man of the house. I'm supposed to be submissive."

"Submissive?" I peered in the rearview mirror to see my daughter's expression, but there was none. Her face looked blank. "Exactly what does that mean?"

"Do what Emmett says," she said.

"What is he asking you to do?"

Lindsey turned her head and looked out the window. "That's pry-vit. It's none of your business, Mom."

Grandma and I glanced at each other.

"What kinds of places does Emmett take you?" Grandma changed the subject in hopes of keeping Lindsey talking.

"I don't wanna tell you." Lindsey pulled her lips inside her mouth and clamped down. This was a new response. Ever since she had learned to talk, it seemed she'd never stopped. As a grade-schooler, when she came home from school, she followed me from room to room, chatting about her dolls, her sticker books, her favorite ice cream, the string hanging from her shorts. If she said something that piqued my interest, I asked a question.

"Mom. You int-rupted me," she'd say, exasperated. "Now I need to start at the beginning. I can't 'member where to go from the middle."

I would correct her pronunciation, saying the words slowly so she'd hear them. "*Interrupted, remember?*"

Ignoring me, Lindsey would start over, like a continuous reel at Home Depot explaining how to tile your floor. As she repeated every minuscule detail, my mind drifted to the list of groceries I needed to write down and pick up at the store, or the meal I planned to cook for dinner that evening. Most of the time, my daughter never noticed.

At fifteen, her habit was pretty much the same. "But I want Tina to stay overnight," she repeated relentlessly one night as I pulled a load of laundry from the dryer. "Mom. Are you listening to me?" She placed her hands on her hips. "You're not listening to me."

"Yes. I. Am. Lindsey." This was the sixth time my daughter had repeated the same words in the last few minutes. Following our counselor's advice, I'd tried setting the timer, allowing her five minutes to get out all her concerns. When the timer buzzed and Lindsey still kept demanding and accusing, I tried another technique he'd also suggested: Stop! Count to Ten! Listen! But

Lindsey wasn't interested in letting go of this subject. I'd even repeated back her exact words so she'd know I'd heard her.

I gathered the warm towels in my arms and carried them through the kitchen, into the living room. "I've already told you. Tina can't." I inhaled the scent of Outdoor Fresh Bounce and dropped the laundry onto one of the plaid love seats. "I've talked to her mother. They have plans Friday night." Our new dog lay curled on the top edge of the sofa. Arthur cocked one eye open, then lifted his head when the towels landed on the cushion. When I started folding, the shih tzu rested his fluffy black-and-white chin back on his petite paws.

"Tina could bring her Cabbage Patch Kid and we could play house."

"It will have to be another time."

"But Michael has a friend coming over Friday. And I only know Tina."

That part was true. As far as sleepovers went, Tina was Lindsey's only possibility. Nine months earlier, John had told me about a student at his school who could use a friend. With her parents' permission, John had introduced Tina to Lindsey. The two girls were similar in many regards. Both talked at the same time, and constantly. I wondered if either one ever heard or answered the other's questions—if there ever were any actual questions between the two of them. But they seemed to have developed a kinship, taking turns inviting each other over for occasional playdates and sleepovers. It was our turn to host Tina. And everything would have worked out fine. If only Tina had been available.

"Lindsey. Tina. Can. Not. Come. Over. Friday."

"Mom. You're not listening to me."

I sighed so loudly, I thought the house might wobble on its foundation. I wanted to cover my ears with my hands. Or take a drive. Or run far away and never return. Lindsey's recent arguing had reached new pinnacles. *Maybe if I were getting paid to listen to my daughter, this wouldn't be so frustrating.* I cracked a smile.

"We've talked about this for over half an hour." I stopped midfold and twisted in Lindsey's direction. "If you want to continue talking, you'll need to pay me to listen." I peered into my daughter's blueberry eyes. "Ten cents a minute. And I want my money up front."

Lindsey's eyes widened. She tilted her head to one side, then sprinted to her room. The sound of coins hitting the dresser interrupted the sudden quiet of our living room. A stack of folded navy and peach towels sat on the love seat. I leaned in and rubbed Arthur's plush, floppy ear. He pushed his soft head into my hand, and I scratched a little deeper. More change clanked together, and I heard my daughter's voice counting aloud.

Lindsey marched out of her room and glared at me. "I'm done talkin'. I don't wanna spend my money that way." She turned sharply and stomped outside to play.

On the drive to the coast, I peered over my shoulder to see Lindsey's face. Now I'd pay *her* if only she would talk to me and give me some information about how Emmett treated her.

Grandma and I told family stories, attempting to engage the birthday girl. Every now and then, when I glanced in the rearview mirror, I saw the corners of Lindsey's mouth turning into a slight grin, but she didn't say another word until we got past the Pacific Coast Range.

"We're gettin' close to the beach. I can tell," she said, clapping her hands.

We took Lindsey to the outlet mall for new clothes. The only piece she wanted was a cartoon-character sweatshirt. I went into the dressing room with my girl and was relieved when no bruises hid under all those baggy clothes. Even though she protested, I found a pair of blue jeans, two pairs of stylish shorts, and a couple of coordinating striped tops. Between the three of us, we walked away from the outlet mall carrying four large shopping bags.

For lunch, Lindsey wanted a cheeseburger, fries, and a chocolate milk shake at Arctic Circle. I requested they make the drink with extra chocolate, the way she liked it, and then we sat in a booth and ate.

I reminded Lindsey about her brother's upcoming high school graduation and party.

"It's at our new house, Linds. We moved in. Remember?" I shoved a straw through the hole in the plastic lid, past the noisy ice cubes, to the bottom of my paper cup and took a long pull of Diet Pepsi. She knew where we lived, but she'd never seen the finished product. John and I had invited her and Emmett to a housewarming we'd hosted a month after we moved in, but she'd told me Emmett said we just wanted gifts. I asked her how that was possible when the invitations specified "no gifts, please." She shrugged and said they couldn't come, "but thanks anyway."

Now, I sat in our booth in Arctic Circle, studying my daughter, wondering what I could say to convince her to say yes.

"We'll come and get you," I added, giving her the date. "Michael came to your graduation, and he'd like you to be there for his."

Lindsey shook her head and slurped the last bit of her milk shake.

Grandma leaned over and stroked Lindsey's shoulder. "Grandpa will be there."

"Besides, Michael misses you," I said. "We all miss you."

"I don't care so much for parties anymore," Lindsey said.

The truth was, Lindsey had always struggled a little with any special event. She'd get frustrated with details like a photo collage I'd made for her graduation party or complain we hadn't made enough shrimp dip. Nearly every holiday or birthday, she'd start the celebration off with a near meltdown. I'd tell her, "Lindsey, you can choose to be happy or to be mad. If you choose mad, you'll need to be in your room." Then she'd paste on a fake grin until she forgot what she'd been upset about. Eventually, she would pull out of her bad mood, usually commenting on how she loved the twisty paper or chips with wiggles or shrimp and cocktail sauce. It pleased me to see her excited about the efforts I'd put into the decorations and her favorite foods.

I wished for some inspiration that would sway Lindsey to come and celebrate her brother's graduation, but she shook her head no. "Tell Michael I love him." Her eyes darted around. My mood flattened. I wanted the entire family to attend, but I also didn't want to ruin my daughter's birthday trip. I let the rejection flit away.

We drove to the beach and walked along the shore, watching the surf crash upon the sand. It was hard to hear over the roar of the waves, so we walked in silence. I reached over and took Lindsey's hand. She held it for a ways, then let go, bent down, and picked up a broken sand dollar.

"I'm gonna save this." She slid the shell into her pocket. "It'll always remind me of the birthday I turned twenty-one."

On the drive back to North Salem, Mom and I tried asking new questions, but Lindsey answered with calculated caution. Then she leaned her head back, closed her eyes, and fell asleep. To me, her pimpled face still looked angelic and peaceful when she slept. She woke a few blocks before I had to turn onto Longhorn Street.

"Emmett never takes me anyplace," she said. "I'm kinda surprised he picked today to take me somewhere special."

"Say the word, Lindsey—I'll keep driving." I didn't want to give her a choice. I wanted to lock the car doors, floor the accelerator, and peel out of that neighborhood. But I remembered our attorney's and the police officer's kidnapping warnings. Lindsey shook her head. So I pulled over on the opposite side of the street, the same place I had parked that first night Lindsey had run away. "You don't have to go in." My eyes pleaded with hers.

Lindsey sat in the car for several minutes. Her eyes darted right and left, her upper body trembled, and her face twitched. I held my breath and said a silent prayer: *Please let this be an ugly memory.*

As Lindsey opened the car door, a movement in the front window caught my eye. Fingers pulled back a section of drape, and two pupils stared at us between the gap. When Grandma and I stepped out of the Camry, the curtain released and swung back and forth.

We helped Lindsey out of the car, exchanged hugs and kisses and "I love yous." We handed her the shopping bags. Lindsey smiled, then turned and walked toward Emmett's salmon-colored house.

With all my heart, I hoped this would not be the last time I'd see my girl smile.

9

ichael graduated from high school without his sister present. He shrugged and looked away, saying he couldn't believe Lindsey wouldn't come.

A few months before graduation, Michael had been notified of his acceptance into the business program at the University of Nevada, Las Vegas (UNLV). The last week in August, John helped him load his Nissan Sentra with clothes, a computer, a printer, and boxes of things he was certain he'd use while living in a dorm.

I thought back to the day I'd hired Michael and Lindsey to help at Country Neighbors, the company I started when Lindsey was a kindergartner. It didn't take long before it grew to 150 sales consultants and a warehouse full of handcrafted merchandise.

The spring after Michael turned five and Lindsey turned eight, I assigned them tasks at the warehouse: sweeping the old wood floor, picking up toys in their play area, and counting boxes of company catalogs into bundles of ten that they rubber-banded together. I demonstrated how I wanted it done. Michael began counting and had a pile of banded catalogs near his feet within a few minutes.

Lindsey's hands trembled as she counted slowly. She talked to herself, shook her head back and forth, and lost count. "I wanna start over." She dropped the catalogs back into the box.

"Do it like this, Linds." Michael grabbed a handful of catalogs out of the cardboard container. He moved one at a time into a new pile. When there were ten, he stretched the rubber band wide enough to slip around the bundle. "See?" He waved the stack in front of his sister's face.

"Okay." Lindsey focused all her attention on counting the catalogs. At the end of the afternoon, her stack was smaller than Michael's, but quantity wasn't the main goal. It was a way for the kids to help out. In exchange, I promised to pay them twenty-five dollars each, two times per month.

When I handed the kids their first paycheck, confusion masked their little faces.

"I want money." Lindsey held the rectangular document in her shaking hands and stared at it.

"Yeah. It's just a piece of paper," Michael said, as I loaded them into our gray minivan.

"We're going to the bank," I told them, explaining they could each keep five bucks to spend right then, "but the rest is going into savings accounts."

At Washington Mutual, the teller pointed to the space on the back of the check where the kids should sign. Michael promptly printed his name and reached up to hand it to the smiling teller.

"Dollars, please. And could I have some quarters, dimes, and nickels, too?" Michael's five-year-old head slid beneath the counter, missing the hard surface by a fraction of an inch. He leaned his body against the wall underneath, waiting for his sister.

Lindsey stood nearby and used one hand to steady the document. She picked up the pen and wrote her name in large, shaky letters that took up most of the backside of the check. I wished the tremors didn't cause her to struggle so.

"I want what Michael's gettin'," Lindsey said. "Please," she added, looking at me and smiling. I nodded and patted her shoulder.

The teller counted out twenty-five dollars twice. Michael put four dollars and the change in his little fabric wallet and stuffed it in the front pocket of his High Sierra jeans. Lindsey stashed her cash in a Hello Kitty purse that she latched and hung over her shoulder for the walk across the lobby to the new-accounts desk.

The kids each counted out two ten dollars piles in front of the bank representative. She picked up the bills and handed them two registers each. I took Lindsey's and printed "Lindsey's Savings" on one.

"You can use your savings account when we go on vacation," I told both kids. "You'll need extra spending money then. Or you could use it for something super special." I ruffled Michael's light brown locks, and he squirmed away from me.

Then I wrote "College Money" on Lindsey's other register, explaining that someday, when she went away to college, the money would come in handy. Michael listened, then held out his registers so I could do the same for him.

Back then, I hadn't yet understood the magnitude of Lindsey's limitations, or that she would never use her college fund for its original purpose. When I finally came to that realization, it stung. Right now though, I was so happy Michael was headed down the path we'd envisioned for him. He wasn't a fair-headed little boy anymore; he was a clear-faced, broad-shouldered young man. His umber hair was cut close to his scalp, although he'd left enough in front to spike upward. Hoping not to cry when my son left, I planned to tell him I loved him, hug him good-bye, then give him some calm, sensible advice.

"I'm proud of you." I choked on the first word, then completely fell apart before the end of the sentence. "So very proud." I babbled on and on, telling him how every decision he'd make from this point forward would make his life easier or tougher. As I said those words, Lindsey's questionable choices filled my head and my body shuddered. I forced myself to focus all my attention back on my boy. "I love you. Be safe." I clung to Michael. "I'm so excited for you," I said between sobs. "College is a new adventure." I told him how I wanted him to graduate, get a job, get married, and have 2.3 kids.

"Mom, you can't have 2.3 kids. It's not possible."

"But that's the national average." I sniffed, more loudly than I had intended to. "So that's what I want. And since Lindsey can't have any kids . . ." My voice trailed off.

"It's okay, Mom. I'm going to be okay." Emotion filled his voice as well. Michael unhooked my arms from the back of his neck and stepped backward. "I love you."

When it was John's turn, my husband choked up, too. He patted Michael on the back in a succession of three quick taps, told him he loved him and to do good out there. Neither John nor I spoke when Michael pulled out of the driveway, his tires bulging from the heft of the load. We just stood in the sunshine, waving and waving and waving, until Michael's car was no longer in sight. We were officially empty-nesters. John started cleaning the garage. I walked back inside the house, sat on the sofa, and stared out the window. Arthur jumped up on the couch and nestled next to my leg.

In my mind, Michael was about to live out everything I used to hope for for Lindsey: college, marriage, children, career. My goals for my daughter had changed with time, especially after numerous junior high and high school counselor and teacher meetings had included the same recommendation: Lindsey should shift from a fully to a partially mainstreamed curriculum and attend more special education classes. I scratched Art's chin. He lifted his head and licked my fingers. Eventually, I had accepted that Lindsey was on her own track and would never fit into the mold of the national average. So the day she had moved into the cottage, then into her own apartment, I'd been ecstatic. Now, even though she was independent of me, her beautiful sovereignty we'd worked so hard for seemed squashed behind the tinfoil taped to Emmett's windows.

Michael, however, had always been easy—easy to raise, easy to teach, easy to play with, and easy to watch grow up. I thought back to the week Lindsey went to Girl Scout camp and Michael became our only child for seven days. The three of us played Risk. Michael acquired all the purple and South American countries. John held most of Europe. Both my guys forgot a player could capture Alaska from Kamchatka, and since Michael hadn't reinforced his armies in that region, I conquered North America, South America, and Europe before they both conceded.

Michael invited Jesse, Tony, and Tyler over. Even four rambunctious nine-year-olds in the house couldn't reach Lindsey levels with their volume. When I asked Michael to set the table, he said, "Okay, Mom," and did it. When we told him it was time for bed, he ran upstairs and changed into his pajamas.

"Thanks for being you," I told Michael, pulling the covers up to my son's neck. Our first dog jumped onto the bottom bunk, turned around in a circle, and snuggled next to Michael's torso. I petted Beethoven's fur, enjoying the alone time with this boy child of mine who tried so hard to follow our rules and requests. I stroked my son's darkening locks and touched his rosy cheek.

"You know, Michael, you don't always have to be so perfect." I leaned over and pressed my lips against his forehead.

Michael nodded, then rolled over and closed his eyes.

⤳

A week after our son left for college, Lindsey's biological father died at fifty-four. His sister called with the news and asked me to tell Lindsey. I wanted to tell my daughter in person and hold her when she cried, but she didn't answer the phone, so I got in the car and drove to Emmett's. No one answered when I knocked. I tucked a note in the front-door frame: "Lindsey, call me. It's important."

She called the next day.

"Marty died." I braced myself for my twenty-one-year-old's reaction. Years before, when I'd told Lindsey her great-grandmother had died, she had wailed. I held her for a while, but it went on for two hours—loud, gagging, racking sobs. We finally told her she could grieve as long and as loudly as she wanted but that she needed to do it in the privacy of her room. Yet, right now, I wished I could be on the other end of the phone, ready to wrap my arms around my girl. "I'm so sorry, Linds."

Lindsey didn't cry or ask questions. The only reason I knew she was still on the line was that I could hear her heavy breathing making its way through the receiver.

"Do you want to go to his funeral?" I asked, figuring Lindsey would say yes and I'd need to find a way to get her to Georgia.

After a long pause, Lindsey said, "He's not my *real* dad. John's my real dad. I don't want to go. Good-bye, Mom." The phone went dead. I stared at the receiver in my hand, listening to the dial tone. I felt the same way as Lindsey. Marty was her biological father, but he had never acted like a real dad. *Any man can be a father*, I thought, *but it takes a special person to be a dad.* John had certainly filled that parental role better than anyone.

I didn't blame Lindsey for not wanting to go to her father's funeral. In all honesty, I was relieved. Farmers Insurance had just offered me a one-year contract to work out of Olathe, Kansas, on its catastrophe team. I would now specialize in weather-related property damage. Handling tornado, hail, and hurricane claims for the majority of the next 365 days sounded like an easier proposition than the unpredictable dealings and disappointments with Lindsey and Emmett. They'd been entangled with each other for fourteen months now, and I hadn't made any progress in getting my daughter back. Cat-team pay was excellent, the travel appealing, and I'd no longer have as much time to dwell on a situation I had no control over. Besides, we intended to use the extra earnings to help with Michael's college expenses.

꘎

After spending four weeks training in Kansas, I was sent to my very first storm, in Marksville, Louisiana. Adrenaline pulsed through my veins as I sped southeast, following five other logo-plastered Farmers vehicles down open highways and freeways and back roads. The bumper-to-bumper traffic evacuating on the opposite side of the road had stopped moving. With no cars in our path, the team of adjusters raced toward the parish where we would estimate hurricane damage.

At a Holiday Inn in Alexandria that night, the storm raged around us. Soon after it passed, hundreds of claims started coming in. We spent the next eighteen days inspecting houses crushed by fallen trees, houses with missing shingles, and damaged sheds and fences. After thirteen, fourteen, or fifteen hours of work every single day, my brain was too spent to think about my daughter's current circumstances.

Every third weekend, I flew home to spend time with John and try to see Lindsey, which was hit-or-miss. By mid-November, I knew neither of my children would be home for Thanksgiving. Since I was still handling claims in Louisiana, I wouldn't be either. John flew in for the four-day weekend, and after I completed my assigned claims, we ate a turkey dinner at a local diner. My one thread of joy: knowing Michael would be home for Christmas.

And so would I. I just hoped we'd be able to convince Lindsey to be there, too.

That hope didn't become a reality. After Michael completed his first semester at UNLV, John and I picked him up at the Portland airport five days before Christmas.

"I got one A and one C, and all the rest of my classes were Bs," he said, tossing his bag on the backseat and climbing into the Camry.

John turned toward our son and patted him on the leg. "Good job," we both said. As I drove toward Silverton, we told Michael that, once again, Lindsey would not be joining us.

I had decided on a different strategy this Christmas: reverse psychology. Begging Lindsey to attend holidays and other special events hadn't worked. Guilting hadn't worked either. Maybe this year, if we acted apathetic, we might have a better outcome. So, although John and I told her we wanted her to spend the holidays with us, we also told her the decision was hers and that we'd respect it. Of course, it was all lip service on my part. I still wanted to kidnap my daughter, throw her into the backseat of our car, and speed away like a bank robber.

"Mom and I delivered her presents last week," John told Michael.

"A few days later, we received her thank-you note," I said. The blue-lined, loose-leaf paper was filled with misspelled words, and the gist was: thanks for the gifts, but she wasn't coming home. "And it had, like, a thousand Hello Kitty, Dora the Explorer, and glitter stickers all over the pages."

Michael smiled. "Sounds just like Lindsey." Then he shook his head. "She should be with family."

"I know. I know," John and I both said. Obviously, indifference hadn't worked either. The brick wall around my heart expanded. It was getting harder and harder to feel anything.

~⋌

Michael flew back to Vegas in the middle of January and started spring semester. At the end of March, right after his nineteenth birthday, we received an envelope with his distinctive handwriting—tiny letters that required us to squint to read them. Inside were two pages of college-ruled notebook paper. Michael was dropping out of UNLV. He'd sold most of his personal belongings and planned to join the military, but for now, he was flying to London so he could backpack through Europe. "While I'm still young," he wrote. He chose not to tell us sooner because he didn't want to be lectured. Michael said he loved us and hoped we'd understand why he had to do things his way.

I stared at the envelope, thinking back to the night I'd tucked him in. "You don't always have to be so perfect," I had said, realizing that all these years later he must have finally taken my words to heart. Why couldn't he have ignored that advice?

Michael told us he'd opened a credit card to buy the airfare. "Go ahead and sell my car and use the money to pay off the Visa bill," he wrote. "And PS: My sleeping bag will keep me warm in below-freezing temps, so no need to worry about me, Mom." By the time we received this message, Michael had already landed in the UK. I immediately tried his cell, but it had been disconnected. I called his roommate at UNLV and several friends. Some had heard about Michael's plans, but most didn't know the specifics, like where he was headed once he landed. No one knew the airline he'd flown or anything else to help us locate our boy. Learning that Michael was somewhere out in the world but being unable to contact him was incomprehensible to John and me.

"I guess he's fully emancipated, then," I told John, marching upstairs and into our perfect son's bedroom. He'd decorated his walls with his favorite American rock band's memorabilia:

autographed Zebrahead CDs, their cases, posters, photos, and even T-shirts. I wanted my kids to have minds of their own, but sometimes I sure as hell didn't like the ones they'd gotten.

I grabbed one of Michael's Zebrahead posters off the wall and threw it onto the floor of his closet. Then another. And another. I took each treasure off the wall, wanting to break it into teeny-tiny pieces, but I stuck all my son's collectibles in a box, out of sight. I rolled up his zebra-striped bedcover and removed the zebra bedsheets and put them in the laundry.

Over the next few days, while I transformed Michael's room into a guest room, the key word here being *guest*, John walked around the house like a zombie. When I asked him to paint over the bright splattered paint we'd used to decorate our son's walls, John took out the paintbrush and did it. When I asked him to go to the store, he went to the store. Other than that, my husband sat in front of the TV with a blank look on his face, jiggling his leg.

We visited the first counselor we could get an appointment with, hoping to understand our son's sudden rebellion. I accused John of having been too lenient. John said I'd been too strict. The counselor said we seemed like loving parents who wanted the best for our son. Neither of us had done anything wrong. Michael was making his own choices, and he'd probably make many more that we didn't agree with.

"Better get used to it," the counselor advised. "He's an adult now."

Yes, Michael was an adult now, and we both believed our son could take care of himself. He had a good head on his shoulders and the smarts to know when someone might be trying to take advantage of him. We raised him that way, so, whether or not we agreed with his recent decision, we had to let go and allow him to determine the best route for this next phase of his life.

Yet that was easier to say than to do. Especially when we didn't believe our children's decisions were wise ones. Lindsey was holed up with an older man, doing who knew what, and instead of attending college, Michael was somewhere in the United Kingdom, exploring on his own. He'd traveled outside the United States many times, but we'd always been present during those adventures.

However, the even bigger issue for us was: What if something bad happened? How could he contact us? How could we contact him? And Lindsey was in a similar situation. After Emmett closed down Sophia's Pizzeria, she often let our phone calls go to an answering machine and returned them only at her leisure, sometimes several days later. But so far, she had always called back. If we had an urgent need to talk with our daughter, John or I could drive to Longhorn Street and pound on the front door. But neither of these methods was ideal. For the moment, we had no reliable way of getting ahold of either one of our kids.

Within two weeks, Michael flew to New Hampshire and got a job at a racetrack. He'd run out of money and wasn't about to ask us to fund his trip. He knew better. When we heard our son was back in the United States, John and I were both relieved, but we wanted him to come home. We talked to him numerous times, coaxing him westward, but that wasn't what he wanted to do.

A few weeks after Michael returned, he raised his right arm during the US Air Force swearing-in ceremony and repeated the enlistment oath. Although this was an honorable decision, my husband appeared as if he were drowning in profound sadness.

I affixed my hands on my hips and blocked John's view of the television.

"I know this wasn't the path we wanted Michael to take," I said, speaking more loudly than the announcer on ESPN. "You and I both thought he would graduate from college." I took one step closer to the sofa, picked up the remote, and hit MUTE. My voice softened. "But wouldn't you feel terrible if Michael followed our dream instead of his own?" I studied my husband's long, blank face. "We want our son to be happy. That's all we've ever wanted," I said, reminding him we'd be flying to Texas in a few weeks. "We'll get to see him then. Graduating from basic training is a huge accomplishment. Don't you think?"

John stared at me and nodded, then went back to watching TV and jiggling his leg, looking as if white noise filled his head.

By the time our suitcases were packed for San Antonio, Lindsey had turned twenty-two. Without a party. She had refused to come to our house or to take another trip to the coast, so we dropped off her gifts at Emmett's place. A few days later, a handwritten thank-you note arrived in the mail. But that was it. Our daughter's situation still consumed my thoughts, but on the afternoon we drove our rental car onto Lackland Air Force Base, I was grateful to be past the angry and depressed funks John and I had been in over our son's recent antics.

The first thing I noticed when I saw my beautiful boy was his hair—or, more accurately, his lack of locks, because they were gone. The only time I'd seen Michael with less hair was on the day he was born. We all hugged and said "I love you." We hugged some more, although hugging was not exactly like it had been before Michael enlisted in the Air Force. His posture was so erect, it felt like hugging a tree. But our son's blue eyes brightened when he saw us.

We were required to attend an orientation briefing, then a parent orientation. It was a hurry-up-and-wait situation.

"Welcome to the Air Force, Mom," Michael said when I complained.

During the heat of the next day's early-morning parade, Michael and at least a thousand other airmen marched in smooth, precise formation. When they stopped, the airmen stood at attention, still as stones, faces forward. I couldn't believe my son could maintain a motionless stance in the Texas heat for thirty-some minutes, but he did.

After the ceremony, there was a base tour and a squadron open house. Although he was our son, Michael addressed us as "sir" and "ma'am" when he introduced us to his Master Sergeant. Then the sergeant presented our son with a town pass, and we took Michael and a buddy whose parents couldn't make it to San Antonio's River Walk. Both nineteen-year-olds looked handsome in their military uniforms, and even though, until now, I'd never seen my son talk or walk in such a formal manner, I kind of liked his new style. More important, I could see that Michael was pleased with and proud of his decision.

At the end of our weekend visit, John and I hugged Michael tight and told him we loved him, that we were proud of him. "Please stay safe," we said at the same time.

As the jet took off from San Antonio International, my husband and I intertwined our fingers and watched the Texas horizon become dusk, then dark. The crescent moon looked like a child's nightlight hanging in the sky. My thoughts drifted to our son's recent journey, a completely different path from the one we'd envisioned for him, but everything appeared to be working out the way he had wanted.

A few stars sprinkled across the midnight canvas, and I hoped someday Lindsey's path would pan out well for her, too. *Could I be wrong about Emmett and his motives?* I pondered for half a second, then pursed my lips and silently damned the short in my girl's neurological system. As confident as I was with my son's lifestyle choices, I sure didn't have the same faith in my daughter's.

10

~⋠ ⋟~

I dialed my daughter's number. *Maybe she'll answer this time,* I thought, pressing the phone against my ear. The rings sounded so distant. I pressed the receiver more tightly against my ear and paced the hallway, excited to tell Lindsey about the uniforms, the shiny brass buttons, and the San Antonio River Walk. Of course I planned to tell her about Michael's graduation, too. She'd always loved her younger brother, but ever since she'd hooked up with Emmett, everything about Lindsey had changed. *Hooked up. What does that even mean? She's twenty-two—why can't she see this is wrong?*

Don't get your hopes up, Linda, I told myself, twisting and untwisting a strand of hair.

The ringing ceased. *Click.* "I'm sorry. This number has been disconnected . . ." blared through the receiver. I jerked the phone away from my ear and stared at it. *Did I misdial?* I dialed the number again, more slowly, making sure I hit every button. Those three detuned ascending beeps and the same recording followed. I slammed the handset into the power base. *Is this another one of Emmett's manipulative ways to keep me from talking to my own daughter?*

I grabbed my purse and drove to Walmart, thinking about how much I hated this man. I wasn't someone who hated easily, but I hated him. Ever since I had first met Emmett and witnessed the excessive attention he paid my daughter, far more than seemed appropriate for an employer, I'd tried to be vigilant, but obviously not vigilant enough. And it seemed as if every time I figured out the rules of the game he was playing, Emmett found some new trick to isolate Lindsey from us. And no young woman should be manipulated into isolation, especially not an intellectually disabled young woman. *Especially not my daughter.*

After buying Lindsey a TracFone with extra minutes, I drove to Emmett's house and pounded on his front door. Lindsey opened it a couple inches. When she saw me standing on the front porch, she scowled. "What are you doing here?"

I caught a whiff of her scent. Dirty socks and onions. Same as last time. I frowned and peeked between the slim gap to see if Emmett lurked nearby. I could see nothing.

"I tried calling," I said, quickening my words, explaining my unannounced visit, hoping to engage my daughter in a conversation. "What happened to your house phone? It says it's disconnected."

"The company forgot to write down our payment," Lindsey said, shrugging her tremoring shoulders, blocking the entrance to their living room.

"Well," I said, pulling the prepaid phone out of the Walmart bag, "I got you your own cell." Lindsey threw open the door and stepped onto the concrete landing, squealing and jumping up and down awkwardly, clapping her hands. I ignored her stained T-shirt and too-tight sweatpants and just enjoyed my daughter's uninhibited joy. Whenever we had given her a gift, she'd generally responded with excitement, but if the gift offered her additional independence and responsibility, her responses were often more animated. "You can buy minutes every month when I give you your Social Security money," I said, grinning, then explained how to use the 800 number.

Lindsey called several times the first week. We chatted, laughed, even scheduled a lunch date. In my head, I was already taking her shopping and buying her clothes that fit, that didn't smell. It was wonderful to hear her former self: the cheerful, talkative young lady she'd been before she met Emmett. I started to feel hopeful that she might be back in our lives on a regular basis.

Then Lindsey canceled lunch and the calls stopped.

I received a letter from her saying she had given the phone to Emmett. "So he can use it for business," she wrote. "Quit bothering us. Leave us alone."

That night I dreamed Emmett cut off my daughter's hands.

I woke in a panic at four a.m., saturated in sweat. Hyperventilating, I hurried into the kitchen and grabbed a lunch sack. For the next few minutes, I inhaled, then exhaled, into a brown paper bag. *It was just a dream. Calm down.* But every time I closed my eyes, images of a handless Lindsey invaded the black space in my head, and I wondered if the dream could be a premonition of something worse.

I continued to snoop in their business, reasoning that if I found proof Emmett had a history of abuse, law enforcement would have to intervene. When I located Emmett's ex-wife online, I didn't know whether she'd confirm or calm some of my worst fears, but I had to find out. I dialed the number and reached his ex's grown son.

"She's afraid of him," he said, refusing to pass on any message. "I'd already left home when my mom got involved with the guy. I don't have any firsthand information."

After the line went dead, my imagination turned feral. I envisioned one violent scenario after another and wondered what could have possibly driven Lindsey into such an abusive relationship. I knew children of abusers often paired up with abusers as adults, but I didn't think Marty, my first husband and Lindsey's biological father, had ever physically harmed her. He'd been distant, absent, maybe even neglectful, but surely not abusive. Once, when Lindsey was two, soon after John and I had married, I'd worried, though.

Marty had carried Lindsey into my parents' house after his weekend visit. She didn't squeal with delight when she spied her grandpa, and she whimpered when I took off her coat. Her left arm hung limp, bruised, swollen.

"Lindsey fell out of bed," Marty said. When I questioned why he hadn't taken her to the doctor, he told me, "She didn't act like she needed to go." I interrogated more, but Marty wasn't sure how or why she'd fallen. "A seizure, maybe?" he said finally, before leaving the house in a huff. *Of course he'd use that excuse,* I fumed. It had been only a few months since her grand mal seizure, and Marty hadn't been around much during that time.

John and I drove straight to Silverton Hospital, where the emergency room technician x-rayed Lindsey's upper arm. Fractured humerus. An ER doctor molded a cast to fit Lindsey's small arm. He didn't believe the injury was from falling out of bed. "If such a scenario actually happened," he said, "it should have broken here." He pointed at her tiny wrist. "So I need to report this to Children's Services."

A week later, the caseworker's investigation found no physical abuse. "The injury was unavoidable," she said.

I never did find out what really happened to Lindsey on that visit. Soon after, though, Marty quit showing up for his scheduled weekends and disappeared from her life until she was sixteen, when he called me out of the blue and said he'd recently had a heart attack and wanted to see his daughter. Their visit went well. Lindsey loved the heart-shaped necklace Marty had bought for her, but she was especially giddy about the promise he made to visit her regularly from that day forward. In fact, he set a date with her in two weeks.

When the day came, Lindsey put on a flowered red dress, white tights, and black flats. She fixed her hair with a stretchy red headband. "I want to look special," she said.

Then she waited.

And waited.

I fussed in the kitchen, checking on Lindsey every few minutes. Marty never called, and he didn't show up, either. Nor did he answer his phone when I tried calling him. Hours later, when Lindsey slipped off the red dress, I saw her tears. I tried to hug her, but she shrugged so hard it knocked my hands off her shoulders. Lindsey kept wearing the heart-shaped necklace, but she never asked to see her father again. And with his next child-support check, Marty enclosed a short note: "I've moved to Georgia."

Years after that day, when I learned Marty had died, I felt no sorrow, no pain, nothing. I'd lost respect for him the moment Lindsey had hung her red dress back in the closet. That would be the last time I'd let him disappoint my daughter.

As much as I disliked my ex-husband, I didn't believe he was an abuser or that Lindsey's current situation was his fault, but my mind spun with possibilities. *Would Lindsey allow someone to harm her physically?* As much as I hated to admit it, I'd struck my daughter once. When she was twelve.

It happened several years before Marty had let her down for the last time. Whenever Lindsey was angry, she tended to fixate on our divorce. I came through the door that evening, my mind ablaze with my to-do list: details for the upcoming photo shoot for the next Country Neighbors catalog, what to cook for dinner, and household chores that had gone by the wayside for far too long.

Although the fall night was blustery, John had gone to the Silverton Foxes football game and Michael was at a sleepover.

As I slipped off my yellow raincoat and hung it in the closet, Lindsey appeared with a demand I'd memorized by then. "I wanna horse!"

"That's not possible." I felt exhausted. I'd already put in sixty-six hours at the warehouse since Monday, and there was still more work to do. There was always more to do. And now Lindsey was demanding a horse. Again. For the fifth time that week. I sighed.

"I wanna ride a horse. I can take care of a horse. I promise!"

"We don't have room for a horse. Horses are expensive," I explained. Just like I'd explained every other time. "A horse needs room to graze, to gallop." My sixth-grader did not seem to grasp the reasons that reinforced the word *no*.

I walked into the kitchen with Lindsey on my heels. My baggy sweatpants were stiff with dried paint splatters from all the custom craft orders I'd painted at the warehouse, but I was too tired to change clothes. The sweatshirt waistband inched upward. I pulled it down, stretching it over my expanding bottom. *I need to go on a diet*, I thought, hurrying into the kitchen.

"You're never around when I need you," Lindsey lectured, arms and head tremoring. With every word, her voice increased in volume. When I stopped moving, Lindsey stood within inches of my body. "Work's more im-por-tant than me!" Her voice pierced the kitchen air. She planted a hand on each hip, then inhaled so sharply, a loud gulp came out of her throat.

"Stop yelling." I yanked a pan from the cupboard, trying to maintain my composure but failing miserably. "Work is not more important." I turned on the water and filled the saucepan, reexplaining that I was busier than normal because, on top of my regular business responsibilities, I was also searching for new crafts to sell, hiring a photographer, designing backdrops, and writing product descriptions for our catalog. "This is temporary, Lindsey. You know that." I pulled a jar of Prego out of the pantry. "I'm going to make spaghetti. You can talk to me while I cook." I hoped food would divert her rage.

"No! You divorced my real dad." She screamed more loudly and stepped closer. Spittle sprayed from her mouth.

"Lindsey!" I wiped my neck with the back of my hand. "You're in time-out! Go to your room!" My voice rose as I washed my hands and snatched a pound of hamburger from the fridge. I grabbed a skillet from the cupboard and slammed it on the stove. "You can come out when you change your attitude."

"You can't make me." Lindsey locked her knees and crossed her arms, holding them tight against her chest. "And why can't I have a horse? I wanna horse." Her eyes narrowed. She glared, refusing to budge.

Rain banged at the dining room window and wind pelted water against the skylight. *My daughter is not going to talk to me this way. Not tonight.* I grabbed her arm. She jerked away, turning her back toward me. I reached out and encircled her torso with my arms. Lindsey stiffened her frame. I held on more tightly, planning to drag her rigid body out of our caboose-style kitchen, through the dining room, down the four-step hall, and into her room. She squirmed and kicked her heel against my shin. I lost my grip. I lunged at Lindsey's waist and tried to hold on. She wiggled from my grasp and tumbled to the floor, chaotically slapping at the air and at me. I stepped back. *This isn't good. Walk away.*

Lindsey's hands flapped until they found my leg. She gripped my ankle and held on tight. When I stepped, her prone body dragged along the laminate flooring. Lindsey pulled my leg to her mouth, and her teeth grazed my calf.

"Let go! Stop it!" I bellowed, more loudly than I remembered ever having done. I felt unbalanced standing on one leg, shaking the other, as I tried to loosen my daughter's grip.

Lindsey scrambled off the floor, tailing me as I took long strides toward the back door. Instead of heading outside, I turned right, into my home office. Lindsey followed, her words taunting me, her breath hot against my neck.

I turned around and stood face-to-face with my daughter. Her eyes darted; her mouth twitched. My body froze. My arms and shoulders felt heavy and stiff, like steel.

"Go. To. Your. Room," I said, low and livid. The throaty sounds came from deep in my gut. The only things moving on my body were my lips. Outside, a rhododendron bush scraped against the window glass. For a moment, the lights flickered in the office.

"No!" she said, her face red, her breath hot. "I hate you! You divorced my bi-logical dad." *Gasp.* "You should not of divorced him." Lindsey loved John. I knew she used this ploy only when she ran out of other things to quarrel about. The wind smacked the siding. The windowpane banged so hard I wondered if it would break. I shook my head. This wasn't the evening I had envisioned. I fixed my hands on my hips and glared. "Go to your room!"

She took one step closer. "You can't make me!"

"Shut up!" I shouted, screaming words we'd forbidden in our home. "Just shut up!" I was the mother, and my daughter was going to mind me.

"You can't tell me that! It's against the rules. I *hate* you!"

My right hand rose.

It swung back, and, in what seemed like a slow-motion film, my hand met the skin on the side of my daughter's face.

Hard.

The lights blinked again; then the room turned pitch black.

We stood in darkness, inches away from each other, silent

and breathing heavily. My hand stung. I no longer heard the wind or the rain.

The house stayed eerily black for several seconds. Lightning flashed. When the lights flickered back on, Lindsey's cobalt eyes widened. Her movie-star lashes fluttered. The skin near her eye flamed red.

"I'm sorry." I felt numb, nauseous. I dropped my gaze away from my daughter. I couldn't bear to see the swelling on the side of her face. My body shook. Lindsey didn't cry. She glared. Her eyes filled with hatred.

"You're in big trouble, Mom," she said, turning and strutting out of the office. When she slammed her bedroom door, the house vibrated.

I stood in the office and replayed the last moments in my head. *I'm definitely in big trouble.*

Lindsey was asleep when I met John at the door.

"I slapped her across the face." When I saw my husband's bleak expression, I averted my eyes toward the carpet. "I think she'll have a bruise." I relayed the events of the evening, and John scratched his chin, but he didn't say anything. What could he say? I'd already mentally pummeled myself harder than he possibly could.

In the morning, shades of black and purple and gray covered Lindsey's swollen left eye. *And I caused it.* I ran to the bathroom and vomited. My stomach churned and tightened. I puked again, curling into a ball on the bathroom floor. *How did I let this happen? I'm a thirty-four-year-old adult. I don't hit my kids.* I'd be lying if I said I'd never wanted to. There definitely had been moments, but I'd never acted. Now I knew why. I felt like I'd abused my child.

I shuffled out of the bathroom, shivering. "Lindsey, I should not have slapped you. I'm sorry."

Lindsey pointed to her face. "You gave me a black eye."

I still felt nauseated, but there was nothing left to purge.

"I know," I said, choking on my words. "I was wrong. I love you." Shamed, I looked away. "May I give you a hug?" I opened my arms. Lindsey nodded, stepping into my embrace. I squeezed her tight, repeating my apologies, afraid to ask for forgiveness. I didn't deserve it.

John and I talked at length. He was worried someone might call Child Protective Services. So far, over his teaching career, he had witnessed only two severe cases of abuse. In one situation, CPS had removed the child from the home. "They did an investigation and determined the boy's home life wasn't safe," John said, jiggling his leg faster. "We'd probably be okay. But you never know."

He suggested I take Lindsey to the coast for a week. My heart raced. Tears pooled in my eyes. I pressed my hands against my face, considering my husband's proposal. His intentions were good, his idea appealing. I could run away until all the dreadful, disgusting evidence was gone. *Yeah, that would be the easy way to handle this situation.*

But I couldn't run away. It would teach my daughter the wrong lesson. Besides, I reasoned, Lindsey could never be sworn to secrecy. Nor should she be. She'd tell anyone who'd listen, "My mom gave me a black eye." I'd rather be honest, take responsibility, and, I hoped, not suffer too-great consequences.

Long before the beginning school bell buzzed Monday morning, I dabbed concealer around my girl's eye, trying to camouflage the bruise, but finally gave up when the makeup made it worse. When we walked through the double front doors and headed to the school counselor's office, Lindsey held my hand. I plodded into the room, terrified the school would call CPS and they'd take my daughter away immediately.

Beneath the fluorescent lights, Ms. Brown moved two blue

kiddie seats directly across from her swivel chair. I'd summarized the situation when I'd made the appointment, so Ms. Brown started the conversation.

"This is unfamiliar territory for me, Mrs. Atwell." Ms. Brown's red lips formed words as they opened and closed. I couldn't take my eyes off her mouth.

When Ms. Brown leaned her petite frame forward, her chin-length pageboy shifted forward too. Her brown eyes focused on my blue ones. "I've never had a parent request a meeting such as this," she said. "Generally, parents wait until they're summoned by the principal or Children's Services." Ms. Brown sounded concerned but tender. I relaxed a bit. She turned toward my daughter and said, "Would you like to tell me what happened, Lindsey?"

Lindsey looked down at her hands and pinched the tips of her fingers. "I wanted a horse."

I pressed my lips together in a straight line and concentrated on my daughter's explanation.

"My mom brought home work to do and I got mad because I can't have a horse and I kicked and hit my mom. I bit her leg, too." Lindsey pinched the tips of her fingers and picked at her cuticles.

I stared at my sweatpant-covered thighs and listened. My index finger drew circles on top of the stretchy cotton fabric.

"I'm not supposed to hit or kick or bite. It's not ap-pro-pri-ate behavior," Lindsey said, her arms and head tremored. "My mom told me to go to my room, but I didn't. Then she slapped me and gave me this black eye." Lindsey's hand went right to her face and pointed at the bruise.

When it was my turn to speak, the only thing I added was, "The lights went out at the exact moment my hand made contact with her skin." I don't know why I felt the need to share that oddity, but I did. "Obviously, I need better parenting skills." My fingertip drew more circles on my sweatpants. "I never want a situation to escalate to this level ever again."

Ms. Brown suggested a counselor we'd used in the past. "Can I count on you to make an appointment soon?" A bell rang in the hall. I nodded as Ms. Brown stood and started toward the door, promising to speak with the principal, as well as Lindsey's teacher, and let them know this was an unusual situation. "I'll follow up with you in about a week," she said, putting her hand on the doorknob and twisting. "Of course, we have to stay alert in cases like this, but I hope I'll never see you in my office again." Her red lips formed a half smile. I shook her hand and thanked her, feeling certain she never would.

And she never did. Although Lindsey and I had other arguments, they never turned physical again. I had learned my lesson, and I hoped Lindsey had learned that anyone who hits has to take responsibility for her actions. If she never learned anything else from me, I hope she learned that.

~~❧~~

My daughter remained tight-lipped about her relationship with Emmett. During our rare, standing-on-their-front-porch visits, whenever I asked questions, she'd say, "Emmett says our life is personal." Once, without any prodding, she told me, "Emmett takes pictures of me. He has video equipment. He likes working on the intranet."

My heart beat faster and faster. "Are you wearing clothes?" I said, sucking in deep, uneven breaths, wondering if he put pornographic pictures of my daughter online. "When he takes your pictures?" My voice filled with alarm. Emmett didn't seem like a skilled Internet guru. On the other hand, why were his windows covered in tinfoil?

"Yes, I always wear clothes." Lindsey scrunched her face, as if the thought of taking naked pictures wouldn't be good. I wanted to feel relief, but I remained skeptical. If Emmett allowed us regular participation in Lindsey's life, if he didn't keep my daughter so isolated, if he let her come around for holidays and birthdays, maybe the lines of communication would open a crack and some of my anxieties would ease.

⌁

My year on the catastrophe team had ended, and I was working claims back in the Willamette Valley when, one fall Saturday, Bonnie, Emmett's across-the-street neighbor, called. I peered through my kitchen window, staring at the red oak we'd planted when we'd first moved in. The leaves were fiery orange and waiting for the first strong gust to knock them off the tree's branches. "I think they're moving," she said, telling me lots of furniture had been carried out of the house the day before. "And today, there's a red truck." She sounded like a private eye as she described the company's insignia. "I wrote everything down," she said, spelling the firm's name. I grabbed a piece of scratch paper and scribbled as fast as I could.

The route to Emmett's place had become familiar to me. I headed west on Hazelgreen, turned left on Cordon Road, ignoring the posted speed limits. I passed a pumpkin field and a maze built with hundreds of bales of hay. A farmer was harvesting a late-season crop on a John Deere tractor, but I didn't try to guess which one or gawk like I usually did. There wasn't time. When I reached the cul-de-sac, the red truck was gone.

I pounded on the door. When Lindsey answered, she opened it enough to stick her head through.

"Are you moving?" My voice trembled as I spoke. "Or did you just sell your furniture?"

"It's none of your business," she said. "That's personal." Lindsey glared at me, and I glared back. The silence didn't last long before she blurted, "We got two hundred and fifty dollars for everything!"

"Everything?" I said, breathless. Many of Lindsey's pieces were gifts from family members. It would cost several thousand dollars to replace them all. How could she have let Emmett sell her things?

"What about Grammy's quilt?" I clenched my fists, thinking how Lindsey's great-grandmother had stitched the rainbow-colored sampler by hand and given it to Lindsey before she died. "And Grandma's photo album?" I gritted my teeth, waiting. My back muscles turned into hot, burning knots. "Did you sell those?" My brow grew tense. I was afraid to hear the answer.

"I still have 'em." Lindsey's body hid in the shadows behind the door. "They're in the house." I asked to see them and suggested she let me take them back to Silverton for safekeeping.

"I don't know where they're at right now." Lindsey shook her head and closed the door.

I stood on Emmett's porch, staring at the faded salmon door. I remembered Lindsey telling me Emmett had forced her to call all of her perceived high school pals. "I'm with Emmett now," she had said. "I can't be part of your life no more." Another time she said, "Emmett doesn't like me to have mem-ries of my past."

I walked back to the car, imagining Emmett towering over Lindsey, ordering her, "Tear up those pictures! *Now!*" I visualized my girl removing a precious photo from the album, ripping it in two, and throwing the pieces into a roaring fire. The thought of her grandmother's album or great-grandmother's quilt being dumped like they had no value tormented me. I wanted to protect my daughter, to save her and her priceless possessions, but I couldn't.

That night I lay in the dark, tossing and turning, agonizing about Lindsey, the quilt, and the photo album.

"If she sold them, it's a done deal," John said Sunday morning. "What can we do about it now?"

Instead of answering my husband's questions, I grabbed the Yellow Pages and looked up the name of a used-furniture store. When I found the address, I drove in constant drizzle to South Salem. The place was closed, but two oversize plate-glass windows displayed Lindsey's pine armoire, denim futon, wicker rocker, and two end tables. Kraft paper tags had been taped to all the items.

I placed both hands on the glass and leaned forward, straining to see the felt-tip-pen prices. The amounts were a fraction of what we'd originally paid. Family and friends had been generous at Christmas, her birthday, and graduation—all so Lindsey's cottage would be furnished with comfortable, beautiful items. My breath fogged up the glass, but I didn't step away from the window. *I'll buy everything back and put it into storage. Then it will be waiting for her—when she comes home.* Tears stung my eyes, and the salty stream reached my lips. Snot ran from my nose. *But why? Why should I do that?* A shudder raced through my body. Lindsey apparently didn't treasure the furnishings any longer.

But she had. Once. I remembered how Lindsey's face beamed when the matching pine dresser and armoire were purchased. She helped place the futon, TV stand, and rocker in her living room. She wrote hand-printed thank-you notes, carefully spelling words, telling the giver what she'd bought and where she'd put it. Most recipients probably had difficulty reading the notes, but she thanked them nonetheless. And my girl had kept the cottage and herself meticulously cleaned and cared for. Everything had had a place.

But now everything was gone.

"I've lost my daughter." I stood on the sidewalk and shivered. I bent over and grabbed my stomach. "I've lost my daughter."

Cars on Twelfth Street whizzed by. I crumbled to my knees, staring through the plate-glass windows at Lindsey's things. I wanted to pound the pavement and yell at the top of my lungs. The long, painful noise that came out of my mouth scared me. I didn't know where it came from.

Why am I so involved? I chided myself. *Why am I taking ownership of things I no longer have control over? This should be Lindsey's pain.* My jaw clenched tightly. My fist pounded on the left side of my chest. *I've truly lost my daughter.*

I forced myself to get up off the cold, hard concrete. I turned and looked through the plate-glass window one last time. Instead of seeing Lindsey's things, I spotted the reflection of a tired, tear-stained, middle-aged woman staring back at me. Snot sullied her upper lip. I swiped my coat sleeve across my mouth. "It's just stuff." I smoothed my frizzed hair, trying to make the female in the window match the picture in my head. It was useless. I turned away. *If the furnishings no longer mean anything to Lindsey, why am I allowing them to mean something to me?* I didn't look back when I walked to the Camry, climbed in, and drove home.

The wall of bricks around my heart turned into a fortress. The emotions behind the clay rectangles hurtled into a dark, cold abyss. My thoughts operated like a broken album, replaying the same unhealthy song over and over. I would never stop loving Lindsey or trying to rescue her, but the torch of constant worry I'd carried for the past two years had to be extinguished or I'd go full-blown crazy. For my sanity, I had to take a step back.

11

❧ ⚜ ❧

or me, taking a step back meant filling up my days with insurance work. That way, I didn't have time to think about how much I wanted things to be different. I rejoined the catastrophe team, and Farmers would send me to Austin or Minneapolis or Phoenix or Denver to pay for hail damage. John continued to teach junior high students and coach three sports. We talked on the phone every evening; then every third weekend I flew home for what we began dubbing "our conjugal visit."

When winter approached, Lindsey refused to come home for yet another Thanksgiving; then she passed on Christmas, too. Michael was stationed at Kadena Air Force Base in Okinawa, Japan. After a bit of begging from me, John agreed that we could could travel for roughly eighteen hours across the Pacific Ocean, just so I wouldn't be childless for another holiday season. Once my husband was in, I tried to tempt Lindsey to go along, too. I found myself again standing on Emmett's front porch, straining to convince my daughter to choose us. Over him.

"You'd see your brother," I said. "And he'd love to see you." Lindsey's expression remained blank. I searched for words that might sway her to my way of thinking and suddenly remembered her obsession with Sanrio's most popular product. "Hello Kitty is made in Japan. They'll be everywhere!"

My twenty-two-year-old smiled for a moment, then shook

her head no. "I don't travel so well," she said. Her words cart-wheeled my memories back to the year Lindsey was fourteen and we drove to Canada. At that time, I didn't quite understand the importance of maintaining a strict schedule in Lindsey's life. I didn't yet understand how much travel disrupted that schedule, and because of the darn short in Lindsey's neurological system, I certainly didn't know how hard it was for her simply to go along with the spontaneous flow of a family road trip.

That particular vacation started off with Lindsey's protest-ing having to sit in her regular place in the minivan. After our fourteen-year-old finally buckled herself into the middle seat, we said she could pick where we ate lunch, hoping that honor would improve her mood. But our daughter sat in the Denny's booth, pouting, whining that nothing on the menu sounded good to her. Later, during a walking tour in Seattle, she lagged behind, and John and I had to nag her to keep up. By the time we arrived at our Best Western hotel in Vancouver, BC, everyone was exhausted. We ate dinner and went to bed, eager for a new day and a fresh start.

At 7:00 a.m., far earlier than my preferred vacation morning start, sunbeams sifted through the cream-colored sheers. I threw back the sheets and placed my bare feet on the paisley carpet.

"Let's go sightseeing!" I touched my son's shoulder, tickling him until he tumbled out of bed. When I rubbed Lindsey's arm, she opened her eyes, sat upright and squinted, then lay back down. "Lindsey, time to get moving."

John, Michael, and I bustled between the room and bath, showering, dressing, and brushing teeth. Lindsey pulled the cov-ers over her head. Nice wasn't working. I tried an approach the counselor had recommended: I counted to ten. I visited an exotic beach in my mind and counted to ten once more. I clenched my teeth. "Linds. You have fifteen minutes."

John shook Lindsey's pajama-covered shoulder. "Get up, sleepyhead," he said. "We're going to breakfast."

"Hurry up." I sat on the bed and waited.

Moving like a sloth, Lindsey gathered scattered pieces of clothing. "I forgot my morning list!" she screeched.

"You're fourteen. You know your routine by heart," I said. It had never dawned on me to pack the laminated sheet of paper; in fact, I hadn't even seen her use it lately. Or maybe she did, but I just didn't know it. "You'll be fine," I said, my patience waning. I forced myself to reach out and touch Lindsey's shoulder lightly before she disappeared into the bathroom. Michael turned on the television. John moved the suitcases closer to the door, then slumped in an upholstered chair. He scratched his chin and jiggled his leg.

Minutes passed. My neck and shoulders knotted. I rapped on the door. "Hurry up! Ten minutes left." Lindsey grunted.

Six more minutes ticked by.

Michael knocked on the door. "Open up, Linds. I gotta go." He crossed his legs and rocked back and forth.

"Leave me alone!" Lindsey's words reverberated through the bathroom door. Someone in another room pounded on the wall.

I stomped over to the bathroom and lowered my voice. "Come out, now." I tapped on the wood casing. "You're disturbing the neighbors."

"Leave me alone!" she screamed. The room on the other side joined in on the pounding. Our walls were being banged in stereo. My teeth clamped together. I tightened my fists. The muscles in my neck and back burned.

"Lindsey. Come. Out. Of. The. Bathroom. Now." My volume increased with every word. John's deep voice mimicked mine. The door swung open. Lindsey stood in the doorway, wearing her Strawberry Shortcake baby dolls.

"What in the world were you doing in there?" I said, my tone frigid as dry ice. I wanted to swat Lindsey but knew she'd scream even more loudly, and the neighbors were already unhappy with us. Besides, I couldn't—I'd promised never to strike my daughter again—so I held my arms tight against my sides.

"Who cares if she's wearing pajamas?" John didn't wait for an answer. "We're leaving." Michael scurried past me and closed the bathroom door.

Bang. Bang. Bang.

"Fine," I said. "You're going in pajamas!"

"No, I'm *not*! I'll change."

Bang. Bang.

I grabbed her Barbie suitcase and stuffed Lindsey's underwear inside. "We're not waiting any longer." Lindsey snatched a shirt from my hands; I tugged it from hers and shoved it into the suitcase. Lindsey held one leg of her pants; I seized the other.

Bang. Bang. Bang.

"Lindsey!" My teeth were clenched so tightly, I worried they might crack. I didn't move any other muscle in my face except my lips when I said, "You've. Had. Plenty. Of. Time. We're. Leaving. Now."

The toilet flushed. Water gushed. Michael sprinted from the bathroom, wiping his wet hands on his T-shirt. He grabbed his duffel and backpack and stood by the exit, shifting from foot to foot.

The blood vessels in my husband's temples swelled. "We're going home!" he said, throwing open the door.

Bang. Bang. Bang.

John jerked two bags off the floor and held one in each hand. He hustled down the hall, and Michael followed close behind, trying to catch his dad's long, angry strides. I rushed out, wanting to leave before the neighbors came out to see who had made all the noise in room 323. Lindsey followed, surprising me. At that moment, I didn't care if she stayed at the hotel forever.

I sat in the minivan, gripping the steering wheel, a silent rage brewing inside me. I felt crazy-angry, the kind that kept me from thinking straight. Days before, Lindsey had appeared excited about this adventure, chatting it up and asking questions, but when the actual day had arrived, she'd turned moody and dragged the entire family into her misery.

I drove the Canadian highway with three properly clothed people and one who wore nighttime attire. Worried, I glanced at John. His eyes stared straight ahead, his lips pressed together. I knew he was furious Lindsey had never gotten dressed. Furthermore, he hated it when she acted disrespectful toward me. I also fretted about Michael. Now he wasn't going to see any of the Canadian sites we'd promised. I felt certain that if he was agitated at all, it was because Lindsey had not come out of the bathroom when he needed to use it. I checked the rearview mirror. Michael held a paperback book in both hands, his eyes riveted on the pages. He wasn't focused on the volcanic rumblings taking place in the front of our van.

Lindsey sat in the middle seat, tremoring. I figured she was angry because we had made her wear pajamas, instead of street clothes. Her eyes darted right and left. Her face twitched. She was probably compiling excuses for her unacceptable behavior, but I wasn't in any mood to hear that same old soundtrack. The lone conversation was the breakfast order yelled into the metal speaker at a McDonald's drive-through. We were going straight home. Spent. No Gastown, no Stanley Park, no zoo, and, if I could help it, there would never, ever be another vacation with Lindsey Jane Atwell.

"Mom, you scare me when you show your alligator teeth," Lindsey said, spreading her Egg McMuffin wrapper flat to lick some melted cheese off it.

"My what?" *My teeth aren't that big. Are they?* I peered in the rearview mirror and forced a smile so I could examine my choppers.

"When you talk with your lips"—my daughter sounded more matter-of-fact than angry—"you show all your teeth."

"You kind of do, honey." John grinned at Lindsey's description.

I thought about her words. When I allowed my daughter to push my buttons, every muscle in my body froze, except my lips. I pronounced every syllable, making sure Lindsey had no chance of misunderstanding my words or directions.

"Thanks, Lindsey." My tone sounded staccato. I hated who I became when my daughter didn't mind. And I hated how she disrupted our family's fun, turning pleasant moments into pissy ones.

But on this day, as I stood on Emmett's front porch, trying to convince my daughter to come to Okinawa with us, I was willing to risk another one of her meltdowns.

"I don't wanna go," Lindsey finally said. "But tell Michael I love him." She closed the salmon-colored door, leaving me standing outside alone.

～

On December 25, the young fellow who picked us up at Naha Airport was an erect-postured airman with a fresh crew cut laced with tiny specks of gray hair, just like his dad had at the same age. Michael loaded our luggage into the trunk of a used Honda Civic he'd bought without any parental guidance. He left the airport, driving on the left side of the road toward Kadena Air Force Base. I clutched the door handle, certain Michael would end up back on the familiar right side of the white line, but our son drove with confidence, and I relaxed a little and peered out the window.

"It's a Hello Kitty haven," I said, as Michael followed a

minivan with a pink decal stuck to the rear window. We passed a billboard advertising the kitten and her friends.

"The local mall is filled with the stuff," Michael said, laughing. "You won't have any trouble finding something for Lindsey."

Okinawa was just as I had imagined it would be, and it made me miss my daughter more. I snapped a couple pictures of Hello Kitty to show Lindsey. I wished she loved to travel. I so wanted to show her the world.

Michael stopped on the side of the road to buy sushi from a vending machine. John and I glanced at each other, scrunching our noses at the same time, wondering if the right kid had picked us up at the airport.

"You eat sushi?" John asked, making a sour face.

"Yep. Want some?" Michael handed the white tray to John, but my guy shook his head. Raw fish had never touched my husband's lips, and due to his finicky eating habits, I knew it never would.

"That's not my idea of Christmas dinner," John said.

"We don't have that many choices on the base." Our son tossed another piece of sushi into his mouth. "We do have a Chili's."

I patted our carry-on. "We brought you a Home Place pizza."

Michael peered into the rearview mirror. "Really?" He raised his eyebrows and grinned. "That's the best Christmas present ever!" Finishing off the last piece of sushi, he tossed the container onto the floor of the backseat by my feet, then slowed for a little Okinawan woman crossing the street, carrying a dog. "I wish you could've brought Arthur, too," Michael said, pointing at the black-and-white pooch lazing in the woman's arms. The dog turned its head in our direction. "He looks exactly like Art." John and I nodded in agreement as our man-child turned the Civic onto Kadena Air Force Base. "Now that Lindsey's living with Emmett, who's taking care of him?" Michael flashed his military credentials at the gate guard, and we passed through.

"The neighbors," I said, wishing we could have counted on Lindsey to help us out. Up until she moved in with Emmett, whenever Lindsey came into the house, Arthur followed her from room to room. "I think he likes me the most," she'd say. We all teased each other about being Art's favorite, but, honestly, whichever family member was nearby at the moment (or was eating and might lose a morsel of food on the ground) was the person Art loved most. Still, there certainly wasn't any harm in letting Lindsey believe she was the dog's best friend.

During the next eight days, Michael introduced us to his superiors and Air Force buddies and showed us the flight line where he worked. Whenever he wasn't on duty, he morphed into a tour guide, driving us to Shurijo Castle, a local craft village, the Peace Museum, and Tomari International Cemetery. One afternoon, as we headed back to Kadena, Michael slid in a Zebrahead CD and cranked the volume so high, I had to cover my ears.

"Turn it down, Michael," John yelled. "It's too loud."

Our son scowled. "My car, my rules," he said. His fingers tapped the steering wheel a couple times. "Isn't that what you've always told me?" Michael was referring to the comments we'd made to him when he was a youngster after he'd complained about our song choices—not about the volume at which we played them. I didn't want to turn this issue into an unpleasant argument, but I didn't want to damage my eardrums, either. I thought Michael should be respectful. After all, we'd flown halfway across the world—or at least it felt that way—to see him. A couple seconds later, Michael grabbed the volume knob and twisted, lowering the racket to a reasonable decibel, low enough that we could hear each other talk. I knew he was trying to prove he was an adult now and could do things his own way, but that wasn't the right way to do it.

That night at Chili's, I shared my thoughts. Our son reluctantly agreed we would never share the same taste in tunes, so he wouldn't listen to music while we were in the car. The next day, though, Michael slid in another Zebrahead CD, picked a song he thought we'd like, and turned the volume to a reasonable level. As it turned out, our son was right. We liked the easy-listening selection he'd found. John and I agreed we wouldn't buy the CD, but at least it felt like we had resolved our first disagreement as adults in a civilized manner.

Time with our boy child was coming to an end. We spent our final afternoon bowling at Emery Lanes on Kadena. John had beat us all—including a couple of Michael's friends who joined in on the fun. Later, we dined off base at Tony Roma's. I was surprised by the number of familiar American restaurants doing business in Okinawa, though, considering how many Americans were stationed at the two military bases on the island, maybe I shouldn't have been. Afterward, we went inside the mall and bought Lindsey a new Hello Kitty backpack to replace the rather ratty one she'd been using for the past few years. Michael helped pick out matching notepads, pencils, stickers—any souvenir decorated with Lindsey's all-time-favorite character—and I tucked them inside.

"She's going to be so surprised!" I said.

"Really?" Michael said. "Don't you always buy her Hello Kitty stuff?"

Our son made a valid point. "You're right," I said. "She probably won't be too surprised, but she *is* going to love everything."

The next morning, with several hours to kill before our flight departed, Michael drove to a viewpoint overlooking one of the white-sand beaches he favored. The skies were clear and blue.

John and I stood on the cliff, holding hands, watching a local family stroll barefoot along the shore. The two kids rolled their pants up above their knees and darted in and out of the surf, screeching and laughing.

"They grow up so fast," John said, using his free hand to rub Michael's back.

"When it's hot, I snorkel over there," Michael said, pointing toward a small reef. It was the perfect place for snorkeling. The ocean was an exquisite aqua color; I would have loved to dive in. "Remember when you taught us, Mom? The day Lindsey bought two hats in Mexico?" Our son laughed, and the Okinawa wind carried the sound toward the sea. "She was so funny."

John and I chuckled, too. I was tickled that Michael still snorkeled on occasion but happier he had positive childhood memories. I'd always worried our boy had felt lost in our family unit, especially since Lindsey required so much parental atten-tion. But the vacation he referred to, cruising to the Mexican Rivera with my parents, had turned out to be one of the high-lights of Lindsey's fourteenth year, and, apparently, Michael's year, too.

"Don't touch. Just look," I had warned, spitting into the face mask and rubbing saliva around. Michael's and Lindsey's faces crumpled in disgust, but both kids copied my actions. I rinsed the mask in salt water and snapped it over my eyes and nose. The kids did the same. Ten-year-old Michael jumped in the water and was off exploring. My dad worked with Lindsey a while longer, but her mask fogged and she couldn't master breathing through a tube. She threw the equipment on the sand. Then, without any eye protection, Lindsey kicked and glided and twirled her slender body in the salty sea, trailing blue and yellow fish. I watched her for a few moments in awe. When my girl was in the water, her tremors seemed to disappear.

Thirty minutes later, we'd all finished snorkeling. Lindsey rubbed a blue-and-white cruise-ship towel back and forth against her skin. "The fish were so pretty," she said, stepping into a pair of lime-green polyester shorts. She pulled them up, stretching the elastic band high above her natural waistline. The knit fabric clung to her damp thighs and wet bathing suit.

A Mexican vendor approached and waved. He flashed sterling silver earrings, straw sombreros, and knockoff sunglasses in our direction. Another vendor opened his arms and displayed his wares, too.

"Blanket, ladee?"

I peeked at my watch. We had to get back to the ship. Lindsey pointed at a sombrero.

"All prices are negotiable," I said, explaining the bartering process. "It's not like back home. Do you want help?"

"I wanna do my own nego-tating." Lindsey shook her head at me, tugging a lime-green T-shirt over her wet head.

"Negotiating."

Her bare feet hopped back and forth on the sand. John pulled a pair of lime-green flip-flops out of her backpack, and Lindsey steadied her body against mine and slipped them on. I hadn't noticed until now, but her outfit screamed, *American tourist.* I chuckled, thinking she apparently planned to add a straw sunhat to her ensemble.

The family posse waited under the shade of a large palm tree, discussing Lindsey's strategy and hoping she'd be quick. Shaking, Lindsey pulled several one dollar bills from her Hello Kitty wallet and counted deliberately. Then she shook her head and turned away, stuffing the bills in the pocket of her soggy shorts.

"Great—we can go." I looked at my watch. We all gathered our beach bags and took five steps.

"Ladee," the vendor yelled. "Okay. Two dolla. Ladee. I'll take two dolla." We stopped because Lindsey stopped. She pulled wet bills from her pocket. Her hands tremored. She counted out two American dollars, shook her head, and stuffed the greenbacks out of sight. I knew my daughter wasn't doing this on purpose. She had just decided not to spend two dollars of her hard-earned money on that hat.

"If you're going to buy one, Lindsey, you need to hurry." I tapped the face of my watch. Lindsey shook her head at the vendor, and we took three steps.

"Ladee, ladee!" the man shouted again. "Okay, ladee. One dolla. Pleeease—one dolla." Lindsey heard this figure, turned, and handed him one wet dollar bill. He gave her a straw hat. Lindsey pulled another crumpled dollar from her pocket, and the peddler handed her a second one.

Michael admired his sister's purchases. "Why'd you get two, Linds?" he said.

She shrugged. "It was a good deal." John slapped her a high five. On the way back to the ship, Lindsey wore one sombrero and carried the other.

As John, Michael, and I stood on the cliff overlooking the Okinawan beach, I smiled. I sure wished all our travels with Lindsey had ended like that one: with a good story.

We sauntered back to the Honda Civic, and Michael drove us to the Naha Airport. John unloaded the suitcases as I wrapped my arms around my son's torso and squeezed, covering his neck and face with kisses. Michael put up with my overt affections until John opened his arms, indicating he wanted some loving, too. They hugged; then John patted him on the back several times before Michael climbed into the driver's seat and rolled down his window. "Thanks for coming. I'm glad you did. Love you."

"We love you, too!" we shouted. Michael shifted into gear, shoved his arm through the opening, and waved for a long, long time. We stood on the sidewalk in front of Departures, watching our son become a speck on the horizon. John and I each grabbed the handle of a roller bag and headed through the glass doors toward the United counter to check in and drop our suitcases. When it was time to board the jet, I held the plastic sack containing Lindsey's Hello Kitty loot, wishing we were already home. I couldn't wait to tell my twenty-two-year-old about our trip and learn how she had fared while we were away.

12

~ᘛ ᘊ~

Once we returned from Okinawa, it took only a few hours to learn what had been going on with Lindsey and Emmett. Several months earlier, although there was no evidence Emmett had any steady work, he had begun driving a shiny, brand-new, red SUV. I'd asked Lindsey numerous times if he'd gotten a job, but she always answered, "That's pry-vit. Stay out of our business, Mom."

John and I unpacked our suitcases, opened the mail, and listened to our answering-machine messages. Three were from a woman identifying herself as a private investigator, asking if we were in any way related to Lindsey Atwell. The air whooshed out of my chest. Had Emmett been caught selling naked photos of my daughter online after all? Had he talked Lindsey into committing some sort of crime? Was that how he earned money? The tightness in my chest increased as I scribbled the caller's information onto a scratch pad and immediately dialed the number.

As soon as the woman answered the phone, I blurted, "Lindsey Atwell is my daughter. Is she okay?" I gripped the phone between my neck and my shoulder, freeing up my right hand to pick up a pen and paper.

"Her name was on the inside of the mailbox at Emmett Hockett's house. He hasn't made the payments on his SUV for four months, and we plan to repossess it."

That's all? I exhaled noisily, and my lungs refilled with air. "You're not after Lindsey?" I said aloud, scribbling notes.

"No. But we hoped you could help us."

"How?"

"With his schedule."

"I don't even know if he has a job. My daughter is living with him. Against our wishes," I said. "And we can't get her away from him. She has special needs. Actually, she's intellectually disabled," I clarified, hoping that information would make Emmett appear as the predator I believed him to be. "What kind of info do you have on him? Has he ever been arrested for hurting someone?"

"No, not that we've dug up," she said, answering only my last question.

My breathing steadied. "He says he's a pastor."

"Well, technically, he is," she said, "if you consider buying that sort of title on the Internet legitimate." She explained Emmett had worked for a nationwide toy store years before but had been fired. He had filed a discrimination lawsuit and won a large settlement. As the woman talked, my mind revisited the inside of Emmett's house on Longhorn Street, and I remembered all the dolls—Barbies, Cabbage Patch Kids, and American Girls—still in their original boxes and stacked in his dark living room. Maybe Emmett had collected them during his employment at the toy store. *Or maybe he stole them.*

The rest of the information the PI shared was information I'd already discovered on my own: two marriages and several unpaid parking tickets.

"Do they ever visit you?" she said.

"No."

"He parks inside his garage. We need the vehicle accessible in order to repossess. Would you be willing to set them up?"

That was a good question. Was I willing to set them up? Not at my house, I wasn't. That would be too obvious—Emmett might realize I was behind the sting. On the other hand, Lindsey had said, "I've always wanted a man with wheels," so maybe, just maybe, if Emmett no longer had wheels, my girl would come home. As I stood there, listening to the woman on the other end of the phone, I realized I might have something that could expedite the whole repossession process: Lindsey's Social Security money.

"Are weapons used? Will anyone get hurt? Will they ever know it was me?" I fired off one question after another without pausing in between.

"They'll never know," the PI promised. She also reassured me that they were not allowed to use weapons, and no one would get hurt. "Ideally, we'd prefer to repossess the vehicle when Mr. Hockett is by himself. It's easier that way."

I thought about her words for a moment, then provided the date on which I expected Lindsey to receive the check I'd be mailing. "Emmett will most likely drive my daughter to the bank that very morning," I said. "The check is written on a Washington Mutual account, so I assume they will go to the branch nearest their home." I twisted a strand of my hair around my finger. "But please don't confront him in front of my daughter."

"That won't be a problem. When Ms. Atwell goes into the bank, we'll approach Mr. Hockett."

"And will you call me when it's over? Let me know how it went, and how Lindsey handled it? Please?"

"Of course," she said.

Five days later, before the clock hands pointed to noon, the phone rang.

"It's done," the PI said. "It went off without a hitch. Once Ms. Atwell walked into the lobby, we surrounded the vehicle, and

Mr. Hockett handed us his keys." As the woman spoke, I pictured Emmett sitting in the Washington Mutual parking lot and two bouncer-built men standing on either side of the SUV. "Mr. Hockett didn't make a scene. He remained calm the entire time. The only thing he asked was, 'Could you take me and my girlfriend back to my house?'" I imagined the repo men hooking the tow truck to the shiny red SUV and driving away with it. "Of course we agreed," she said. "We weren't about to leave them stranded several miles from home."

Now that Emmett didn't have "wheels," I figured I'd hear from Lindsey. Surely she'd want us to pick her up. When a week passed and she still hadn't called, I drove over to Longhorn Street to check things out.

"Would you like to come for dinner Sunday? Emmett can come, too, if you want." I knew they'd never come, but I wanted to hear the repossession story from Lindsey. I stood on the front porch in the rain, peering into the sliver of an opening, wondering if Emmett was nearby.

"We can't."

"Why not?"

"It's pry-vit." Lindsey parroted the same words she always did, then abruptly added, "We don't have trans-por-ta-shon."

"What?" I covered my mouth with my hand, hoping my face portrayed shock. "You don't have a car?"

"It's the bank's fault," she raged, defending Emmett. "They didn't write down his payments."

"Then Dad or I will come and get you?"

"No," Lindsey said. "We don't need your char-it-ee."

Charity? I'd never heard Lindsey use that word before. Did she even know what it meant?

Lindsey closed the door, and I drove back to Silverton, rehashing the day Emmett had lost his vehicle. My involvement hadn't helped get my girl back. What would it take to bring her home? After Lindsey sold all her furniture, I'd promised to step back, to quit focusing on things I couldn't change, but that wasn't turning out to be so easy for me.

Lindsey turned twenty-three in May, and as far as I knew, without any candles on a cake. Since I was working on the road, John and I mailed her some new clothes and a Lisa Frank activity set. A few days later, a handwritten thank-you showed up in the mail. I sent letters, and she reciprocated at irregular intervals. Whenever I wasn't on the road, I stopped by Longhorn Street. The curtains were always drawn, and the side windows were still covered in foil. Many times no one answered the salmon-colored door. Every time that happened, I buried my worry deeper, building a taller, thicker wall of bricks around my heart.

In early August, Lindsey called our house on a weekend I was home. I couldn't believe my luck. She shouted into the receiver, but there was so much noise in the background, I could scarcely hear her words.

"Listen, Mom." Her voice sounded louder and terser than normal. I attempted to decipher the racket coming through the receiver and decided she might be in a bowling alley. "This is im-por-tant," she said. "I have a new address." Lindsey painstakingly spelled "Mail Boxes Etc.," then "P-O b-o-x," like someone might do for a child learning to write. "Send my Social Security there."

"Did you move?"

"That's pry-vit. Just send me my money." Lindsey hung up the phone.

One of my worst fears had just come true: Lindsey no longer had a physical address. As I stood in the kitchen, staring at the dead receiver, I didn't yet know Emmett's mortgage company had foreclosed on his house. When I found out, Lindsey would make another excuse, telling me, "It was the bank's fault. They didn't write down his payments." At that moment, all I knew was that I would no longer be able to drive to Longhorn Street and pound on the door until someone opened it a sliver.

When my year contract with the catastrophe team finished, I asked my supervisor if I could roll off and back into the local office. I needed to be in the Willamette Valley so I could track down my daughter's whereabouts. I mapped the address Lindsey had given me and drove to a small white house on a quiet residential street. When I walked through the front door, I saw a row of private mailboxes to the left. To the right, a woman stood at a counter, rolling UPS tape across the end of a small box. She glanced in my direction, and I noticed her dark, brown eyes. *Sympathetic eyes*, I thought, strategizing about how to convince her to help me.

"I can't find my daughter," I said, explaining the situation. I described Emmett and my daughter's physical features. "She's having me send her mail to this address." The woman's eyes looked confused. She shook her head no, saying she hadn't seen them, though she added, "Maybe my husband rented them the box."

"I'm worried," I said, handing her my business card, begging her to call if she saw anything concerning.

For the next two months, I sent Lindsey's Social Security checks to that address. I sent letters, too, and she wrote back sporadically, but her letters never disclosed where she was staying. "I'm OK. I'm happy. I hope your happy," she wrote over and over.

One winter morning, John left for work at his usual time: 6:20. I fell back to sleep. At 6:32, someone pounded on the door inside our garage so loudly that I woke, confused. *Did John lock himself out?* The pounding continued, matching the beats in my chest. I threw off the warm quilts, grabbed a terry-cloth robe, and hurried down the hall, past the den. I looked out the front window. The sky was charcoal, the sun taking its ever-loving time to rise that morning.

My breathing quickened; I started panting. "John?" I hollered through the solid door. The response was muffled. My body started trembling uncontrollably. I asked again and realized it was Lindsey. I opened the door slowly, not sure if she was alone. No one ever used the garage door at this time of day. *Why didn't she come to the front of the house? And why visit so early in the morning? Is Emmett with her? Will he shove the door open and push his way in? Will he try to hurt me? Steal money?* I didn't know if he could brainwash Lindsey into committing crimes, like Patty Hearst, the heiress who'd been kidnapped by a left-wing radical group, then isolated and threatened until she agreed to hold a semiautomatic rifle and help them rob a bank. Did Emmett have that kind of power over my daughter?

I had an embarrassing secret, which I hadn't shared with a soul, not even John: at times I feared my own child. She'd changed so much. Now she appeared disheveled, greasy, sneaky. Often hateful. I wanted to believe in Lindsey, but I wasn't willing to place bets on either her or Emmett at 6:33 a.m.

Lindsey stood on the upper staircase landing in the garage. Emmett wore his flannel shirt and lurked at the bottom of the wooden steps. My heart thumped hard in my chest, and goose bumps pricked my arms. My hands shook. Sweat trickled between my breasts.

I invited Lindsey and Emmett in, flipping on every light switch we passed on our walk from the hall to the kitchen, through the dining room, and into the family room. I hoped to create a brightly lit fishbowl so the neighbors could see in—in case of an ambush. Once we all stood in the family room, I wrapped my arms around my torso, trying to disguise my fear.

"I want my Social Security money." Lindsey held out a shaking hand, steeling two icy eyes on me. I shouldn't have been surprised by this request. Lindsey had recently called and said, "Don't mail my money next month." She had told me Mail Boxes Etc. refused to accept their mail any longer, and I wondered if that company had "forgotten" to write down Emmett's payment, too. Lindsey said she would call back, "as soon as I get a new address." But she didn't call. As it got closer to the day I should have mailed her check, I worried, *Will Lindsey be able to buy groceries? Will she be able to pay rent at her new place?* That is, if she even had a new place yet.

I glanced at Emmett. He stood near the wall, with his hands clasped together where the flannel met his black sweatpants. He tipped his face toward the hardwood floor.

I massaged my arms, trying to rub away the goose bumps. "Give me a hug, Linds." I opened my arms, pulled her close, and squeezed tight. She felt soft and squishy and smelled the same as she had the last time I'd seen her. I'd never get used to her new stench. Her hair hung loose, looking greasier than ever. A man's plaid coat—something Emmett had discarded?—hung on her shoulders, the zipper ripped on one side. Her hands disappeared beneath the sleeves. Faded denim jeans covered her pudgy butt. She wore the cartoon-character sweatshirt Mom and I had bought for her twenty-first birthday, but now the navy neckline crimped from overstretching.

Emmett asked to use the bathroom. Without looking at him, I nodded and pointed in the right direction.

When the bathroom fan turned on, I sat Lindsey on the sofa and took her right hand in mine. "Where have you been?" I whispered.

"Emmett got a new van." Her eyes darted right, then left. "It's white. We've been living in it." My insides sank. I wanted to cry. I shook my head, trying to comprehend her words. My *daughter is homeless.* "Emmett says it's none of your business." I knew she wasn't supposed to tell me anything, so I changed topics.

"Have you ever seen Dad treat me poorly?" I said, as quietly as possible. A thousand blackheads covered her nose, her forehead, her chin. I wanted to clean her face. "Why do you allow Emmett to treat you this way?"

Lindsey pulled her hand free of mine, and her blue eyes widened. "Mom. I just want to be loved." She gasped. "I don't want the same things you do. Emmett loves me, and I love him." Lindsey stopped for a moment, her arms and head shaking. She gasped again. "We're married."

She lifted her left hand and splayed her fingers. The sleeves of the coat slipped away, exposing a gold band with a tiny diamond that could have been cubic zirconium, for all I knew. It wasn't the size or the quality of the diamond that mattered to me, though; I just believed the man who married my daughter should make her feel valued and loved. And in my mind, that started with his taking proper care of her—by ensuring they had housing, for instance. "Emmett's an intranet pastor," Lindsey reminded me, turning her mouth into a wide smile.

I didn't correct her pronunciation. I stared at her slender, dainty hand. Every single nail had been gnawed below the plate, leaving ragged edges. Her cuticles were chewed and torn. Two appeared fiery red. My eyes fixed on her ring finger and the shiny metal, already losing its luster. Lindsey told me Emmett had married them in a "pry-vit ceremony at his house." My body froze, feeling gutted, numb. She talked and talked about this being "real love" and how great Emmett was and how happy she was. My mind wandered, zinging question after question that my daughter would never answer. *How could she marry him? Was the union legal? Were there any witnesses?* There had to have been witnesses! My heart plummeted to my toes.

When Emmett stepped back into the room, I wrote Lindsey a check, held my breath, and hugged her again, unable to make myself offer congratulations or "I'm happy for you" or any other expression of joy. I ushered them outside to the driveway, where they'd parked a dented white utility van. Emmett turned the key in the ignition, and the van sputtered. He backed out of the driveway, then drove away, leaving behind a trail of gray smoke.

Nine days later, a thick letter with a return address on the Oregon coast arrived in our mail. Depoe Bay was almost two hours away from Silverton, so I couldn't drop by and check on Lindsey very often. My head filled with dread as I removed the six sheets of paper and smoothed them out on the counter.

In handwriting barely legible to me, Lindsey wrote that she hated me for being her representative payee and that she wanted to be responsible for her own money now that she was married. I turned one page, then another. Large, misspelled scrawl spelled out: "We want a baby. You should not of let me get my tubes tied. Emmett said so." My body folded in two, and I held my gut. Tears stung my eyes. I stayed in this position for several minutes, terrified to read further.

When I finally stood upright, I read: "We're getting my tubes reversed. As soon as we can."

Rage, anger, and spite filled the next three paragraphs. When I finished reading, I folded the papers twice, tore them in half, and tossed the bits in the trash.

Another one of my fears had come to fruition: Lindsey blamed me for her tubal. I fretted about her accusation, wondering why Emmett wanted kids now. Maybe for the increased Social Security payments that would come with a baby.

For days, I walked around the house like a zombie, replaying Lindsey's words in my head. My heart still believed my daughter had made the right decision. *Emmett is messing with her.* I was so caught up in Lindsey's recent blame game I didn't recognize that the letter was actually a forewarning.

When the phone rang, I answered, feeling numb.

On the other end of the line, a Social Security agent identified himself, then quickly explained he'd stepped away from his desk to tell me Lindsey and Emmett sat in his office.

"They say they're married," he said, rushing his words. "They want to change the representative payee from you to him. Is that okay?"

"Absolutely not," I said, grateful that this man saw through Lindsey's charade but angry that Emmett continued to try to control my daughter. If the representative payee designation changed, I might never know where Lindsey lived.

I slid the phone into its cradle, grabbed my car keys, and drove to Marion County Records in Salem to investigate marriage licenses. I gave the clerk Lindsey and Emmett's full names and tapped the counter with my fingers until she completed the computer search.

"No applications for those last names," she said, explaining she had access only to Marion County, not records for the entire state. The air I'd unconsciously held in my lungs released, and I felt a slow burn. They might have applied for a license in a different locale, but Lindsey said they had married at Emmett's house. I doubted he would travel far for a license.

I knew Lindsey believed she and Emmett were legally married. I knew she wanted to be loved, and if my daughter had been adored by a man who genuinely cared for her, one who didn't isolate her from family, I'd have supported such a union. But to me, Emmett's actions screamed, *User! Abuser!* And since he didn't appear to earn any money, I wondered how they survived. *On Lindsey's Social Security?* That seemed impossible. The amount was scarcely enough to sustain her, but whenever I asked where Emmett worked or what he did to make money, Lindsey always said, "That's personal, Mom. Stay out of our business."

13

Emmett and Lindsey moved again—to Newport, another coastal community, thirteen miles south of Depoe Bay. When Farmers assigned me a wind claim near that town, I typed Lindsey's new address into MapQuest, printed out the directions, and planned a detour to their place on my way home.

As I steered my logo-plastered company vehicle into the driveway, the first thing I noticed was the huge slab of barren asphalt, as long and wide as the turquoise duplex, as if someone had initially thought they'd build in that spot but then had decided to move the structure back into the space that could have been a yard. *Asphalt jungle* came to mind. All the window coverings were drawn, and when I knocked on their unit's door, no one answered. I walked around the end of the building and found a fishing-tackle business in the parking lot behind the duplex.

The man inside was reading a magazine, but when the bell on the door jingled, his head tipped in my direction.

"Have you ever seen the couple in the duplex back there?" I pointed in the direction of Emmett and Lindsey's unit. "The first one? They just moved in."

He set the magazine on a Formica counter the color of a Milky Way candy bar. "I'm their landlord," he said. "Why?" I handed him my business card and told him I was Lindsey's mother and that she'd run away with this man. I asked him to call me if he ever saw anything concerning.

"All I care about is them paying their rent on time." He smoothed the whiskers in his beard. "So far, so good. But they haven't been here long. They seem nice, though." As I left his shop, I fidgeted with my car keys, wondering how they could suc-cessfully fool people so easily when Emmett seemed so dangerous for my daughter. *Obviously, they've duped the landlord, too.* I drove across the Yaquina Bay Bridge and stopped at the Newport Police Department. *New jurisdiction, new results,* I thought, as I shared my fears with an officer.

"Choosing a bad partner isn't a crime." The officer showed no emotion. My jaw locked. Did the academy teach all cops to basically say the same thing? "But I'll do a welfare check within the week," he finally said. He shook his head and frowned. "I have a daughter, too."

Three thousand, one hundred twenty minutes crept by before the officer called. "I didn't see any bruising or evidence of abuse. She acts like she wants to be there."

Am I misreading all the signs? Is my imagination running wild? My gut told me different, and I gripped the receiver more tightly.

"But I never met the guy. He wasn't there. So I didn't get to see them together."

Well, how helpful is that? I wondered, wishing Lindsey dis-played some sign of distress or indicated a desire to leave. The police would help then. Wouldn't they?

To stay in her life, in addition to continuing to send my daugh-ter cards and little notes, I invited Lindsey for Easter, Thanksgiving, birthdays, and every other family celebration. Now it was Christ-mas again—her fourth one away from home.

Emmett refused to come, which translated to Lindsey's refus-ing to come, too. Celebrating another holiday without my girl threw me into a depression. I didn't want to decorate or bake or buy gifts. But John and I planned to host the extended-family festivities, so I prepared the house, the meal, going through the motions, knowing Lindsey would be missing but hoping for the remote possibility she'd change her mind. I'd even procrastinated mailing her gifts. Just in case. But on Christmas Eve morning, it was obvious Lindsey wasn't going to show. I called Mom to see if she wanted to drive to Newport with me. We loaded Lindsey's gifts in the Camry and calculated the driving time, the visiting time, and the return time. We had to be home by early afternoon, when family would arrive.

I drove across the Yaquina Bay Bridge with Mom in the passenger seat. We'd talked the entire time, but once we spotted the turquoise duplex, we both turned silent. The huge asphalt driveway was vacant except for Emmett's dented white utility van. We parked next to it and stepped out of the car. An inlet bordered the north end of the driveway, and several seabirds circled above us. The unit faced an enormous sand dune covered in beach grass, preventing a view of the Pacific Ocean. Even if there had been a view, it would have been hard to see anything. The thickening gray skies were weighted with so much moisture, it could have poured at any minute.

I knocked on the door. To the right was a small picture window with a damaged turquoise mini-blind. Lindsey's fingers, the nails still chewed to uneven edges, spread a small opening between a couple of broken slats. Two eyes peered through the space; a blur of blue darted right, then left. When they rested on me, their expression turned icy. The fingers and eyes disappeared. No one answered the door, so I knocked again, feeling jittery.

"Merry Christmas," Grandma and I yelled in unison, our voices loud and cheery, my insides tense. We shouted at the door and at the mini-blind-covered window.

"We have gifts," I said, hoping Lindsey heard us. I wasn't leaving.
"We want to see you," Grandma added.

Emmett cracked the door two inches. The whites in his eyes
had yellowed.

"Go away," he growled, his breath shallow, his glare menac-
ing. "You shoulda called first."

"I didn't think you owned a phone." I froze a false smile on
my face and reminded him we didn't have a number to call. After
I gave Lindsey the TracFone and she turned it over to Emmett,
I continued to call, but no one ever answered—till one day,
when I got a recording that the number was no longer in service.
"Emmett, you told me we'd be welcome anytime." Grandma and
I stood on the large concrete step outside the front door. Fog
from the inlet crept closer. A fine mist sifted onto our coats. "It's
Christmas Eve. Can't we see Lindsey?" I shivered, realizing my
anxiety magnified the quivers.

Emmett flashed his brown eyes at Lindsey, at us. He opened
the door slowly and waved us in with a flannel-covered arm. The
gesture wasn't warm. He stepped backward, and I noticed he was
wearing black sweatpants again.

"I just got home from work," he said. "I was gettin' ready for
bed."

"You have a job?" I asked, stepping through the threshold.

Emmett glowered at Lindsey. "Yeah," he finally answered. "I
work the night shift. At a hotel."

"Good for you!" My voice sounded as if I were talking to a
five-year-old instead of a grown man. Emmett rarely offered personal information. But, I figured, if I gave over-the-top praise,
maybe he would share some this time. "Which hotel?" I asked,
trying not to sound like I was interrogating him.

"Mom, that's pry-vit!" Lindsey stood behind Emmett, dressed in
low-slung, dark-colored, baggy pants. The blue-and-white-striped

sweatshirt she wore was faded but clean. Her thick brown hair had darkened; some strands now touched her butt.

Nothing simmered on their stove, and no Christmas tree cheered the small space. My daughter had been raised with holiday traditions that included tons of food and lots of activities. I wondered if any part of her missed our celebrations, but for the moment I didn't want to think about how she lived or ask Emmett any more personal questions that would probably cause angst. I just wanted to give my girl some loving.

"Come here, Lindsey." I grabbed her shoulders and wrapped my arms around her torso for a long squeeze. My hands barely touched each other. Lindsey felt squishier than last time. She smelled like perspiration and dirty socks. I was glad the onion smell was missing. After hugging Grandma, Lindsey turned away, bent over, and rolled onto the couch. Her pants exposed the crack of her behind.

I tried not to stare at her greasy hair, but I couldn't help myself. I wondered if she had rinsed out all the conditioner.

"I only take a bath a couple times a week," she said, watching me. "We don't need a high water bill." Emmett fidgeted, shook his head, acting like Lindsey had misunderstood his words.

That was possible, I realized. Many times over the years, I'd wondered if Lindsey's neurological short caused her to hear a different message than was actually said. I recalled the time when Lindsey was fifteen and we'd adopted Arthur, several years after we'd given Beethoven to a family who owned a large farm. Our busy road had turned out to be too dangerous for a big pooch that bolted whenever we opened the front door. Lindsey begged to take our new, twelve-week-old shih tzu on walks, but she struggled with learning how to treat him. If Arthur sniffed a bush, Lindsey yanked on the leash, causing the collar around the five-pound puppy to tug against his neck with force.

"Lindsey, don't do that," I scolded, explaining that Arthur was smaller than Beethoven. "It'll hurt him. And you shouldn't pull on any animal like that." Most of the time, she'd pet the puppy gently and give him tons of kisses. But when it came to walking, she would forget his little legs couldn't maintain her pace.

"Lindsey!" I wagged my finger in my daughter's face when I caught her tugging on the leash, dragging Arthur behind. "Stop it! How would you like it if we put a leash on *you* and dragged you around?" Lindsey picked up the puppy and carried him into the house.

The next afternoon, John arrived home from school with a smirk on his face. "Guess who called me today?" He set his grade book and the papers he planned to correct that night on the kitchen counter.

I shrugged. I couldn't even attempt a guess.

"The high school counselor." He breathed slowly, prolonging the suspense. "Lindsey told him you planned to put a leash on her." John paused again, letting his words sink in. "And tie her up in the backyard." My husband howled. He found it easier to be amused by Lindsey's harmless antics than I did.

My eyes widened; my mouth hung open. *Why would Lindsey say that?* My heart drummed inside my chest. Then I remembered. A sudden heat hit my cheeks and spread toward my neck.

"You told him what really happened?"

"Yeah, I told him." John leaned against the kitchen counter and scratched his chin.

"Lindsey's so literal." I felt my shoulders tighten. A huge knot settled in the back of my neck. *Why does she do this?*

My fifteen-year-old took her time sashaying into the kitchen. She wore purple slacks, a purple sweater, and a purple headband. Everything had to be purple back then. I thought she looked like a giant eggplant at the time, but I was nostalgic for that attire now.

That day, though, my face flushed a bright red. "Did you really think we'd put a leash on you?" I positioned my hands on my hips and glared at my daughter, bombarding her with questions. "Why'd you say that to the counselor? What else did you tell him?"

Lindsey mimicked my stance. Her eyes darted. "Because you said it." She talked so fast, she gasped. "You said you were gonna tie me up in the backyard and make me eat dog food." *Gasp.*

"Do you believe that?"

"Well, you said you would."

I had never said that I would tie her up or make her eat dog food, but I wondered, *Is that really what my daughter hears?* Anyone who knew us could see that our family treated Lindsey well, that we genuinely loved her. That was the big difference, I realized. If Emmett's actions had shown love and care for Lindsey, even if she misrepresented the details of their conversations, my gut wouldn't have been churning. The landlord and police officer's comments replayed in my head. *"They seem like a nice couple." "She acts like she wants to be there."* When I'd heard those remarks, for one fleeting moment, I'd questioned my instincts. Standing in Emmett and Lindsey's living room right now, I didn't doubt my suspicions one bit.

I changed the subject away from Emmett's rules on showering. "Let's open your presents," I said. Lindsey tore into her presents like a toddler. *Why can't life still be that simple, like it was back then, when Lindsey was three years old?* My mind somersaulted back to the first time my girl crawled onto Santa's lap and asked for something specific: a Cabbage Patch Kid. I smiled to myself, remembering how I'd thought such a request would be easy.

I drove to Toys "R" Us.

"We sold our last one three days ago," the clerk said, moving his hands and arms wildly in the air as he described the number of mothers hunting down Cabbage Patch Kids that holiday season. "And we're not getting any more for a week." My quest kicked into high gear: I checked Mervyn's, J.C. Penney's, and Meier & Frank. All had sold out. Two days before. Yesterday. "You just missed the last one," a perky young sales associate told me. "I sold it fifteen minutes ago."

I started calling stores, saving the time it would take me to drive between them.

"I'm not supposed to tell you," the salesman at Montgomery Ward said in a hushed voice after I whined and pleaded and explained that a Cabbage Patch Kid was the only thing my three-year-old had told Santa she wanted. "Be here tomorrow when the store opens. We're not putting out the stock until after we close the doors tonight."

I arrived the next morning twenty minutes before Montgomery Ward opened and was shocked to see other parents already in line outside the locked doors. As the seconds ticked away, a crowd formed. By the time the salesman opened the doors, it was clear this would be no ordinary shopping trip with an orderly line. I prepared to sprint, grab, and wrestle if I had to. Inside, someone shoved me, an elbow butted my cheek, but I moved forward, faster, closer to the back wall. My arms reached out. My fingers touched cardboard. I grabbed a box, tucked it to my chest, and wrapped my arms around the package. I felt more like a professional football player who'd caught a pass and was protecting the pigskin than a mother trying to make her daughter's Christmas wish come true. I hunched forward; my hands tightened their grip. I guarded the doll with my body, stepped slowly backward, and studied my prize. Her birth certificate said Darby. She had blue eyes and red hair and a face full of freckles. Another customer approached me and asked to trade, but I shook my head. Darby was perfect. I paid for the doll and drove home smiling.

Lindsey's shaky hands tore the wrapping paper away from the package on that long-ago Christmas morning, and the moment she glimpsed the doll, she squealed. I snapped pictures on our 35 mm camera. John ripped the Kid from the box and plastic wrap while Lindsey jumped up and down, clapping her hands. He handed her the doll. She clasped Darby to her chest and squealed some more.

That night, as I tucked Lindsey into bed, she told me, "I love Darby." She kissed the doll's freckled face and squeezed its squishy body. I opened the covers and tucked Darby in with my daughter. "I'm gonna sleep with her forever," she whispered, and closed her eyes.

As Grandma and I stood in the middle of Emmett and Lindsey's Newport living room, I realized I'd give almost anything for my girl to ask for something specific again—just so I could have the opportunity to make another one of her wishes come true. She never asked for anything anymore—except for us to leave her alone.

We watched Lindsey unwrap two new pairs of jeans. "Thank you! Thank you!" she said. "I needed these!" She stood awkwardly for a moment, held one pair against her waist for a couple seconds, then tossed it aside. I hoped they'd fit her. Grabbing another package, Lindsey plopped back down on the sofa, tore off the paper, and found four new tops. One had two kittens playing on the front.

Lindsey's face lit up just like it had when she was a child. "I love aminals." She pressed the shirt against her cheek. My daughter had been mispronouncing this word ever since I could remember. My previous corrections had never worked. I saw her so rarely that I didn't want to spoil the moment, so I let the mispronunciation slide and watched Lindsey open the box with a new pair of pink Nike tennis shoes. "Yay!" she said, waving them around in the air. "These are perfect, because I sure do walk a lot."

Her physical appearance didn't support such a claim. She was the heaviest I'd ever seen her. Our family gene pool was full of hefty people, so Lindsey came by this trait naturally. I struggled to maintain the recommended weight for my current age and height, and that goal was getting harder with each passing year. A reasonable weight gain wouldn't have bothered me, especially if she made healthy food choices, but I suspected Lindsey consumed excessive quantities of junk and fast food.

When Lindsey opened a jewelry-making kit and a Lisa Frank sticker set, she squealed even more.

"This one's from Grandpa, too," Grandma said, handing Lindsey one last package, filled with a dozen coloring and activity books and a Safeway gift card. "So you can buy some groceries," Grandma added.

"This is the best Christmas ever!" Lindsey said, hugging her grandmother and me.

"We brought you a sample of everything, Lindsey," Grandma said, opening a large paper Safeway sack. "We should put these in the fridge."

Lindsey walked into the kitchen and opened the icebox, and Grandma set margarine containers filled with ham, mashed potatoes, gravy, rolls, green salad, and corn on the empty shelves.

"When you're ready, you can warm them in the microwave," Grandma said.

"Here are a dozen of your favorite Christmas cookies," I said, opening the small tin and showing her the frosted stars. "And this container has a little bit of shrimp dip." Lindsey clapped her hands again.

"I'll give you a tour," she said. The duplex was sparse and tidy, the complete opposite of their Salem home. I didn't recognize one item in the room and wondered if the place had come furnished.

"This is the stove." Lindsey pointed at the stove. "And here's the refrigerator." She paused and pointed at the large white box, sitting in the corner, that Grandma had just filled with food. "We have a microwave, too." She pointed at the unit sitting on the counter, as if we wouldn't have recognized a microwave if she hadn't pointed it out.

Every time Lindsey pointed, Grandma and I smiled and nodded and said, "That's nice, Lindsey. Nice."

"This is the bathroom door." Lindsey didn't offer to let us go inside, so we looked at the closed door and nodded.

"Most nights I sleep on the couch with Darby." She *did* still have her Cabbage Kid! My daughter continued to surprise me. I wrapped my arms around my torso and smiled. It was heartening to see a glimpse of the innocent little girl I thought we'd lost forever. "I fall asleep watching TV," she continued. She pointed to another closed-off room. "This is the bedroom door."

When we circled back to the living room, Grandma said, "What do you do all day, Linds? Do you still like coffee? Does Newport have a Dollar Tree?"

"I like to walk on the beach and pick up bottles and cans."

Emmett lurked nearby, head tilted in our direction.

"Sometimes I go for coffee. There's a coffee shop on the other side of the bridge." Lindsey chatted as if Emmett weren't in the room.

"It's Lindsey's money," Emmett said.

Lindsey turned her head toward him.

"The money you send. Lindsey spends that however she wants," he said. *Another lie.* Lindsey had written me that she gave Emmett money for a storage unit, electricity, and water. I knew she also bought food. "And she buys coffee," Emmett said. "I take her to the Dolla Tree so she can buy colorin' books and other stuff." He sounded puffed-up and proud. Didn't he think it even a little odd that a twenty-three-year-old still slept with her Cabbage Patch Kid and bought coloring books?

I filled my lungs with air, then asked, "Emmett, why don't you let Lindsey come home with us? We'll bring her back in a couple days." I watched him fidget. "That would be such a great Christmas gift!" He looked at Lindsey. Lindsey looked at him. "Wouldn't you feel good knowing you made my day special?" No one spoke. "Why don't you both come? We have lots of food." I patted my daughter's knee. "All your favorites."

"I have to work," Emmett said. "The night shift."

"I'm not coming if Emmett can't." Lindsey's eyes lowered and fixated on the tan carpet. Her head and arms tremored.

"Lindsey, if Emmett's working, you'll be all alone." I attempted to reason with my daughter, explaining the proposed plan one more time.

"I want to spend Christmas with Emmett," she said, unwavering. "I won't leave him alone." It was impossible to persuade her to come with us. Nothing I could say would convince her Emmett would either be at work or sleeping, so she'd be the one spending the holiday alone. Unless she counted sleeping with Darby.

~✹~

One week later, on a sunny but chilly New Year's Eve Day, a thick envelope came in the mail. I unfolded the chaotic wad of blue-lined, loose-leaf paper and smoothed the stack flat. The words on the first page were not contained within the lines, but they were inscribed with Lindsey sweetness. "Your kind, thoughtful, and caring. I love you. Thank you for the stickers and clothes and shoes." My fingers lingered on the page, tracing her shaky handwriting. A smile crept across my lips. Even though Lindsey was two and a half hours away, reading her words made me feel closer to her and I wondered, *What is she doing right now? Having coffee? Walking on the beach? Going to the Dollar Tree?*

I turned over the first page to read the next sheet. The second through seventh pages were covered in gigantic print with only two words on each sheet. In a few places, the blue ink pen had pressed hard enough to gouge the paper. Some words were misspelled and illegible, but the gist was: Don't come without calling. Stay out of our business. "Your mean," she wrote. "Don't come unless your invited." Other words were so clearly written, I suspected Emmett had actually inscribed them. I shook my head, restacked the wide-ruled papers in a neat pile, stapled the pages together, and tucked them in our old, punched-tin pie safe with the rest of the correspondence I'd recently started saving. If something bad happened, my girl's letters were the only things I had left.

14

❧ ❧

t was March when Lindsey and Emmett's landlord called and
told me they had moved out in the middle of the night.
"They owed me three months' rent," he said. My cheeks stung.
This wasn't the way John and I had raised our daughter. "And
they must have spent the rent money on pot, because there were
leftover roaches in an ashtray."

I cringed. *They're doing illegal drugs?* "Are you sure?"

"It smelled liked marijuana to me," he said. "Do you have a
new address for them?"

I shook my head slowly, processing his words. "No, I don't,"
I said. But I certainly wished I did. I would've given it to him.
At least that's how I felt at the moment. If sharing their contact
information could help me get my daughter back, I'd sing like a
canary. Yet none of my "tough love" tactics had worked so far.
Why should I think this would work either?

Upon learning Lindsey might be doing drugs, I felt my anxiety accelerate into overdrive. Amid all of her mental and physical
challenges, she didn't need to complicate her life by operating in
an altered state.

As I entered another year of this ordeal, the movie reel that
played through my head felt like a Stephen King horror film,
with scenes of rape and mayhem. Now those scenes incorporated

illicit drugs, too. I tried to turn off this flick, but my brain wouldn't cooperate.

Feeling frantic, I told John about the phone call with Lindsey's landlord. The month before, I had agreed to rejoin the Farmers catastrophe team because I missed the excitement of traveling. Moreover, the pay was excellent. The very next morning, Farmers expected me to head toward Sherman, Texas. But how could I leave town when I didn't know where my daughter was?

"I'll be here," John said, giving me a hug. "If Lindsey calls, I'll get her address. Or she'll send another letter. She always does. Besides, what can we do until then?"

Nothing. There was absolutely nothing we could do. Work was the one thing that kept my brain busy. It kept me from thinking about my daughter and trying to fix problems that couldn't be fixed. And ever since Farmers had given me my Texas assignment, I'd been giddy. Michael was now stationed at Sheppard Air Force Base in Wichita Falls, only two hours west of where I'd be working. My mind was already brewing up ways to sneak away from Sherman to visit my son.

I nestled my face against John's soft T-shirt. "You're right. I'll go," I said, realizing Lindsey's drama shouldn't disrupt an opportunity for me to see my boy. Eventually, Lindsey would need to receive her Social Security money. Certainly, she'd contact us before it came time to send the check next month. She always had in the past.

Five days later, I was climbing on roofs and estimating damaged shingles, when my last inspection of the day canceled. I called Michael and said, "I can be there by dinnertime."

"That would be great, Mom. I'm getting tired of eating on base." Maybe I should have been offended that my son seemed more excited to be taken off-site to eat than to see me, but my heart knew he appreciated the fact that I would drive that far just to treat him to a meal.

Between Sherman and Wichita Falls, the highway medians were besieged with Indian paintbrush and bluebonnet blooms. I'd never witnessed such dramatic color on the sides of any road. It probably didn't hurt that the Texas skies were a crisp, clear blue that afternoon. By the time I reached Sheppard AFB, I'd stopped three times to pick wildflowers and arrived a few minutes later than planned.

"Here, son." I handed my twenty-one-year-old a mixture of stunning blue and red-orange flowers. "I picked some for you."

"What am I supposed to do with these?" he asked, shaking his head. "I don't have anything to put them in." Well, there was at least one difference between my boy child and my girl: Lindsey always loved flowers. She wanted flowers after her tubal ligation. "And if I die," she had instructed us, "I don't want to be burned. I want to be buried. But don't put any dirt in my grave. And don't forget the flowers. I want lots and lots of pretty flowers."

"You know, Mom," Michael said, "I think it might be illegal to pick the flowers here."

My face froze. I'd never thought of that. I hadn't intended to break the law and stashed the bouquets in the trunk of my car until I was back at my hotel.

We ate at a barbecue joint not far from the base. I sat across the table, admiring Michael's broad shoulders, his quick smile. Both my kids had beautiful smiles, although Lindsey's was totally natural. We'd never had to pay for orthodontic treatment for her.

Michael told me about leaving Okinawa and how he'd sold his Honda Civic to another new recruit.

"That's how it works, Mom," he said, reminding me that since Okinawa is an island, the cars have low mileage. He lifted a bottle of spicy barbecue sauce and smacked the bottom with one hand, and a splash landed on his brisket. "I drove the Honda for two years, then sold it for almost what I paid. Pretty good, huh?" He picked up his sandwich and took a bite.

As Michael talked about his life, I nodded and grinned. "Are you going to buy a car here?" I dipped a piece of turkey into the sauce and bit into it.

"No. Lots of guys already have cars," he said. "I bum rides all the time." He told me he planned to wait until he was transferred to his permanent duty station before buying another vehicle. "By then, I should have enough rank to live off base, and I'll need a car to get back and forth."

My son had everything figured out. He was working hard and moving up in rank. He wasn't sure where he'd be stationed next, but he anticipated Nellis Air Force Base, near Las Vegas. That sounded good to me. It would be much closer to home.

"Dad's envious," I said with a giggle, explaining how badly John had wanted to come, too. As a middle-school teacher, my husband didn't have the flexibility that I did with my work, so I was feeling pretty darn smug. I wanted to call him right this minute and tell him how well Michael was doing.

Our conversation turned to Lindsey and her recent move. "In the middle of the night," I said. "Can you believe that? We didn't raise either one of you to act like that."

Michael picked up a french fry and tossed it into his mouth. "Well, it doesn't sound like Lindsey," he said a few seconds later. "Sounds like Emmett is a bad influence."

After our meal, I dropped Michael off at Sheppard and headed back to Sherman without seeing a single wildflower in the dark night. I had hoped to get together with Michael at least one more time before I was assigned to a different storm, but that didn't happen. The days my son was free, my schedule was packed, and vice versa. Two weeks later, I flew home for my weekend with John, uncertain where Farmers would send me next.

Then Lindsey finally called.

"My Social Security check didn't come yet!" she yelled, sounding angrier than Emmett had in his driveway three years earlier. "Why are you holding on to it? You need to send me my money—"

"Lindsey! Stop yelling." I thought about hanging up, but I wanted so badly to talk to her, even if she was being difficult. "You didn't give us your new address. How am I supposed to send it if I don't have a place to send it to?"

"We're in a 'partment on Oak Street." *Gasp.* "In Lincoln City."

I scribbled down the address, then repeated everything back.

"Yes. Now send my—"

"Lindsey," I interrupted. "I have something I need to talk to you about. Are you listening?" I knew what I was about to say would make her angrier than she already was, but that was okay, because I was mad, too.

Back when I owned Country Neighbors and Lindsey worked for me, she'd opened a college savings account for herself. The account had both our names on it and didn't require two signatures. John and I matched the kids' college contributions, figuring they'd need a lot more money for their higher education than they would be able to deposit on their own. Once Lindsey started Silverton High, we recognized college was an unrealistic expectation for our daughter. Yet in order to receive Social Security benefits, Lindsey couldn't have more than $2,000 in all her bank accounts—the program required her to spend down her savings. When we suggested using a portion of her college money to turn the shed into a cottage, she agreed. "I bought the windows," she told everyone who visited, pointing at the vinyl Milgards and grinning. "Aren't the stripes nice?" she added, referring to the white grids between the panes. We liked our kids to have owner-ship in the things we did, and Lindsey certainly seemed to derive a lot of pride from her contribution to her first place.

The remainder of the monies sat in a Washington Mutual savings account, earning interest. At the end of every quarter, when the statement arrived, I thought, *We'll do something special. When she comes home.*

But those weren't my thoughts when I came back from Texas and found the final statement sitting on the counter, waiting for me. Lindsey had withdrawn $923.80, wiping out the account. After seeing the zero balance, I called Washington Mutual. The manager explained Lindsey had legal access to this money and nothing could be done. Emmett had driven Lindsey to a bank branch where the tellers had no familiarity with our family. If they had gone to the one in Silverton, this never would have happened.

Now that Lindsey was on the line, I scolded her, told her how disappointed I was that she took the money without asking. I twisted and untwisted a strand of my hair.

"It's my money, Mom. Emmett said so."

My daughter was partially right. Fifty percent of it had been hers. Since we had matched both our kids' contributions as gifts, I thought our portion would be used for something we'd all agree on. Now it was gone. *Maybe it went toward putting a roof over my daughter's head,* I silently reasoned, hoping that was the case.

Lindsey gasped. The sound of her sucking in air brought me back to the moment. I tightened the grip on the phone as my daughter demanded I send all her Social Security money. "The minute it goes into the account," she said. Her words sounded urgent, as if she needed the funds yesterday.

She switched topics and told me Emmett wanted her to keep the drapes drawn because he didn't like any light in the house. "I prefer the night, too." My girl's voice sounded disconnected and strange. "I like living at the beach in the dark, but sometimes we like to go to the casino." *Gasp.* "And I like that even better."

Is someone after them? Do they owe a loan shark or a drug dealer a bunch of money? Could they really be using drugs?

"Is everything okay? Is anyone after you? Are you smoking pot? What's going on?" were the rapid-fire questions that came out of my mouth.

But Lindsey wouldn't answer any of my inquiries. "It's pry-vit," she said, and hung up.

Waves of letters arrived in the mail. One on one day. Three on another. One every day for six days in a row. First the angry ones: "Stay out of our lives. Leave me a lone. I hate you." Then the love letters: "I love you. Thank you for the stamps. I'm happy. I hope your happy." All the words she wrote were sounded out and spelled phonetically, with shaky hands. Most of the words were barely legible, but I'd had years of practice, so I could decode most of the messages.

One of Lindsey's letters included the name of the motel where Emmett worked. I figured she must have slipped by divulging this information, since everything was "private" and none of our business, but I was grateful. None of the new letters spewed any anger about her not being able to have a baby, and I felt grateful for that, too. I tucked the page that mentioned Emmett's workplace in a special spot in the pie safe. Then I sent Lindsey cards with pictures of kittens and puppies and baby chicks, with notes that said, "We miss you. We love you. Please come home."

When Lindsey's birthday approached, I pulled the saved page out of the pie safe and did a Google search for the Sea Odyssey Motel. After the antique clock in the hallway struck midnight, I dialed the motel's number. When Emmett answered, I asked if we could visit on Lindsey's twenty-fourth birthday.

"I'd like to bring her grandparents." I reminded Emmett that

Lindsey and Grandpa shared a birthday. "Grandpa misses her. He'd really like to spend May tenth with his granddaughter." Even though this strategy had not worked in the past, I tried to use words that would touch a soft spot in his mind or heart so he'd agree to a visit. But I refused to beg. "We'll buy dinner," I said. "Anywhere you want."

He said nothing. Seconds of silence ticked by.

"Please, please, pleeeease!" I begged, irritated at myself for having so little restraint.

"We'll meet you at Taco Time in Lincoln City," Emmett said, his voice flat. "Do you know where it's at?"

"Yes," I said, confirming the hour. "We'll be there."

⤳

Dad, Mom, John, and I sat on the concrete benches outside Taco Time on a typical seaside afternoon: overcast, cool, the air a mixture of sea and salt. A red truck, a blue minivan, a black SUV, a navy PT Cruiser—a steady line of vehicles pulled up to the drive-through microphone. People shouted orders, pulled forward, and disappeared behind the back of the business.

Seventeen minutes passed. Dad looked at his watch three times but didn't say anything. "Late's a sign of disrespect," he'd always said when people were tardy. I panicked. *That bastard*, I tagged Emmett. *They're not coming.*

Then it dawned on me. It was my dad's birthday, too. And this year he was celebrating at Taco Time, certainly not the restaurant of his choice. But ever since Lindsey had been born, his birthday had taken a backseat. I remembered my daughter's second-birthday party. I got so caught up in buying Lindsey a new red trike and making sure the party favors matched the Big Bird theme, I totally forgot we were celebrating another birthday, too. When I picked up the cake at Roth's grocery store, it had been prepared the way

I ordered it: "Happy 2nd Birthday, Lindsey." I quickly asked the decorator to add "and Dad" after Lindsey's name. The yellow bird took up so much space on the top of the cake, Dad's name looked like the afterthought it was. And it didn't really make sense, since my dad wasn't turning two, but when he saw the cake, he didn't seem to mind. He raced past it and over to Lindsey, picked her up, and tossed her into the air as she tee-heed and begged for more.

After our picnic, we lit the two candles on *their* cake and Dad helped blow them out. Lindsey clapped her hands and chortled. She tried to eat the cake with a spoon, but her hands and arms shook. John cut the cake into little squares. Lindsey dropped the spoon and picked up a lump. It squished between her fingers, but she ate every square, sucking the remaining sweet mess off her hands. When the cake was gone, Lindsey's teeth and face and fingers and shirt were all stained Big Bird yellow, and everyone said, "Doesn't she look adorable!"

Yep. Year after year, my dad had sacrificed his special day for his granddaughter, without complaining. Now, I leaned over and gave him a kiss on the cheek. "They'll be here. I know they will." Dad patted my hand and nodded. "And in case I forget to tell you later, happy birthday, Dad. I love you."

Finally, a white utility van approached loudly, roaring like its muffler had failed. As it pulled into the lot, the van stalled, backfired, and released a cloud of disgusting gray smoke. The van lurched forward. Emmett coasted into the first parking spot before turning off the engine. No one got out. We all stood and stared at the van. Thirty seconds passed. I couldn't wait any longer and walked toward their parking spot. Lindsey stepped out. Her face looked sullen, her gait slow. She wasn't the same granddaughter who used to greet her grandpa by jumping up and down and shrieking with joy. Lindsey's eyes darted to Emmett, to us, and back to Emmett.

The four of us rushed toward Lindsey, huddling around her, hugging and kissing and shouting, "Happy birthday!" She pulled back and watched Emmett. When we opened the door to go inside, Emmett said, "Let's eat out here."

We zipped up our coats, and Emmett sat down. His rear end took up all the space on one bench. John and I alternated standing, since the other three seats were mostly occupied. I went inside and placed the orders. We ate our beef and chicken soft tacos listening to people yell their orders into the microphone, smelling a mixture of salty sea and exhaust fumes. Lindsey didn't relax until she finished her meal. Then she smiled at us, at Emmett, and opened her presents.

"You know, Lindsey," Grandpa said, as she finished opening her last gift, "you were my very first grandchild. You were the best birthday gift ever." Lindsey beamed.

I still remembered Dad holding my hour-old infant in his hands. His blue eyes were round, wide open, and misty. "Hello, little baby. Hello, Lindsey. I'm your grandpa," he cooed in a low voice so soft, so gentle, I wondered why I hadn't wanted the two of them to share a birthday. But I knew why. Living with him during my teen years had been difficult. He thought I was defiant; I thought he was ridiculously strict. I was an Aries; he was a Taurus. Ram and bull. We were like oil and water, and I didn't want to have the same tumultuous relationship with my girl. So, throughout my pregnancy, whenever Dad suggested May 10 as the perfect day to deliver, I teased back, "I'll hold my legs together, rather than have my baby on your birthday!"

Grandma unwrapped confetti-frosted cupcakes and put one candle in Lindsey's and one in Dad's. John struck the matches, and after three tries he lit the two wicks. We sang "Happy Birthday," and Dad's voice still belted the most loudly when it came to the "dear Lindsey" part of the song.

When we couldn't prolong the visit any longer, we exchanged a lot more hugs, kisses, and "I love yous." Emmett led Lindsey back to the van. Before she got in, Lindsey turned and waved, grinning widely. I wondered why she always seemed so reserved when she first saw us. Did Emmett read her some riot act beforehand?

Days later, a letter arrived in the mail and addressed us as Linda and John, instead of Mom and Dad. "Don't call Emmett at work ever again. I don't want to see you. Stay out of our business. I got a life with my own husband. I don't like my mom. I don't get along with her. I hate her. I want her to leave me alone."

I wrote back: "We'll never leave you alone, Lindsey. You're our daughter. My mother is involved in my life, and I intend to stay involved in yours as often as I can. We love you. We'll always love you."

On the front side of the envelope, I printed "Lindsey Atwell" in block letters, then added her address. I licked a stamp and stuck it in the upper-right corner, placing a return label in the upper-left one.

Before I slid the notecard into the envelope, I reread my response, replaying Lindsey's angry words in my head. They sure did sting. No one would deny Lindsey and I had to work at a harmonious relationship, but we'd always worked hard, and in my mind, it had paid off.

My mental movie reel showed scenes from her twenty-four years. On her second birthday, she grinned, with Big Bird–yellow frosting smeared across her face. I could almost feel the huge hug she gave me after she discovered her newfound independence from her Get Ready for School List. I loved the way her eyes glittered when I first mentioned converting our outbuilding into her very own cottage. And my heart beat faster with the pride I felt when she settled into her first real apartment.

It wasn't easy. Not even half the time. My mental movie reel also replayed one particularly difficult scene, one week before Lindsey's tenth birthday, when my mom and I had taken the kids to see Mount St. Helens. We'd had an interesting day talking about volcanoes and how the scenery had changed since the major eruption eight days after Lindsey was born. We planned to stop for dinner, but I wanted to go to the souvenir shop first, since the kids had been saving part of their Country Neighbors earnings to spend on a keepsake.

A bell on the door jingled when we entered the one-room store. Families gathered around postcards, ash-filled souvenirs, jewelry. A thin woman stood behind the counter, pursing her lips, the red of her lipstick feathered into the deep lines around her mouth. She smiled only when she took money from a customer.

Lindsey examined every item in the store, moving from one glass counter to the next, fingering trinkets within reach. Her head and arms tremored.

"Be careful," I reminded her.

"I can't make up my mind. I can't make up my mind," she said to herself.

Seven-year-old Michael selected a volcanic-ash hourglass, paid for it with his allowance, and said, "Let's eat!"

My fingers touched his shoulder. "Not yet, Michael." I turned to chat with the cashier as I waited for Lindsey to find the perfect treasure, hoping she'd find it soon. "I used to live in Longview," I told her. "Went to high school there. I've spent a lot of time on the mountain. It's sad to see it in this condition."

The clerk nodded and said she'd lived in Castle Rock all her life. "I opened the store a few years ago." Her expression remained serious, her mouth pressed into a straight line. "I was in Vancouver when she blew."

"Me too! This is my Mount St. Helens baby." I stroked Lindsey's bouncy, chin-length curls.

"Don't touch my hair!" Lindsey said, slapping my hand off her head. "I have head lice!" Her voice sounded loud, screechy, as if her words were amplified over a public address system.

"What?" A smile froze on my face. *She doesn't have lice.* My cheeks stung. Heat spread down my neck, into my torso. A customer sprinted toward the exit, dragging her son behind. The gift shop owner shifted her glare between Lindsey and me.

"I have head lice!" Her voice sounded louder and screechier the second time.

A man backed away from the counter and headed for the front door. One lady grabbed her child's arm, putting distance between her daughter and mine. Another woman whispered something to the lady standing beside her. They turned and sprinted out of the store. Michael's eyes widened; then he dashed outside on the tail end of another family.

"No, you don't." I forced a laugh, hoping laughter was contagious. But no one joined in.

"Well. I had head lice once."

"Lindsey." My smile faded as my shoulders stiffened. I pulled a single breath inside my chest and lowered my voice. "You had them well over two years ago." I didn't want the man in the big blue jeans to hear. Maybe he would keep shopping. The decorative doorbell repeated its ding-a-ling as customers exited. The clerk narrowed her eyes and scowled. Through the plate-glass window, I watched Michael standing by our gray van, shifting from one tennis-shoed foot to the other, waiting. I bet he hoped no one recognized he was the brother of that loud girl in the store.

I clenched my teeth, bent over, and lowered my face to the same height as my daughter's. My eyes drilled into hers. The only things moving were my lips. In the slowest, firmest, most

I-mean-business manner, I told her, "You. Do. Not. Have. Head. Lice." I grabbed her arm and lugged her toward the door.

"You're pinching me!" Lindsey's tone should have been reserved for someone receiving an unmedicated arm amputation. No customers remained inside the souvenir shop. Even the man in the big jeans had waddled out. The owner frowned. Mom snatched a handful of postcards.

"Let go! You're hurting me! *I do too have head lice!*"

I yanked Lindsey outside, dragging her toward the parking lot. She kicked and tried to smack my face with her free hand. I held her away from my body. Families in the parking lot watched my normal-looking, almost-ten-year-old daughter act like a tantrum-throwing two-year-old.

"What a brat," someone murmured.

"If that mother would just smack her, she wouldn't act that way," a man grumbled.

I would have cared what they said and what they thought, but at that moment I was too damn mad.

Later I retold this story and people laughed. I tried to find the humor in it, too. It wasn't easy, though. I was embarrassed, disappointed, frustrated. And I knew I needed to talk to someone.

Dr. Duane, a licensed clinical social worker, worked with kids in the Silverton School system, as well as with families in his private practice. He'd met Lindsey at her elementary school, and his office was a mere three miles from our home.

When I first saw Dr. Duane, I wondered if he had traveled in a time machine. He wore his hair wild and shaggy, similar to styles sported by the guys in my 1976 high school yearbook. I followed him through his living room, kitchen, and back hall toward the rear of his house, into a smaller-than-normal bedroom that had been converted into an office. The blinds were half-closed. The overhead light had one bulb, instead of two, giving the room a hue somewhere between dark and light. Dr. Duane scratched his beard, then lowered his stocky, middle-aged frame onto a brown recliner and motioned for me to sit on the green sofa.

The minute my butt touched the cushion, my lips moved.

"I wanted a daughter, but not the one I got." I covered my mouth with both hands, shocked I'd said those words out loud. A sob caught in my throat. I swallowed hard. *What kind of mother says such a thing?* For one moment, I didn't move, didn't speak. Surely Dr. Duane would scold me. But the counselor's face didn't change or appear to judge me as he sat in the recliner, head tilted, listening.

"It's not one specific thing Lindsey does that makes me crazy," I added, attempting to justify my confession and recognizing it was impossible to do so. "It's the accumulation of everything." I shared how Lindsey followed me from room to room. I knew that trait wasn't normal. None of my friends' ten-year-olds required that type of attention. Michael was three years younger, and he hadn't followed me around since he was a tot. "And my daughter jabbers," I added. "But the worst part is the arguing." I fidgeted with my hands, trying to control my emotions. "She's like a pit bull that locks its jaw on someone's leg and won't let go. My daughter doesn't give up. She just gets angrier and louder."

I tapped a fist against my chest, telling Dr. Duane that as far as Lindsey was concerned, I'd built a huge, invisible wall of protection around my heart. "I didn't realize I was doing it at first." Recently I'd peered inside my soul, to the place that used to house my affections, and the space felt hollow. I pictured a thick wall of imaginary bricks, to which I'd added one or two (or five or ten) every time an unpleasant incident occurred.

I wrapped my arms around my torso, hugging and squeezing myself as I rocked back and forth. "I go through the motions of parenting Lindsey because that's what mothers do, but I don't enjoy it." I pictured wild ivy digging its roots into the wall's mortar and climbing the bricks, tangling, strangling any fondness I harbored for my daughter. "Sometimes I feel as if I'm standing on the rim of a deep canyon and if Lindsey says one more word, I might hurl myself over the edge." I covered my mouth with both hands, trying to hold back words I'd never shared with anyone. Not even John.

"I dream of running far away," I said, my voice so soft I wondered if the counselor could hear. "And never coming back." I knew escaping would be the easy way out. Abandon my husband and kids. Leave John to deal with all the chaos. The idea tempted me, growing more appealing, more urgent, every single day, but I knew I'd never really run away.

"It's not uncommon to have these thoughts," Dr. Duane said, handing me first one tissue and then the entire rectangular box of Kleenex. "Many clients have communicated similar feelings when they've suffered a major life change like yours."

I nodded, shredding a piece of tissue balled in my hand. Dr. Duane coached me on grieving the loss of what I'd hoped for my superstar daughter. He suggested making time for self-care, and for John and me as a couple, so I wouldn't hit a breaking point. Dr. Duane also offered tips for dealing with Lindsey's arguing, something he'd do often in sessions to come. Sometimes the tactics worked for a while, but then more arguments would come up, no matter how I responded to them. But somehow, Lindsey and I always managed to come out on the other side of the squabbles.

While she was growing up, we both saw counselors to learn how to communicate better and reach resolution more easily. It had been years since either of us had been in counseling, and although I continued to hold out hope for a better relationship with my adult daughter, another difficult letter arrived in the mail. As I read it, I realized Lindsey's mental movie reel played the hard scenes, editing out our family's unconditional love.

"Stop treating me like a little kid. I'm not a chiled. I don't won't her on my porttiey. Stop lieing and putting things in my head. Stop playing games. You hurt my feelings. I don't like how you treat me. rude and mean. Stop being selfish. I'm verry busey. Don't have time two see you. I'm sereous. I'm taking you two Judge Hattchet or Judge Mathes. It's a court room. Serious. It just depeind whitch one I get in two First. I want to take you two Hattchet if I can. If not it will be Judge Mathis. PS. No joke."

If the letter hadn't been so hateful, some parts might have been comical, and I instantaneously felt desperate.

On a fall girls' trip to Lincoln City, I mustered enough courage to visit Emmett's work. I strode through the door with confidence and peered around the Sea Odyssey office. There were two more people behind the counter than I had hoped. A tall, athletic man dressed in slacks and a pressed Ralph Lauren button-down shirt stood near the wall at the rear of the office, talking with another woman about the correct way to fill out a time card. I couldn't read the name on his tag, but I saw MANAGER spelled out boldly beneath it. Instantly I felt out of sorts and uncomfortable, but it would have been awkward to turn around and bolt, so I stepped closer to the counter. A stick-thin woman with a flaming red mane pressed numbers into an adding machine. She looked up and smiled. I lowered my voice and asked if Emmett was employed there. When she nodded, I told her about my daughter. My pitch rose uncontrollably as I spoke. The manager and other woman raised their faces to listen.

"She's only twenty-four." I angled my body away from the two people at the rear of the office and more toward the redhead. I spoke faster and faster. "She has a disability. He won't let me see her. She's holed up in his apartment. He's a predator." I rattled off one accusation after another. What did I expect from these people? Sympathy? Yes, that was exactly what I expected. But the stiff body language of the woman with the flaming red mane indicated she didn't believe a word I said.

"The Emmett I know isn't like that." She tossed long, loose strands of hair over her shoulder. A thick frown formed on her freckled face. "I've seen them together. They seem fine." The redhead's tone turned heated as she continued to defend Emmett.

I've made a huge mistake. She's his friend. The manager cocked his head in my direction. Would he fire Emmett based upon my allegations? I didn't want that. Did I? How would he and Lindsey live if he was unemployed again? Emmett had charmed his coworkers, like he'd initially charmed John and me. But these people hadn't seen the foil taped to his windows or read the hateful letters my daughter sent. They hadn't seen the way Emmett lurked nearby or how he manipulated Lindsey.

I started backpedaling.

"Hey, I shouldn't have interrupted your work." I stepped backward out of the office door and hopped into my friend's waiting car, feeling like a criminal. I'd gone way too far. I knew the redhead would give Emmett my description and repeat every ugly accusation I'd made.

My friend's tires squealed when I told her, "Get out of here!" As we sped away, I remembered Emmett had once sued a toy store for discrimination. He wasn't afraid of a lawsuit. I wrung my hands until they hurt. *Could he sue me? For defamation of character? Would he have a case?* My accusations were only my beliefs. I had no concrete evidence he'd abused Lindsey, physically or mentally—and Lindsey wasn't talking. If this ever went to court, could I convince a judge and jury to see things my way?

At 2:12 a.m. three days after my visit to the Sea Odyssey, I answered a ringing phone, confused and groggy. "Who's calling?" I asked, gradually recognizing the man's voice.

John positioned himself on an elbow and mouthed, "Who is it?"

I covered the mouthpiece and whispered, "Emmett." John shook his head and lay back down.

"Don't ever come to my business again!" he said, yelling at me for trashing his good name. My mind tuned in, alert, hyper-sensitive, but my body shuddered from the tone of Emmett's voice—the same one he'd used years ago while standing in his driveway with balled fists, batting the air.

I rolled out of my warm bed and trudged from the bedroom, down the hall, through the kitchen, and into the family room. The chilly air caused goose bumps to appear on the skin my flannel pajamas didn't cover. I pulled a blanket off the couch and wrapped it around me as Emmett's angry voice came through the receiver.

I rocked back and forth, listening, worrying about what I'd done. Arthur jumped up on the sofa, and I wiggled my fingers through his soft fur, petting furiously. When Emmett paused, I told him I wouldn't go to his business if he'd let me talk to Lindsey once in a while. "I want to see my daughter." I sounded whipped. "I need to spend time with her, make sure she's well."

"She's fine," he said gruffly. "She's happy." I didn't believe him. She wasn't the same girl she used to be. Emmett changed the subject. "She's my wife. Why don't you write 'Mrs.' on the mail you send?"

"I haven't seen a marriage license." I gritted my teeth and swallowed hard, trying not to call him a liar.

"I love her," he said.

My stomach clenched.

"She loves me." He switched topics again and talked about

Lindsey's challenges. "She argues and goes on and on when I just want a little peace and quiet. She sure needs a lot of attention."

For the first time in my life, I hoped Lindsey was driving someone crazy. *Him.*

When Emmett terminated the call without agreeing to a visit, the only comfort I felt was the weight of my dog's head pressed against my thigh. I scratched Art behind the ear, visualizing images of my slender, fit daughter, her face clean, smooth, soft, her curls freshly washed and fashionably styled. I pictured her wearing a swishy blue skirt and a crisp white top, smelling good, like baby powder. "That's an old memory," I mumbled, shaking my head. The last time I'd seen Lindsey, she'd looked unkempt and frazzled. "The two images just don't jibe," I said aloud. Arthur raised his head and licked the back of my hand. "Nope," I said, looking at my furry companion. "They just don't jibe."

15

~≈ ≈~

As December approached, I scheduled an extended amount of vacation time so I could spend two whole weeks at home during the holidays. There were moments when I questioned this decision because this Christmas would be the fifth one without Lindsey. Michael had used all his leave for a family wedding in Hawaii the summer before. We'd understood the trade-off when he made that choice, but a mother's heart is anything but rational. I wanted my kids home for the holidays.

I went through the motions of preparing for Christmas: decorating, baking, and shopping. Michael was easy. He had told us, "Cash is king," and ever since he'd made that declaration, we had ordered a couple of Zebrahead T-shirts from the UK and sent them, along with a check. In Lindsey's case, so far I'd bought a grocery store gift card and a Lisa Frank activity case. I still fantasized my girl would come home for the holidays, but if she didn't, I planned to make another trip back over to the coast.

On December 19, the phone rang. John lifted the handset and mouthed, "Emmett," and I picked up the extension.

"Would you like Lindsey for Christmas?" he asked, sounding nervous. "Actually, till after New Year's?" He rambled on about how he'd be working at least ten days in a row. "We won't have no time together. She might as well be with family."

"Great," John said, arranging to meet Emmett in two hours.

I covered the sugar cookie dough with plastic wrap and slid the bowl onto a shelf in the fridge. John turned off the oven. I snatched my coat and purse. He grabbed the car keys and tossed them to me when we stepped into the garage.

"I can't believe she's coming home in time for Christmas!" I jumped into the driver's seat of our new Kia Optima.

"I think this is it," John said, sounding confident.

Please let this nightmare end, I begged the universe.

As I drove the highway toward the coast, John and I dissected Emmett's words.

"He said till after New Year's?" I asked, although I'd heard him loud and clear.

"Yep. I got the impression he's tired of her."

"You think?"

"I do. I think he's giving her back."

We both fell silent, lost in our own thoughts. If we didn't make any stops, we'd get to Lincoln City in exactly two hours. When we hit the mountain pass, drizzle spattered the windshield. It could have been worse—there could have been snow.

"Our hopes have been shattered before," I finally said. "And Lindsey decided not to come home." I didn't want to sound skeptical or jinx our chances, but I didn't want to suffer further disappointment, either.

"I know," John said, pausing for a few seconds, then reminding me that Lindsey had been the caller in the past. "This time Emmett called." That was true. He'd never called and offered up Lindsey before. "I think he's done. He sounded exhausted." John looked out the window, then slid a Marc Cohn CD into the car's stereo system.

I couldn't help but absorb some of John's hopefulness, but my heart still felt protected by all those layers of bricks and ivy. I couldn't let myself imagine Lindsey coming home for good. Not yet, anyway.

When we pulled into Lincoln City's public parking lot, "Walking in Memphis" filled the inside of our car. The coastal skies remained thick with clouds. All of a sudden, a sunbeam squeezed through an opening. I spotted Emmett standing next to his utility van, and the shadow of someone sitting inside. I pulled alongside the van, put the Kia in park, and turned off the engine. John and I jumped out.

Lindsey opened the door slowly and climbed out slowly. She lumbered toward Emmett slowly and stood beside him by the van. Watching my daughter move was like viewing a slow-motion movie. Was she injured? Then I saw she was large and stiff, wearing another pair of baggy jeans. An oversize khaki coat was zipped all the way to the tip of her chin. The one change was her hair. It had been cut and now hung to her shoulder blades.

John and I ran up to our daughter and took turns wrapping our arms around her torso for quick hugs. Lindsey pulled away and stepped closer to Emmett. Instead of seeming excited, her eyes appeared cloudy and dull.

"This is awesome!" I said, twisting a strand of hair around an index finger, hoping I wouldn't say something to cause Emmett or Lindsey to change their mind. "Home for Christmas! What a treat! I'm so happy!" Exclamation marks punctuated every one of my sentences.

"Grandma and Grandpa are going to be surprised," John said. "I'll get your stuff."

I reached out, slid my fingers around the upper arm of Lindsey's coat, and gave her a gentle nudge in the direction of the Kia. At first she didn't move. She stood as if her feet were glued to the asphalt. I squeezed my body behind hers and placed one hand on each shoulder blade. When I added a little more pressure, Lindsey probably would have said she felt as if I were shoving her. And she would have been right. I wanted to get my daughter moving in the direction of *us*. At the same time, I wanted to block any view she might have of *him*.

"The house is all decorated, and I was getting ready to bake sugar cookies when Emmett called."

Lindsey turned her head, trying to glance over her shoulder. *Why did I say his name?* I put my face in front of hers, then slid my arm around Lindsey's shoulder so I could point her toward the car. "This will be the first Christmas you've spent with us in years! Dad and I are so excited!" I said, walking alongside her, speaking loudly enough to obscure any conversation between John and Emmett. I opened the rear door of the car. Lindsey sat her bottom on the seat, keeping her legs outside the vehicle.

Emmett opened the utility door on the back of the van and removed three large Fred Meyer shopping bags overflowing with Lindsey's belongings. He handed them to John. John put them in our trunk. Even in the salty air, the clothes smelled musty and sour, like old dishrags. I was glad they'd be locked out of sight and smell range.

"Thanks for coming so quick." Emmett walked around to the driver's side and opened the van door. He put one foot inside. He didn't hug Lindsey or tell her he loved her or say good-bye. Lindsey sat in the backseat, staring in Emmett's direction, opening and closing her palms, waving like a small child. Emmett backed out of the parking spot, revving the engine and grinding the gears. Then he peeled out of the lot, leaving a trail of blue-black exhaust.

"Guess he didn't see me," Lindsey said, her face blank. She turned her body, bringing one foot at a time inside the Kia. Her heavy frame slumped against the backseat. John closed the door, then looked at me across the roof of the car. He raised his eyebrows. I twisted a strand of hair around a finger, then climbed into the driver's seat.

"We're going to have a great Christmas." I turned the key in the ignition, wishing Michael hadn't used all his leave for the Hawaii trip. "Are you excited?" I peered in the rearview mirror. My daughter didn't look excited. In fact, she showed no emotion at all, so I kept talking. "We'll be going to Aunt Beth's tonight, because Tenley is leaving for Japan tomorrow. She's dancing for Disney," I said, hoping something I shared would start a discussion. In the past, Lindsey had liked hearing about her aunt and cousin, but this news didn't change her facial expressions one iota. "Uncle Rob and Grandma and Grandpa and Karley will be there, too," I added.

Lindsey nodded her head and stared out the window. "Emmett says he wants a quiet Asian woman," she said. "And I'm not either one of those."

John and I glanced at each other and fidgeted. I didn't know what to say. Maybe John was right. This could be it. Although logic told me not to get my hopes up, my heart felt a few tiny fissures weakening the mortar in between the bricks.

"We'll go shopping, Lindsey. Get you some new clothes." I couldn't wait for her to bathe, to wash her hair. In this enclosed space, she smelled like the clothes John had locked in the trunk.

"Mom has the guest room ready for you." John shifted in his seat so he could look at Lindsey.

"Emmett works a lot," she said. "I don't see him much. He's very busy." She laid her head back against the leather headrest and closed her eyes. I wondered when she'd cut her hair. It didn't look quite so greasy. "Sometimes I don't do what he wants, and he yells."

"Does he hurt you?" John asked. My back stiffened. My hands gripped the steering wheel more tightly, and I looked straight ahead, preparing for my daughter's answer.

Lindsey turned away. A long silence filled the car. "No.

Emmett never hurts me. Sometimes I hit him. He holds me on the bed so I can't." I'd held Lindsey down myself when she hit or kicked, but I thought she'd outgrown those behaviors.

I changed the subject. "Do you remember Charmaine and Mark?" I referred to our family friends. "They're coming for Christmas Eve."

"I can't 'member." Lindsey shook her head. "You know, Mom, most of the people I meet, the things you say, they just go out one ear and through the other."

"Don't you mean in one ear and out the other?" I glanced in the rearview mirror in the direction of my girl. She didn't answer, and I saw that she'd closed her eyes. Her mouth was sagging, and her breathing was rhythmic.

John switched CDs, then twisted the volume knob. The rest of the way home, we listened to James Taylor sing Christmas carols, cautious smiles gracing both our faces.

16

When Lindsey walked into the house, Arthur yipped with excitement. "Down. Stay down," she ordered, as he circled around and around her feet. Slowly, she bent down and stroked the pooch's fur. "Good dog," she said.

"See, we're not the only ones who have missed you," I said, leading Lindsey up the stairs to the guest room. It took a long time because she had to pause on every step before proceeding. When we finally got upstairs, I walked into the room first. "Here's where you'll be sleeping," I said, surveying the space. The walls were painted moss on the bottom third and ivory the rest of the way to the ceiling. A floral design in green and blue and lavender was stenciled just above where the moss color ended. The pattern resembled the bedroom in Lindsey's cottage. I'd liked what we'd done so much, I'd repeated the adornment after Michael dropped out of college. This was the first time in years Lindsey would spend a night in our home. I hoped the familiar setting would make her feel comfortable.

John carried the three Fred Meyer bags into the room and set them on the floor. Arthur ran over to the bags and sniffed them, then curled into a ball on the floor and watched.

"I'll wash your clothes." I lifted each item, holding my breath, looking at the set-in stains.

"They're clean," Lindsey said, but she agreed it might be good to wash them again. "I didn't use soap."

It took two cycles in the Maytag with an extra scoop of Tide and two Outdoor Fresh Bounty dryer sheets to reduce the unpleasant odors. Before Lindsey showered, I gave her a half a cup of vinegar mixed with water.

"After you wash your hair, rinse with this," I said. "It will help get all the soap out." When my daughter came out of the bathroom, her body smelled like lilacs and her hair transformed from dull to silky and shiny. We picked out the best outfit, a pair of jeans and a dark blue T-shirt. I hugged her, noticing she again smelled faintly of dirty socks and onions. *Must be the clothes. They'll never come clean.*

At Aunt Beth's house, ten voices hollered, "Hello! We're glad to see you." Twenty arms reached out for hugs. Lindsey sat in a chair outside the circle of family, fiddling with her hair, her hands, the lint on her T-shirt. Her head and arms shook.

"How long will you be staying with your folks, Linds?" Uncle Rob asked when everyone gathered around the dinner table, passing bowls and plates of food from one person to the next.

Lindsey gulped for air. "Till after New Year's, I think." Then she stared at her hands in her lap, acting uncomfortable and shy. "I love Emmett, and he loves me."

Everyone at the table fidgeted for a few moments, glancing in John's and my direction. I sucked in a breath.

"You look beautiful, Lindsey," Grandpa said, reaching over to pat his granddaughter's shoulder. "I sure have missed you." I expected Lindsey to giggle like she used to, but she just said thanks, picked up one of Aunt Beth's homemade yeast rolls, and shoved an end into her mouth. She ate a full plate of food and asked for seconds, then thirds on mashed potatoes. When it was time to leave, Lindsey said, "Aunt Beth, you're the bestest cook." It was the happiest tone we'd heard from her all evening.

"Tomorrow we'll get you some new clothes," I said on the drive home. Lindsey nodded, leaned back on the leather head-rest, and fell asleep.

The next morning, I crawled out from under an inch of warm quilts, remembering my girl was sleeping in our house. I slipped on a white terry-cloth robe and grinned. My toes touched the hardwood floors; the oak planks felt warm and solid beneath my feet.

I shuffled out of the bedroom, down the hall, and into the kitchen. I made a mug of hot tea, snatched a fiber bar from the pantry, then walked into the family room and sat on an oversize leather chair, kicking my feet up on the ottoman to read the *Oregonian* and wait for Lindsey to wake. Arthur jumped up on my lap and snuggled into a tight ball.

Christmas had always been one of my favorite times of the year, and I loved the traditions that went with it. Growing up, Dad never allowed us to open even one gift until Christmas morning. Santa had to slip down the chimney and leave our presents under the tree before any wrapping could be torn from a package. Whichever one of my siblings woke first, anytime after midnight, he or she ran through the house, hollering, "Santa's come! Santa's come!" I loved it when it was me. But unless I roused first, I felt groggy and disoriented, at least until the gifts had been passed out. My two sisters, brother, and I opened ours in an all-at-the-same-time frenzy, tearing paper and ribbons with such vigor that the year long anticipated event ended in a matter of minutes. Then we'd go back to bed and sleep late.

John had told me his family opened most of their presents on Christmas Eve. Once the gifts were handed out, everyone watched as each family member took a turn opening his or hers, one at a time. Their experience sounded more civilized, more structured, than the bedlam at my house.

When we first married, John and I were at an impasse because I wanted our kids to carry on my childhood tradition. John thought it fine if they opened their gifts on Christmas Eve.

"We don't have to do everything the way your family or my family did it," John said during the middle of a quarrel. "Why don't we create our own traditions?" His question stopped me midsentence. *Why should my way be the only way?*

"I guess you're right." My sudden concession surprised even me. Instead of feeling tired, I'd be rested on Christmas Day.

Our customs evolved over the years, and eventually we opened all gifts except the ones from Saint Nick on Christmas Eve. On Christmas morning, the kids checked out their stockings and opened whatever Santa had brought. I wondered if Lindsey had upheld any of our traditions while she was with Emmett. It didn't seem so, based on the times I'd visited during the holidays. *Does she even remember ours? What will she be like this year?*

Forty-five minutes later, the *Oregonian* had been read, the noble fir's lights twinkled, and Boney M. was singing "Mary's Boy Child" as Lindsey clomped down the stairs loudly enough for me to look in her direction. She stood in the kitchen doorway, draped in a thin, dingy robe, the ties barely knotted around her waist.

"Dad says he doesn't think it's a-pro-pree-at for me to just wear pajamas, so I put on a bathrobe. I want to be a-pro-pree-at," Lindsey mumbled to no one in particular.

"Thanks. Dad will appreciate it." I nodded and smiled. Lindsey wore lingerie that verged on sheer. John insisted on a robe when his daughter's nighttime attire fell into the no-respectable-dad-should-be-seeing-that category. Even I was relieved in this instance.

"Would you like me to make you some breakfast?" I asked.

"I'll make it myself," Lindsey said.

"Okay, then. There's cereal or waffles or toast."

Lindsey jerked a stool away from the island. "I'm good, Mom!"

Instead of sitting, she opened the freezer door and stared inside. Mist drifted from the cold compartment. *Hurry and pick something,* I thought, wanting to jump from my comfy perch and help. But I knew she would not appreciate any interference. After all, she'd been living on her own for over four years. Without interruption, Lindsey's movements were slow and methodical. With interruption, her pace would slow and be accompanied by extreme agitation.

"Oh, and Lindsey . . ." I paused. "When you're showered and dressed, we'll go shopping." Lindsey didn't answer. She picked a box of waffles and removed two. Her hands shook wildly. *Early-morning tremors,* I thought, realizing the shaking had not improved during her years away.

The first time I had noticed Lindsey tremor was shortly after her grand mal seizure. She was sitting in her high chair, eating breakfast. A large white tray locked her in place, and she moved her head from side to side, swaying, like I do when I hear a favorite song on the radio and try to keep time to the beat. Lindsey sang a nonsensical tune, scooping spoonful after spoonful of Cheerios. By the time the utensil reached her mouth, two pieces remained on the spoon. Most of the milk sloshed off, and oat circles fell back into the bowl or onto the white tray. Lindsey forced her shaking fingers to pinch the wayward circles until every last Cheerio had disappeared into her mouth. Back then, her actions looked like a giddy search-and-rescue mission. She wasn't frustrated that day, but she exhibited exasperation a few months later when she tried putting together a wooden puzzle.

"*Aaaaargh!*" my eighteen-month-old daughter howled. "*Owwwww! Nooooo!*" I ran to the living room and found her eyes scrunched tight, tiny tears staining her flushed cheeks. Lindsey's lips puckered. She clutched a wooden ear of yellow corn, forcing it into a My First Puzzle opening.

"Lindsey!" I dropped to the floor. "What's wrong?" Her hands shook. The puzzle piece wouldn't slide into the wooden slot. I grasped her hand, and together we guided the corn into place. She snatched the apple.

"*Urgh!*" she grunted, trembling, pounding on the apple, trying to make the piece fit. I took her hand and helped slide the red apple into the slot, and her face relaxed. She grabbed the green pepper. Odd. She'd never been frustrated with this puzzle in the past. Maybe she was too tired to do it today. I took the pepper from her hand and diverted her attention to Mr. Rogers, who sang the last lines of his theme song, "Won't You Be My Neighbor?" My toddler's eyes watered. Her bottom settled on the carpet as I watched for a minute.

When Mr. Rogers suggested taking a walk to visit the neighbor's cat, Lindsey clapped with glee. I put the puzzle back together and stored it in the bottom of the toy box. After that, Lindsey didn't seem so troubled by the tremors.

Now I watched my adult daughter unplug the toaster and pull the appliance tight against her torso. Her other hand clumsily guided two slim waffles into dual slots. Watching her struggle still pained me, but I couldn't take my eyes off her. This task was simple for John, for me, for almost any other person on the planet, but the tremors had been a part of Lindsey's world for so long, she'd evidently learned to compensate even better than I remembered. I smiled at my girl's ingenuity, her stubbornness, which did come in handy in these situations but was annoying as hell in others. After she loaded the toaster, she plugged it in, jabbing the metal prongs several times before the ends slipped into the electrical socket. I worried she would shock herself if she poked the wrong way, but so far she had never complained of that to me.

My daughter picked up a small round prescription container and clutched it in one shaking hand. Her eyes focused on the white top as her other hand pressed and turned, then pressed and turned the lid some more. The white cap sprang open. I was surprised the pills didn't explode from the bottle and spray in all directions like an ocean wave hitting a huge rock. I could have removed the lid in one swift move. Lindsey fought to open three more bottles. She stuck a trembling finger inside each tube and removed one tablet, before twisting the cap back on. She organized her daily dose of pills on the tile counter.

"One, two, three, four." Lindsey rested an index finger on each pill for one shaky moment. She had to focus all her attention on this task.

The waffles popped from the toaster. Lindsey selected a red plate from the cupboard and stacked the waffles on top. She opened the fridge and removed a small carton of milk, then found a tall drinking glass and set it on the tile. The tumbler clinked when it landed. Holding the tumbler firmly, Lindsey filled the cup halfway. A small amount of liquid sloshed over the rim. She grabbed a waffle between her fingers and thumb and took a big bite.

"Help yourself to syrup or jam." I told her the syrup was in the pantry and the strawberry jam was in the fridge door.

Lindsey rolled her eyes. "I like my waffles dry," she said, taking another bite. Dry didn't sound appetizing to me, but at twenty-four, she could eat her breakfast the way she wanted. She took a bite of waffle, a gulp of milk, developing a rhythm: eat, drink, eat, drink. She changed the rhythm and added a pill: eat, drink, pill, drink.

The pills, the waffles, were all gone. So was the milk. Lindsey rinsed the glass. Her hands trembled when she tried to put the plate in the bottom dishwasher carriage. After several tries, the plate slid between the plastic guides. The cup fit easily on the top shelf.

"I'm taking a shower, Mom." Then she clomped back up the stairs.

I got off the leather chair and readied myself—in less than thirty minutes—for a day of shopping. Two and a half hours passed before Lindsey was ready to leave for Walmart. I'd forgotten how slowly my daughter moved.

Lindsey needed everything: bras, panties, socks, jeans, pants, shirts, hair care products, headbands. I filled a shopping cart with possibilities and put Lindsey in a dressing room, handing her a few items. Eleven minutes later, Lindsey had on one outfit and what seemed like seventy-nine more to go. I wanted her to try on everything so we could find clothing that flattered her current figure, but at this rate, we'd be here all day.

"Do you need help?" I asked. A merry chorus of "Rudolph the Red-Nosed Reindeer" played over the loudspeaker.

"Yes." She unlocked the door and let me enter the fitting room. Lindsey's bulk left little space to shift around. She had trouble climbing in and out of the pants and taking off the shirts. Her tremors didn't help. She stood on one leg, lost her balance, and fell against the side wall, landing with a loud thud. The room felt stifling.

"Lift your arms," I said, more gruffly than I intended. I was thrilled Lindsey was home, but she was twenty-four. I'd forgotten how much work it was to help her try on clothes. Lindsey thrust her arms in the air and glared at me. She sat on the seat and kicked off the pants, grunting. Perspiration pooled between my breasts. My forehead percolated beads of sweat. Water trickled into my eyes and burned. I rubbed hard, mixing sweat and Mary Kay face cream. My eyes burned more.

"Emmett made me leave," Lindsey said, halting our progress. "I didn't want to go. I should be with him." Her words pierced my heart. She could have used a sharp knife and it wouldn't have hurt any worse. I couldn't believe she'd rather be with *him*. Lindsey pulled a sports bra over her shoulders; it tangled in her hair. I tugged, and the bra broke free.

"What do you do on Christmas?" I stared at the rolls of skin around her middle. No bruises, no scratches. Thank goodness. Her breasts dangled to her navel, swinging to and fro when she moved. They reminded me of the song "Do Your Ears Hang Low?" She must not have been wearing good brassieres. She needed one with a lot more support.

"Sometimes we go to Taco Time." She sported a half smile. "That's my favorite. I don't like Taco Bell. Their food makes me sick." I nodded, tossing in a comment now and then, as Lindsey talked about all the fast-food establishments she frequented. "Purple's still my fav-rit color, Mom." Then she told me about the ten tacos she consumed during one meal, and in the next breath, she said, "And I need pull-on tops, too."

Lindsey didn't iron, so she needed clothing that didn't wrinkle. A few buttons were okay, but because of the tremors, it took longer for her fingers to maneuver the spheres through the tiny fabric slits. She liked zippers if they functioned effortlessly. I rummaged through the items left in the shopping cart outside the fitting room and pulled a few stretchy tops and a purple one with miniature screen-printed bows off the pile. There weren't a lot of choices in women's fashions that would appeal to my daughter.

"Where do you normally shop, Linds?"

"I don't shop very often. Are there any shirts with aminals? You know I like aminals."

I walked through the women's section one more time and couldn't find even one T-shirt in her size with an animal decal.

"It's okay," she said, after two hours of trying on clothes in a cramped space. We'd found a pair of black flats, numerous undergarments, a pair of modest pink flannel pajamas, and enough outfits to last several days. Now that I knew her size, I could check out a couple more stores for things to put under the tree.

"I like what we got," Lindsey said, helping carry two of the plastic bags to the car. "Emmett's sure going to be surprised to see all my new stuff."

I rolled my eyes and hurried to the car.

～

John's brother, my two sisters and their kids, my brother and his boys, and my parents arrived for Christmas Eve. Lindsey greeted our guests with a cool "hi" and stood stiff as a statue when everyone hugged her. She positioned herself at the kitchen island and loaded Wheat Thin after Wheat Thin with a shrimp, cream cheese, and cocktail sauce dip. "I should save some for the rest of you," she said, scooping another bite of dip and shoving the loaded cracker into her mouth.

"You should save room for dinner, Linds," John said, patting her on the back. Lindsey frowned. "But I like this dip. And Emmett never makes it." John raised his eyebrow, Grandpa poured himself a glass of Beringer white zinfindel, and Mom opened the oven and peered inside. I wished Lindsey wouldn't say Emmett's name. It sucked the holiday spirit from the room. I pulled in a quick breath and said, in the cheeriest voice possible, "You also like ham, and it will be out in a minute."

John grabbed a Lay's Wavy potato chip and plunged it into my dad's famous onion dip. "If you're still hungry after dinner, you can have more then," he said, tossing the whole chip in his mouth.

I shifted the appetizers and dips off the island to another counter to make room for the broccoli salad and green salad and Mom's cranberry salad. "We're going to make ham sandwiches with Aunt Beth's rolls." All the women added their contributions to the growing spread on the island. I pulled the honey-glazed pork out of the oven, the plates from the cupboards, the silverware from the drawer, and lined everything up in a neat row. We all held hands while Dad said grace.

"Grab a plate, Linds," John said, putting Lindsey at the front of the buffet line. "I'll help you dish up your food."

In between the smorgasbord and gift exchange, Michael called from Sheppard Air Force Base. We passed the phone from one person to the next. Lindsey screamed into the mouthpiece, "Hello-Michael-I-love-you-Merry-Christmas," like it was all one long word, never waiting for her brother to answer. I didn't know if she heard anything he said, because after she finished speaking, she handed the phone to Grandma.

When it was time to open presents, Lindsey tore into her first one with gusto. I never got tired of her enthusiasm—the same enthusiasm she had when she was three and received her Cabbage Patch Kid. The same enthusiasm as when she was six-teen and we rented a limousine so that she and a few family friends could ride in style to Home Place for pizza. Even when she turned eighteen, the over-the-top happiness she expressed after receiving a bouquet of flowers didn't include an ounce of self-consciousness.

"Thanks, Grandma! Thanks, Grandpa!" she said, clapping and giggling, then holding up three oversize coloring books and a new box of crayons. "I needed these!" A VHS movie tumbled out of the box and onto the hardwood floor. "*Garfield!*" She picked it up off the floor. "That cat's funny! I love everything. Thank you! Thank you!"

Finally, we were seeing snippets of the old Lindsey. Grandpa winked at me as I handed her a package wrapped in red and white snowflakes. There were still six more to go. I'd wrapped each item in its own box so she'd have more to open and so I could prolong the glee filling our home for the first Christmas Eve in five years.

"Another one?" Her hands shook as she ripped the wrapping paper from the box and lifted the lid. The white lights on the noble fir blinked on and off. Grandma and Aunt Kandi and I pointed our digital cameras in Lindsey's direction and pressed the shutter buttons. "I love purple! Thanks, Mom. Thanks, Dad," Lindsey said, pulling a rich-hued, two-piece sweatsuit out of the box.

Everyone took a turn opening a gift, but no one's excitement matched my daughter's. When the last present had been opened, the uncles helped John pick up the torn ribbons and wrapping paper from the family room floor. "Why don't you model your new clothes?" John said, stuffing the ruins in the kitchen garbage can.

"Yes," Aunt Kandi said. "I want to see them on you."

Grandpa turned toward his granddaughter. "Me too."

The aunts helped gather Lindsey's purple sweatsuit, a pair of black pants with an elastic waist, a pair of dark blue stretch jeans, one pink and one white turtleneck, a zip-up black vest, and a sweater with black and white stripes and stacked them in Aunt Kandi's and my arms. We carried the new clothing to Lindsey's room, where she'd have privacy to change. I showed my daughter how to coordinate the different tops and vest with the pants.

"I know how, Mom," Lindsey said, grabbing the pink turtleneck and black vest from my hands.

"Your mom is just trying to help," Aunt Kandi said. "She wants you to be a fashionista!" My sister pulled Lindsey into her arms and gave her a big hug. "I sure have missed my niece. I'm so glad you came home this year," Aunt Kandi said.

Twenty minutes later, I waited at the foot of the stairs as Lindsey descended in the same step-pause method she had used going up. She gripped the handrail tightly and placed both feet on the same tread before moving down to the next one. She'd never felt stable on stairs, and her slowness made for a dramatic entrance into the family room, where everyone gathered and waited. She grinned and twirled around awkwardly. The festive space erupted in applause, and Lindsey's grin broadened.

"You look beautiful, Lindsey," Grandpa said, wrapping his arms around her. She giggled like she used to. It was the best sound I'd heard in a long time.

Uncle Bob stood and extended his elbow. "I'll escort you back to the stairs. I can't wait to see the next outfit."

Lindsey placed her hand on Uncle Bob's arm and giggled again.

The fashion show went on for the rest of the evening, not because Lindsey had so many new clothes, but because it took her a long time to navigate the stairs, undress, and then redress. But whenever she entered the room, the family halted their conversations, applauded, and offered compliments. Certainly, this had to be very different from her last few Christmases. For me, the only way this holiday could have been better would have been if our son were home, too.

After everyone left and Lindsey was in bed, I knocked on her door. "Can I come in?" Lindsey's response was so soft, I barely heard it and assumed she said yes. She was under the covers, and the light from the hall cast the outline of the door's shadow halfway across the room. I sat down on the matelassé and scooted closer to my daughter's blanketed form.

"We're so glad you're home," I said, stroking Lindsey's soft, dark curls. "Why don't you stay? You know you don't have to go back."

"I'm going back, Mom. You can't stop me."

"I realize I can't stop you, but you should be a part of our lives. Especially on holidays. Everyone misses you."

"But I don't like crowds. I didn't have any fun tonight."

I abruptly lifted my hand from Lindsey's hair. The mortar between the bricks hardened. How could she possibly say she hadn't had fun? She'd eaten great food, giggled, opened presents, and seemed to love them all. She sure had looked like she was having fun.

"Tonight wasn't a crowd," I finally said, adding some mortar and a couple more bricks to the fortress around my heart. "It's family. *Your* family."

"Emmett's my family now," Lindsey said, rolling over. "Good night, Mom."

17

~⋗ ⋖~

y nighttime bedroom visit hadn't gone the way I'd hoped, and on Christmas morning, after Lindsey unloaded her Christmas stocking and opened three presents from Santa, her mood soured. She stomped into the bathroom and slammed the door.

When she came out, I was cleaning up from the previous night's festivities, wiping down the sticky countertop.

"Is something wrong, Linds?" I said.

Our big celebration was held on Christmas Eve, so Christmas Day around our house tended to be low-key, lazy. I still wore pajamas and had no intention of changing out of them in the near future. Squeezing lemon-scented dish soap into a cloth, I scrubbed the tile a little harder. John was watching football in the den. After I finished cleaning the kitchen, I planned to read the newspaper, then serve leftovers for lunch—and maybe even for dinner, too.

"You don't want me to be with Emmett." Lindsey planted her hands on her hips and stood in front of me, tremoring. Her eyes darted right, then left.

She's picked up on that? Even a hearing-impaired person should have recognized the contempt dripping from my voice whenever I said his name.

"We need to talk." I tossed the dishcloth in the sink. "Let's sit." I motioned in the direction of our nook.

Lindsey pulled the Windsor chair back, banging its wooden legs against the trestle supports underneath.

"Please be careful, Linds."

Her blue eyes glared into mine as she positioned herself in the seat and crossed her arms.

I leaned forward. "You're right. Dad and I don't want you to be with Emmett. We've never wanted that. Do you know why?"

Lindsey scowled. "You're prejudice," she said. Her arms tremored. She stiffened her stance and glared at me.

"We're not prejudiced. He was your boss, and he lied to us. We didn't like that. He should never have started a relationship with you. It was inappropriate because he took advantage of you. We didn't like that, either. Besides, he's too old for you."

"I don't care much about age." Her eyes darted again. *Gasp.* "Age doesn't matter."

It felt like Lindsey was parroting Emmett's words. "You're right. Sometimes age doesn't matter," I said. "But in this case, it does." I studied my daughter's angry face, focusing on her eyes, hoping to feel some connection, but this conversation wasn't going any better than the one the night before. I decided to change strategies. "A few days ago, we asked if Emmett hurt you, and you said sometimes he holds you on the bed."

"He makes me mad, and sometimes I try to hit him, so he holds me down so I can't."

"What do you do to make him mad?"

"I'm not submissive. The Bible says I should be submissive."

"What does that mean, *submissive?*"

"When Emmett tells me to do something, I'm supposed to do it." Lindsey's blue eyes widened. "You're always getting in my business, Mom. I love Emmett." She didn't try to control the angry pitch in her voice, and it got louder and louder. "I'm not talkin' anymore." She pulled her lips inside her mouth and glowered in my direction.

"I want to make sure you understand that you have choices." I reached out to run my fingers along the side of Lindsey's face, but she jerked backward as if I'd slapped her. I dropped my hand, feeling great sadness. Did she remember what I had done all those years ago? Maybe Emmett touched her cruelly and this was how she reacted. I softened my voice and said, "We just want you to be safe. We want you to be happy."

ᴗ

After Christmas, Lindsey slept a lot. She watched *Garfield* several times, and her laughter made its way from our upstairs bonus room, down the hall and stairway, and into the kitchen. I searched through one of our closets and found three more movies. When I handed her *The Lion King*, *The Land Before Time*, and *The Little Mermaid*, she said thanks but offered no other conversation. She talked kindly to John but avoided lengthy discussions with me. Her face soured when I asked a question or reminded her over and over, "We love you. You have choices. You don't have to go back." After a few days, my words sounded grating. Even to me.

"Don't you miss working?" I asked, telling Lindsey about my job and how rewarding it was to help people after they'd suffered a weather loss.

"Women aren't supposed to work outside the home," Lindsey said. I raised my brow and twisted a strand of hair around my finger. "Sometimes we have bad storms at the beach," she added. "I don't think we got any damage."

"Don't you miss us?"

"I'm supposed to only pay attention to my husband."

"Do you have friends at the beach?"

"Emmett don't believe in having friends. We just have each other."

"Are you two really married, Linds?"

"That's pry-vit."

"What kinds of things do you do with Emmett?"

"I don't see him much anymore. He's hardly ever home anymore 'cause he works all the time."

"Aren't you lonely? Is that really how you want to live?"

Lindsey awkwardly turned on her toes, yelling as she stomped away, "Quit gettin' in our business, Mom!"

John suggested I let her be. "You're putting too much pressure on her." He pulled me in for a hug and gave me a quick kiss on the lips. "It has to be her decision. Otherwise, staying here will never work."

I knew John was right. Several times I'd overheard him telling Lindsey we wanted her to stay, so I recognized he was working on her, too—in his own calm way. She didn't snap at John like she did at me. I didn't want my daughter to go back to the coast and live with Emmett, yet having her in the house wasn't how I had envisioned life, either. She lived at our place as if she were on vacation: eating whenever she wanted, sleeping much of the day, and watching movies until the wee morning hours. When I suggested she join us for dinner, she glared at me and said, "I'm not hungry now, Mom!"

We definitely had not developed the rapport I'd dreamed a mother-daughter relationship should have—more like the one I shared with my mom.

Early on New Year's Eve, Farmers Insurance called a catastrophe in San Diego County. Torrential rains had caused extensive damage, and a few homes had slid into canyons. Rainwater and earth movement were not covered perils under Farmer's homeowners' policy, but an adjuster had to inspect the property before a denial letter could be written. I was ordered to leave that afternoon. As I packed my suitcase, the phone rang. John and I picked up two different extensions at the same time. When I heard Emmett's voice say hello, my body froze. I let John talk, eavesdropping on the bedroom line.

"It's snowing," Emmett said. "The roads are too icy. Don't try and come over the mountain. Better wait a few days."

"Sounds good," John said. "I don't want to drive in this kind of weather anyway."

Both men hung up the phone at the same time, and I stood in the bedroom, gripping the handset. *A few more days. Lindsey gets to stay a few more days.* As snarky as my daughter had been, I had to try one more time. *What if this is my last chance to talk her into staying?*

I found Lindsey sitting in the recliner in the family room, staring out the window, her hair wet from her morning shower. The drizzle that had started a couple of days earlier had not let up, and I wondered if the dreary weather reminded her of Newport.

"That was Emmett," I said. "He says it's too icy to drive and we should wait a few days before Dad brings you back."

Lindsey cocked her head to the side. *"He called?"* Her voice contained a hint of surprise, but not the happy kind of surprise—more like shocked disbelief, like maybe she had never expected him to call for her. Her mouth didn't form a smile, nor did her eyes fill with delight.

"Do you really want to live with Emmett?" I asked, standing in the entryway, still clutching the phone in one hand. "Especially if he wants a quiet Asian woman?"

Lindsey looked at me, hesitated, then turned her head to peer back outside. My heart pounded.

"We're not really married," she said.

I wanted to reach out and touch Lindsey, let her know every-thing would be okay, but she didn't seem receptive, so I stood there and waited for her to continue.

"I wanna stay." *Gasp.* "But I like the ring. I want to keep it."

My heart did a little dance. *She's staying. She's staying.* "Good decision, Linds. That makes me happy." The smile on my face must have exposed every single tooth in my mouth. Then I remembered one more question, and my expression turned seri-ous. "Do you want to tell Emmett, or do you want us to tell him?"

Lindsey's eyes widened. Her face turned white. "Could you or Dad tell him?"

I nodded so hard, I dropped the phone on the floor. "Yes! Dad will do it!" I opened my arms in the direction of my daughter. "Can I have a hug?"

Lindsey stood and let me wrap my arms around her torso. "Dad's going to be so excited. Do you want to tell him?"

Lindsey nodded, but her body language didn't exhibit any enthusiasm. In fact, her body only trembled harder as her eyes darted right, then left.

～�

Lindsey and her few personal belongings occupied the guest room in our house when I drove south on I-5 in my logo-plastered company vehicle. I hoped everything would be exactly the same when I returned in three weeks. John said he would drive over to the coast and get the rest of Lindsey's items while I was away on my assignment; that way, when I came home from San Diego, I could devote my time to helping her settle back into our community. My mind raced with the things she would need: counseling, a caseworker, a job, maybe even her own place someday. I couldn't imagine living in the same house with Lindsey for too long a period. That wasn't the kind of independence either one of us had striven for on her behalf. She needed to make friends in the community and learn to socialize again.

I tried to focus on the things that would expand my girl's life in a positive way, but my mind played devil. *Lindsey has changed her mind before. What if she goes back to Emmett?*

Every night, John and I talked on the phone. He told me he hadn't heard from Emmett. "Which means," John said, "this is really it. Emmett doesn't want her any longer."

My husband's words lingered long after our phone call ended. Every night, as I tried to go to sleep, I replayed his soothing, reassuring sentences over and over in my mind. But, I reminded myself, Lindsey might still change her mind.

When a week passed and we hadn't heard anything, John called Emmett late at night at the Sea Odyssey because it was the only number we had for him. Emmett started in with his commentary about dangerous roads and how we should give it a little more time before we drove over the mountain pass.

"Lindsey is staying here," John told Emmett. "She's not coming back."

John said he quit talking and no one spoke for what seemed like a long time. My husband wondered if the line had gone dead. Then Emmett snorted.

"She's a lotta work," he told John. "She should stay."

18

H e schmoozed me till the end, Linda," John said, his husky voice coming through the receiver of my company cell phone. "Emmett told me, 'You and me, we're thinking exactly alike, John.'"

I sat down on the bed at San Diego's Residence Inn and untied my nonslip, roof-climbing Cougar Paws, kicking off one boot and then the other. "Emmett sounded like the decision wasn't possible until he gave permission," John said.

"Probably because of all that women-must-be-submissive crap he spews," I said.

"It's over." John sounded relieved. "This ordeal is finally over."

I wanted to jump up and down like Lindsey, clapping spastically. Sitting on a hotel bed with no one looking, I could easily have gotten away with an uninhibited display of joy, and believe me, I was tempted. But until Lindsey's things found their way back into our home, I didn't totally trust her not to go back to Emmett.

"He wants her things out of the house," John said. "As soon as possible." That tidbit of information felt encouraging. Even if Lindsey wanted to stay, maybe Emmett had no intention of allowing her to. *Maybe he's already found a quiet Asian woman.* "We're going to wait till the weather gets better," John said. "Probably after you get home."

My three-week assignment in Southern California ended at

the same time the Oregon cold snap ended. John had arranged the meeting time at Emmett's apartment in Lincoln City and was planning to leave the next morning.

That night, John and I snuggled in bed, holding hands. "Are you nervous about seeing Emmett again?" I asked, vacillating about whether I should go, too.

"Not really," John said. "Now that James has agreed to come along." Our friend had known Lindsey ever since John and I had started dating. At six foot seven, James stood several inches taller than Emmett. Besides, he owned a truck with an extended cab, so we could get all of Lindsey's things in one load. "I don't want a repeat of that one confrontation," John said, without adding anything more. Neither one of us had ever forgotten the angry image of Emmett standing in his driveway, shaking his fists, yelling at the top of his lungs. It was enough for John to travel with backup this time. "James will make Emmett think twice before doing anything crazy."

"You don't think Emmett will try to stop her, do you?" I asked. I hadn't allowed myself to consider that option until now. From what John had said, Emmett sounded genuinely ready to rid himself of Lindsey and her stuff, but maybe I should be there to make sure things went the way I wanted.

"I don't think he will. But you never know." John shifted under the sheets and squeezed my hand more tightly. "No matter what, this time Lindsey is coming home with us." I liked how determined my husband sounded, and now that Lindsey was going to stay with us, I wasn't sure I could treat Emmett well. I fantasized about poking out his eyes, scratching his face until it bled, and kicking him in the groin. In my imagination, my fingernails were long, like Morticia Addams's, and I wore my pointiest shoes.

When I told John how I felt, he said, "Maybe you'd better stay home."

I pulled our intertwined fingers onto my stomach and covered them with the palm of my other hand, thinking about his comment. "You're right. I shouldn't go." The main reason I'd wanted to go was to make sure a few treasured items came home. "You promise you'll get them?" John nodded; then his breaths turned even and deep.

The next morning, Lindsey chewed her fingernails and paced the family room until it was time to leave. She'd pulled her hair back with a white, stretchy headband. Her complexion had started to clear up, and she wore her matching purple sweatsuit. "I like to be com-ter-ble," she said, hugging her torso in an attempt to control the tremors raging in her arms.

"It'll be okay, Linds. Dad and James are going to go in, get your stuff, and leave. That's it," I said, watching my daughter pace. "He can't hurt you."

"Emmett never hurt me!"

"Ever?"

"I don't wanna talk about my pry-vit life, Mom."

John sauntered into the family room with James. Lindsey and I tilted our chins toward the ceiling and waved at our friend.

"We're not playing games with Emmett, Linds." Then John repeated everything I'd already said. "You don't even have to talk to him. Just point to your things, and we'll load them into the truck."

Lindsey chewed on her index nail until the cuticle ripped off, but that didn't stop her from moving on to the middle finger. Watching my daughter made me angry. Why did Emmett have so much power over her?

"I don't think I have very much left," Lindsey said. "I gave Emmett my big TV and my bike."

I pictured the purple, female-styled frame we'd bought Lindsey years earlier. "Why would Emmett want your bike?" I said.

Lindsey jerked her head in my direction, steadying her angry eyes on my face. "Because he needed it for business, Mom."

⤚

At the apartment in Lincoln City, the drapes were all drawn, and it didn't look like anyone was home. John pounded on the door for several minutes before Emmett opened it a sliver.

"You shoulda called first," Emmett said, blocking the entrance into his home. "I just got outta the shower."

"This is the time we agreed on," John said, stepping forward. James stepped forward, too. Emmett opened the door wider, letting the two men and Lindsey pass through.

Lindsey pointed a shaking finger at a VCR; a twelve-inch television; a gray boom box; ten CDs, twelve cassette tapes, and fourteen animated movies; a liquor box full of crayons and coloring and activity books; two sacks of assorted stuffed animals; and three more Fred Meyer bags of smelly clothes. She picked up her Cabbage Patch Kid and tucked it under her arm. John and James carried items out as quickly as Lindsey pointed.

"You can stay, Lindsey," Emmett said, scratching his bald head. "If you want."

Lindsey remained focused, pointing at her belongings.

"It won't be the same around here without you," he said. "I still love you."

"Knock it off, Emmett," John said, glaring at Lindsey's old lover. "You told me things haven't been good. Quit manipulating her. This is the end." Lindsey stared at the dirty brown carpet. "How 'bout the Tweety Bird cookie jar?" John asked. "Mom wants you to bring that."

"I don't think it's here," Lindsey said, never looking in Emmett's direction. She picked up a broken sand dollar and slipped it into her pocket. "I haven't seen the cookie jar in a long time. Maybe it's in storage."

When all of Lindsey's items were in the extended bed of our friend's big truck, John realized they didn't need quite so much space. Most of Lindsey's items had been sold to the secondhand store a couple years before, and about many of the things we thought she would take, Lindsey said, "It's not mine anymore. I gave it to Emmett."

Emmett stood against the wall, smirking. Lindsey hugged Darby, but she didn't ask to hug Emmett or say good-bye, and he didn't say anything further. As John placed the last items inside the extended cab, Emmett slammed the apartment door. Lindsey and her moving crew turned their heads in the direction of the noise, but there was nothing to see besides a large brown slab of wood. John helped Lindsey climb clumsily into the cab; then all three headed back to Silverton.

At home, the guys unloaded the truck, carried the few boxes and items into the house, and put them in our daughter's bedroom. Lindsey carried Darby inside and headed up the stairs, too. I followed along, bombarding her with questions as she took the steps one slow movement at a time.

"How did it go? Was Emmett there? Was it hard? Are you glad to be gone?"

Lindsey concentrated on climbing. "He wanted me to stay," she said when she reached the midway point between the lower and upper floors. Then, once both of her feet touched the last step, she added, "I still love him, but I'd made up my mind to leave. So I did." Lindsey walked into her room and laid Darby on the bed. She adjusted the pillow so Darby's head was a little higher than the rest of her cloth body. Then she pulled the broken sand dollar from her pocket and set it on the bedroom dresser.

My heart omitted a beat and my lips curled into a grin. *She saved the sand dollar from her twenty-first birthday.* I reached over, closed my eyes, and squeezed my girl tight. When I opened them, my eyes landed on Mom's photo album and Grammy's quilt.

"You protected them." I turned one page at a time to make sure nothing was missing. My eyes watered when I closed the album. I lifted the quilt to my cheek and sniffed. *Dirty socks and onions.* "Let's put this in the wash right now." I jerked the quilt away from my nose, but my heart soared.

~⋗

It had been several weeks since Christmas break had ended, and John had resumed teaching junior high students and coaching a girls' basketball team. Farmers told me to pay some invoices out of my home office until the next catastrophe occurred. Once Lindsey and all her things were back in our house, she slept most of the next three days and nights. John and I gave her space so she could transition back to the way we did things in our world, but I was beginning to worry she might be depressed.

On her fourth official morning home, Lindsey came and stood in the doorway of my office. "I wanna move back. I don't like it here." Her eyes darted right, then left. "I still love Emmett, and he still loves me." Her words made my skin crawl. I looked at my arms, expecting to see creepy insects swarming my limbs.

"I'm sorry you miss him, but that's not a reason to move back." I bent over my computer, trying to read the tiny print on a fax scanned into the file. "Dad and James wouldn't have gone over and picked up your stuff otherwise." I pressed the plus sign on the keyboard to enlarge the print. "So we won't be taking you back." Lindsey stormed out of my office, and I heard her clamber into bed. Later, when I checked in on her, the pastel quilt was pulled over her head, and she didn't answer when I said her name.

Around 1:00 a.m., the sound of Lindsey's voice woke me. *Who would she be talking to this late?* I crawled out of bed, pulled on my terry-cloth robe, and tiptoed upstairs into the bonus room to investigate. The table lamp was on in the corner of the room. My daughter sat in the green wingback, wearing her new pink pajamas and talking on the phone. When she caught me standing in the doorway, her eyes got big. "I gotta go," she said, and hung up.

"It's after midnight, Lindsey. Who in the world—"

"Emmett told me he might come back for me in twenty years. He wants me to wait for him." She stared at my face. "I promised I would."

"Twenty years is a very long time," I said, my voice weary. I glanced at the clock on the wall, and a loud sigh erupted from my mouth. "Why would you want to go back to someone who wanted you to leave? Who asked you to leave?" I crossed my arms. "Who says he wants a quiet Asian woman? You need a man who loves and cherishes you like Dad does me."

"Emmett didn't hurt me so bad."

So bad? "I thought he didn't hurt you at all."

"Sometimes he forced me to do stuff I didn't want to do. Sometimes I said no. And no means no."

"Yes, Lindsey. No does mean no," I said, explaining that whatever a person is doing at that time, "no" means they should stop immediately. My body began to tremble. I tried to lock eyes with my daughter, but hers darted around the room. *Is she telling me what I think she's telling me?*

While growing up, Lindsey often took conversations out of context, recounting a discussion that sounded worse than it had actually been. More than once, more than one hundred times, really, I'd listened to my daughter's retelling of how someone had done her wrong, convinced I would have to rush in and save the day. I was certain that was how the school counselor felt when

Lindsey told him we planned to put a leash on her and tie her up in the backyard. There wasn't a snippet of truth to the story. It was a total misunderstanding, but I figured Lindsey told it with such intensity that the counselor believed the situation needed to be investigated.

And it wasn't just conversations Lindsey had difficulty with. Conceptualizing length of time and degrees of pain were issues, too, and I blamed them all on that damn short in her neurological system. I remembered a time when she tripped on a city sidewalk and wounded her head. A Good Samaritan called and told me Lindsey was headed to the emergency room in an ambulance.

I arrived at Silverton Hospital in time to see the EMTs wheel a metal bed holding my daughter through two oversize doors. A big hunk of gauze was pressed against Lindsey's temple. Remnants of gauze, an ACE bandage, and strands of bloody hair had been twisted together into a point that stuck straight out of my daughter's forehead like a unicorn's horn. Blood had dried on her nose and cheek and chin. Fresh droplets skirted the gauze bandage, dripping along the side of her face. Lindsey's head was elevated, and she chattered as the EMTs guided the bed down the hall. When they passed, I stood flat against the wall. *She's okay.* I inhaled deeply, then released the air in a long and steady exhale. One EMT laughed at something my daughter said. Lindsey giggled, and her head and arms tremored.

"Are you impersonating Gwen Stefani or Madonna?" the ER doctor asked my girl. Lindsey laughed again but didn't pick one of the singers. I knew she wasn't familiar with either of them. "Where do you hurt?"

Lindsey pointed to both knees, her right ankle, her head. She seemed in remarkably good spirits for her condition. I was doing pretty darn well myself, considering I couldn't handle the sight of blood, especially when it originated from one of my kids. I called

John from my cell phone to let him know where we were.

Lindsey noticed me standing outside the room and waved. "My mom is not brave. But I'm brave, just like my dad." The dark-haired, handsome doctor looked a lot like George Clooney. He smiled and nodded. Lindsey seemed infatuated with him. Heck, *I* was infatuated with him.

The nurse asked me questions about Lindsey: allergies, tremors, developmental delays, address, full name, and the other times she'd been to Silverton Hospital. Then she permitted me to step into the room.

When Clooney removed the bandage, I looked away.

"Mom, I tripped on the sidewalk. I fell face-first, and my soda can went flying." *Gasp*. "My hands couldn't stop me. My leg hurts bad, but I'm being brave."

"You have an abrasion," Clooney said. "But it can hurt a lot more than a laceration. More area needs to heal." He asked the nurse to clean the scrape on the upper-right side of Lindsey's face and forehead.

She wetted a clean, square cloth with saline solution and wiped away the dried blood, the dirt, and pieces of grit from the wound, then placed a fresh bandage over the oozing opening. "The doctor ordered X-rays," the nurse said. "We need to find out if you have any broken bones."

"It really hurts—"

The nurse interrupted my daughter. "On a scale of one to ten, how bad does it hurt?"

"All tens. Everything hurts like a ten."

"Ten is pretty bad pain," I told Lindsey, hoping to clarify the level.

"Generally, a person with pain in that category can hardly talk and wants medication to make the pain go away. Are you sure your pain rates a ten?" the nurse asked.

"Well, I guess it would be a six or an eight or a five, then." Lindsey held up several fingers, none matching any of the figures she had just shared.

The nurse wheeled my girl to X-ray, but the films showed no broken bones.

Clooney turned Lindsey's head in his hands. He lifted the bandage and examined the wound. The socket around her eye had turned pale shades of purple. "You're going to have a black eye," he said, smoothing the bandage back in place.

Now, standing in our bonus room, I stared at my daughter, processing her recent confession. At that moment, I wished Lindsey's comment of "no means no" was a simple case of confusion, like being unable to estimate her level of pain. Now I worried the past four and a half years might have been even worse for my girl. If what Lindsey had insinuated was true, there was likely going to be a lot of internal pain, the type of pain I had no clue how to help her with. And if her implications were true, could we have Emmett arrested? Would Lindsey be willing to press charges? Testify? I shook my head. Lindsey hadn't told me anything concrete, and even if she had, her accusations in the past had been suspect.

"You know, Lindsey, now that you're home, maybe it would be good to talk to a counselor, someone who would listen and help you sort out things that happened while you were gone."

"I'm not talkin' 'bout my business." Her tone sounded strong, inflexible. "You can't make me. Emmett says it's personal." She pulled her lips inside her mouth, and I thought she might lock them and throw away the key, as she had a few years before. Instead, she sat stiffly in the wingback, the silence of the wee hours engulfing us both.

I felt as if we were opponents in a verbal boxing match. I didn't have any fancy language left to spew—any words that would coax my daughter into my way of thinking. I studied my girl and realized that years earlier, when the OHSU doctors had told me people with similar intellectual disabilities eventually lived out their lives in group homes, I'd been afraid that Lindsey would end up there. As she grew up, the teachers at Silverton High told me Lindsey demonstrated above-average social skills for someone with mental challenges. But when Lindsey applied for Social Security, a Salem psychologist warned that our daughter had a "propensity for difficulties with social judgment." Yet what I heard (or wanted to hear) was that Lindsey possessed enough abilities to live independently, without the support of a group home. Now I wasn't so sure my ears had been as tuned as they should have been. Maybe a group home would have been a better option. If Lindsey had had full-time supervision, maybe she wouldn't have run away with Emmett.

"Well, when you *are* ready to talk, I think it should be with a professional." I tightened the belt on my terry-cloth robe and searched my girl's blueberry eyes, knowing if I said anything further, Lindsey might dig her heels in deeper and never agree to seek therapy. It was better to retreat to my corner of the house and let Lindsey retreat to hers. "I'm going to bed."

As I moved down the stairs, my mind replayed Lindsey's statements. The oak treads beneath my feet were cold and hard. I wanted my daughter to live a mentally and physically healthy lifestyle, so I needed to determine the best ways to handle all the potential issues that might lie ahead. Even heavier on my heart was the fear Emmett would return to Silverton unannounced and entice my daughter to hop in his van, and she'd leave willingly with him once more.

Fortunately, Emmett vanished from our lives, and we never heard from him ever again.

19

~ ~

Y ou can't stay up all night and sleep all day," I finally told my twenty-four-year-old. She'd been staying with us since before Christmas but officially living in our house for about ten days. "It isn't good for you. Dad and I have to get up, and so should you. By nine o'clock."

I wasn't sure what I wanted Lindsey to do after she got up and ate and showered. A few chores seemed reasonable. If she lived in our home, she should contribute to the running of it. She didn't need to sit around and watch Disney movies for hours on end. I made a list: make bed daily, keep bedroom tidy, clean bathroom, wash clothes once a week, clean up kitchen counter after using, and put dishes in dishwasher. That was enough for now. I'd add more tasks as time went on.

I figured these requests would irritate my daughter, so I prepared myself to hear, "You're not the boss of me," but when Lindsey looked at the list, she just said okay. I remembered her childhood Get Ready for School List and how structure seemed to suit her. Now that she was older, the same technique seemed to be working once again.

On the third of the month, Lindsey's Social Security money was deposited into her bank account. Based upon Social Security guidelines, we were obliged to collect a reasonable amount of rent from our daughter, and, as uncomfortable as this regulation made us feel, John and I had a plan. Someday, when she moved out, we would use the money we collected to help buy new furnishings for her apartment.

"I'm already dreaming of her moving out," I told John, twisting a strand of hair around my finger. "What kind of mother am I?" During Lindsey's long absence, all I thought about was getting my daughter back. I believed I'd be so ecstatic to have her home that I could put up with whatever bullshit she flung my way. Yet in the few short weeks Lindsey had been back in our house, the difficult relationship between my daughter and me hadn't improved. My neck and shoulders were in constant pain, and I often held my breath in anticipation of our next battle.

"Well, she's not very easy to live with," John said, jiggling his leg. "That's for sure."

❧

Lindsey and I sat on barstools at the kitchen counter, talking about her budget. When I asked how she and Emmett had handled their finances, she pulled her lips inside her mouth and shook her head.

"That's pry-vit, none of your business, Mom," she finally said. No matter how they had managed their funds as a couple, I knew from past experience Lindsey hadn't always managed her money well. The same spring break we cruised to the Mexican Riviera with my parents and Lindsey bought two sombreros, she learned a second financial lesson, too.

"It's a cashless system on the ship," I said, during lunch on the Lido Deck. I showed both our kids the cruise-ship charge cards they would use over the week. "Whenever you want something, like a soda or a souvenir, you give them this card." I handed one to Lindsey, and her eyes grew wide. "At the end of the week, we'll get a bill."

"I get my very own charge card?" my thirteen-year-old girl asked, holding the rectangle tightly between two fingers. She flashed those movie-star lashes; then, using her free hand, she picked a french fry off her plate and pushed it into her mouth.

"Yes. And don't lose it." I set my fork on my plate and handed Michael his card. "We'll buy your drinks, but you're responsible for any souvenirs." I reminded them the money they withdrew from their Country Neighbors savings accounts was for extras on the ship and at port.

Michael slurped the last bit of his soda through a straw. Everyone at the table turned toward my son. "Sorry," he said, shrugging. "I remember how it works, Mom."

My mind flashed back to the time Michael and I had taken a cruise with Mom and Dad to the Caribbean. I'd never traveled solo with my son before and wanted the chance to focus all my attention on him, for a change. I'd been impressed with how my ten-year-old interacted with staff, like a little English gentleman. It warmed my heart when he tried escargots and lobster and politely asked for seconds. He made friends with kids from Minnesota and California and Idaho and became a pen pal with a girl from Canada. "It's easy, Linds," he reassured his sister.

"It's like money," John added between bites of pepperoni pizza. "Don't spend more than you can afford."

"And don't spend it all at one time." I added. "Budget so your thirty dollars will last the entire week."

Lindsey opened a pocket on her Hello Kitty wallet and slipped the card inside. "Now I'm ready to explore. Do you think I'll get lost?"

"Nah," Michael said, acting as if he were captain of the SS *Minnow*. "You can't get lost." That wasn't totally true. John and I had become disoriented on past cruises, believing we were aft when we were actually forward, but being confined to the boundaries of a floating resort helped. We didn't always know exactly where we were, or how to get where we wanted, but we always found our way around. Eventually.

"Stick together," we told the kids.

"That's a good idea." My mother nodded and patted Lindsey's shoulder.

"But she'll cramp my style." Michael waved his hands in the air, rejecting our suggestion. *What style? He's only ten.*

"Whatever, Michael," John said, wiping his mouth with a napkin. "You need to keep an eye on Lindsey." Michael shrugged and rolled his eyes.

"You're the experienced cruiser," I said, hoping a compliment would encourage him to help.

"Yeah. Right." Michael stood, then moved from one foot to the other, looking over his shoulder—for an exit, I presumed.

"I don't wanna do what Michael's doing." Lindsey picked fry salt off her fingers. For all of her challenges, she possessed a keen sense of direction. "I don't wanna be rushed. I wanna explore on my own."

"Okay, then," I said, though I worried this might not be such a good idea. "As soon as we finish eating, Dad and I are going with Grandpa and Grandma to the Sun Deck for the sail-away party. When you're done, come find us. If you get lost, ask a crew member for help."

John, my parents, and I walked toward the music. The reggae band was jamming to "Hot Hot Hot." I twirled, walking, dancing, and shaking my booty to the Caribbean beat. A waiter shimmied nearby, holding a tray filled with a dozen frozen, fruity concoctions high above his head. Whiffs of coconut and citrus drifted in our direction.

"To a week of fun in the sun." I clinked my glass against John's, then sipped my slushy margarita. The lime puckered my mouth; I licked the salt from my lips, already treasuring the time I'd get to spend with my family. *I'm so lucky.* One short blast of the ship's horn signaled our departure.

"I have some for Michael, too," Lindsey said, appearing out of nowhere and handing me a silver-and-gold key chain and a blue-and-gold pen, both imprinted with the Princess Cruise Line logo, as well as a bag of chocolate candies. "They were free." She distributed identical trinkets to John, Grandma, and Grandpa.

"Where did you get these, Lindsey?" I said, not bothering to thank her. I knew they weren't free.

"In the gift shop. They wouldn't take my money. The lady gave them to me." Her huge smile exposed the small gap between her two upper front teeth. My parents cocked their heads and smiled, their gazes darting between Lindsey and me. I mentally calculated the value of the items and realized she had spent most of her thirty dollars in one shopping spree, and we'd just set sail. I turned the souvenirs over in my hand. Neither was something I wanted or would use, even if they were free.

"Lindsey, don't you remember? We talked about how the ship doesn't take cash . . ." I started to say.

"Yes, but these were free."

"Did they ask for your card?"

"Yeah, but the lady said I don't need to worry 'bout paying."

"That doesn't mean they're free. She meant you didn't need to pay right now." I explained and reexplained the cashless system, like I'd explained and reexplained millions of other things her mind didn't digest on the first or second or third attempt. It wasn't her fault the short in her brain messed her up, but boy, it sure could be aggravating. For both of us. Lindsey crossed her arms and stared at me as if I were speaking French instead of English. "Is this really how you want to spend your money?"

"All the stuff was free." Lindsey's arms and head tremored.

She clenched her jaw. We were at an impasse. I thought about using a statement our counselor had suggested—"I disagree with you"—but those words infuriated my daughter. "Don't you like your presents?" she asked, her voice tinged with hurt.

"It's not that," I said, her sadness tugging on my heart. "You can keep all these treasures"—I paused, then gestured like a game-show hostess in the direction of the gifts Mom, Dad, and John held in their hands—"if you want. But let's go back to the room and add everything up." Lindsey scowled.

"Let Mom help you," John said, extending his hand so Lindsey could take back the gifts. She gathered the rest of the treasures, followed me down the steps, and through the long corridor to stateroom 2112. I pulled a calculator from my purse and added all the prices. "You spent twenty-six dollars and thirty-five cents. If you keep all this stuff, you'll have less than four dollars for the rest of the week. Is that what you want?"

"It's not free?"

"Did the salesperson take your card?" I asked again. Lindsey nodded, fury evident on her face. "If she scanned your card, you'll pay when the bill comes."

"You don't know what you're talkin' 'bout, Mom!" Lindsey's hands flew around in the air as she described her understanding of the transaction. She was verging on a meltdown, and I didn't want to start our vacation that way.

"Stop!" I held out my hand like a school crossing guard. Lindsey froze in place, like a child playing freeze tag. It was as if she had an invisible barrier around her. "Listen!" I wished I'd thought to use this second counselor-suggested technique earlier. Before I'd finished the final command, my girl started counting. Loudly. Once she reached ten, I offered a new solution.

"Let's go to the front desk and talk to the purser," I said, hoping she'd be more receptive if a neutral party confirmed the news.

"You're wrong, Mom." Lindsey shoved the gifts into a plastic bag. She followed me out of the room, along the corridor, and up the stairs.

I frowned. "Let's wait and see."

"Twenty-six dollars and thirty-five cents," Alex at the purser's desk said. He spoke with a thick, Austrian accent. I only knew his nationality because of his badge—under Alex was his country of origin. I studied my daughter to make sure she understood his words. Cruising exposed my kids to people from a variety of countries. I loved that about this mode of travel. Alex bent his body forward and handed my daughter a printout.

"I have to pay this?" Lindsey turned away from me and leaned closer to the purser.

"Yes, ma'am," he said. "At the end of the cruise."

"What do you want to do, Lindsey?" I asked. "Do you want to keep the items and give them away as gifts, or keep them for yourself?" I exhaled slowly. "Or do you want to return them?" I stated that option last, hoping she'd pick that one.

"Can I?" Lindsey said, the anger snuffed from her voice.

"Let's go see."

Lindsey retraced her steps and arrived at the gift shop doors without any detours. *Guess she won't have trouble finding her way around*, I thought, seeing Greta standing at the cash register, smiling. She was from Sweden. "I thought I might see you two," she said, her voice cheery, her blond ponytail bobbing as she spoke. "I tried to explain the process to your daughter." Lindsey stacked the key chains, pens, and chocolate on the counter.

"I know." I nodded and inquired whether everything could be returned.

"Of course." Greta took Lindsey's card and scanned a credit.

Lindsey thanked her; I thanked her. Several times. We climbed the stairs toward the Sun Deck.

"It's nice you wanted to bring us gifts." I wrapped one arm around my girl's shoulders and squeezed. "You're a very considerate young lady."

"I thought they were free."

"We all make mistakes. Now, let's go have some fun."

Ever since that cruise, Lindsey had used the envelope method to keep track of her finances.

"Cash works best," she said, confirming she and Emmett had never used credit or ATM cards. Given his repossession and foreclosure history, I could certainly see why. I handed Lindsey two thick white envelopes filled with small bills, just as she'd requested. Just as we had done before she'd left. "Food Money" and "Allowance" were written in block letters on the outside.

"Next month you can go to the bank on your own," I said, reminding her we weren't always around, so she'd be responsible for filling her envelopes. "As far as groceries go," I said, watching Lindsey open the flap of the envelope that contained her allowance, "you need to buy some meals that can be microwaved."

Lindsey nodded, removing several single dollars, laying the greenbacks in a row on the tile countertop.

Her finger touched each bill as her mouth counted aloud. "Ten, eleven, twelve dollars," she said. "I keep this money separate from the rest." Lindsey stacked the cash in a haphazard pile. "I still sponsor my child from the Philippines. I've never missed a payment, even when I was with Emmett."

My hand went to my chest. I thought my heart might explode from pride. I didn't know if I would have been as dedicated as Lindsey was in this area.

"I gotta go to Safeway and buy a money order." Lindsey scavenged through our junk drawer for another number 12 envelope, printed "Children International" in her large, uneven scrawl on the outside, and stuffed the twelve single dollars inside.

Then she shoved all three envelopes into her faded Hello Kitty pack, slid the worn straps over her shoulders, and headed toward the back door. "See you later."

My daughter's arms trembled as she clutched the handrail in the garage and made her way down the wooden steps. Her gait was uneven as she ambled through the garage and down the driveway. I so wished everyday activities were easier for her. I closed the door and sighed. Lindsey still had not agreed to counseling, but John and I both held out hope she would change her mind soon—if we could just crack the secret combination to the short in her brain. I didn't want to crack the short only so she'd agree to therapy; I also longed to experience lively adult conversations with my daughter, like the ones I had with my son. Many of Michael's opinions differed a great deal from John's and mine, but we respected the fact that he could defend his views with sound arguments. I wanted that for Lindsey, too.

Once, I had coffee with a mother whose son flapped his arms for the entire hour. "He's my gift from God," she said, smiling at her boy. "I wouldn't change his autism for anything. He's perfect the way he is." I looked at her as if she'd come from Mars. I couldn't understand her way of thinking. Certainly, all kids are unique gifts. There's no arguing that point. And if I thought really hard, I could probably conjure a time when I did believe Lindsey was a gift from God—maybe during those years when I still embraced my Southern Baptist upbringing. Yes, I was grateful for my girl, but I also knew that if I owned a magic wand and could remove Lindsey's challenges, I'd be waving that mystic stick like a madwoman.

⌐

Later that afternoon, Lindsey came home, sipping a Snickers iced mocha and carrying a thin plastic bag. Boxes of Lean Cuisine meals spilled onto the counter when she set the bag on the island.

"You cut your hair!" My hand reached out to touch the clean, dark curls coiled against my daughter's scalp. It was the first independent decision she'd made since she'd come home. "You look adorable!"

Lindsey grinned as she stuffed her meals into the tightly packed freezer compartment. She quickly closed the door so they wouldn't fall back out.

"My backpack broke today." She held the black-and-pink bag open for my inspection. "I unzipped it at Safeway, and it came apart."

"Definitely time for a new one." I recognized it as the one we'd purchased on our trip to Okinawa. "Would you consider a nice new leather one, more like a purse you can carry on your back?"

"I prefer Hello Kitty," she said, pulling two Dora the Explorer coloring books and a packet of stickers, covered in sparkles, from the broken bag. Lindsey barely took a breath before continuing, "And tomorrow I wanna get a job." *Gasp.* "So I have to look pro-fes-sion-al." She broke the word into four distinct syllables. I wasn't sure how Hello Kitty would help her do that, but if she wanted Hello Kitty, there wasn't any point in trying to talk her out of it.

Upstairs in our storage room, I located the kelly-green three-ring binder Lindsey and her special education teacher had compiled in high school. Lindsey lifted the cover. Inside the binder pocket was her resume for Goodwill.

"I'll update it if you like."

Lindsey nodded and grinned. "Can you do it right now?" she asked, flicking the paper against my arm.

The next morning, after showering, combing her hair, and

putting on a pair of khaki slacks and a plain white T-shirt, Lindsey slipped on a coat and the new Hello Kitty backpack we'd found at Target the night before and walked downtown to deliver resumes to local businesses. She repeated this routine for weeks. John and I were amazed at her persistence. Our girl wasn't giving up.

"I've always wanted to work with kids," Lindsey said, when a day care owner finally hired her to clean up after toddlers. My daughter clapped her hands like a six-year-old, and her voice rose several octaves when she shared the news. Lindsey hurried into the kitchen, packed a turkey-and-mashed potato microwaveable meal in a brown lunch sack, and stuck the bag in the freezer for the next day.

But within six months, the owner had trouble making payroll.

"She's a liar," Lindsey said, using the same inflammatory language she had when she'd lived with Emmett.

"If payday falls on Sunday, it's not lying if she waits till Monday," I said, thinking my explanation clarified the situation.

"You're not listening to me, Mom! She didn't pay me on time!"

"I *am* listening to you," I said. "I just disagree with you. Since you don't work Sundays, she can't pay you until Monday. Your boss is not lying." Twenty minutes later, after Lindsey had repeated the same accusation over and over and I'd repeated the same responses, the conversation started to feel like I was trapped in the middle of the movie *Groundhog Day*. I pinched my lips together, put my hands over my ears, and walked away.

Things got worse at the day care. The next pay period, the owner paid my daughter several days late, then begged Lindsey to hold the check until after the weekend.

Lindsey stomped through the house, saying, "I need my money." The truth was, she didn't really need the money—she *wanted* the money—but I didn't have words to defend her boss's request. Years ago, when I owned Country Neighbors, I never would have considered asking my employees to hold their checks, nor would I have been pleased if Farmers Insurance had asked me to hold off cashing my paycheck, either.

Then the owner called and confided in me. "Lindsey is bossing the kids around, and she doesn't listen very well," she said. I sighed, shaking my head. "I can't seem to get through to her," she added. "Could you talk to her?"

"The teachers are in charge," I reminded Lindsey later that afternoon. "You were hired to clean and pick up toys."

"Rules are rules." Lindsey planted her hands on her hips. "And some of those kids don't mind the teachers. They need my help."

"No, they don't. They need you to clean up, so they can take care of the kids."

"Mom, you're not listening to me."

But I was listening to my daughter. I listened while standing at the kitchen island and in my bedroom and outside the bathroom door. I definitely couldn't help but listen when my twenty-four-year-old followed me around the house like a toddler. In fact, I felt as if I was doing a lot more than my fair share of listening. In between Lindsey's pauses or gasps for air, I offered advice, but she didn't want to hear anything I had to say.

Two and a half months later, the owner called and told me she was terminating Lindsey. "Your daughter doesn't listen," she said. I hung up the phone as Lindsey walked through the back door with her final paycheck. "I didn't want to work for a liar anyway," she told me, shrugging her shoulders.

~~⋗

Lindsey returned to her routine of delivering resumes around town.

"I'm gonna help wash dogs," Lindsey said three weeks later, when the owner of Lotsa Bubbles hired her. "I've always wanted to work with aminals."

I cocked my head to the side, smiling, eager to hear more. My girl reached into a drawer, found a brown paper bag, slid a microwaveable meal inside, and stashed the lunch sack in the freezer until the next day.

Soon it was apparent that Lindsey's tremors made the canines nervous. "One dog poked a hole in my skin." She lifted the bandage wrapped around her thumb and pointed to a scratch. "The owner says the dogs think I'm afraid of them. But I'm not."

"Give them time. Maybe the dogs will get used to you. Just like Arthur did."

One morning, Lindsey packed two Dr Peppers in her lunch sack before she headed to her job. Two days passed. I was scrubbing the stovetop when Lindsey marched into the house and threw her backpack on a barstool. "I stored them in the work fridge!"

"What?" I squirted some Cerama Bryte onto a dishrag and rubbed at a burned spot on the stove's ceramic surface. "What are you talking about?

"My Dr Peppers!" Lindsey's arms moved animatedly in the air. "And I only drank one. I was saving one for later. But when I went to get it, my Dr Pepper was gone!" Lindsey's blueberry eyes grew wide. "The boss's boyfriend drank my Dr Pepper!" Lindsey's mouth moved and her arms jerked as she told the story of how her employer planned to replace the soda. It was obvious my daughter was having none of her boss's explanation. "I told her it was stealing," Lindsey said.

I cringed. Why did she have to use such provocative language? I blamed it on Emmett. He was such a bad influence! "*Stealing* is a strong word, Linds. If she plans to replace it, I think the word is *borrow*."

"Not if they didn't ask," Lindsey said, grabbing her backpack off the barstool. "Then it's stealing!"

⌣

After weeks of working from my home office, I was sent to Minneapolis to handle hail claims, and it was a relief to be gone from Lindsey's drama for a while. Three weeks later, when John picked me up at the airport, I was surprised to learn that our daughter still had her job at Lotsa Bubbles.

The next afternoon, John was slathering butter on a loaf of sourdough bread and I was sprinkling the final layer of mozzarella over a deep dish of lasagna when Lindsey slammed the garage door and marched into the kitchen.

"I lost my job," she said.

"Why?" I suspected the answer without asking: Lindsey was too difficult. While I'd been on the road, handling insurance claims, Lindsey and I had talked on the phone several times. One evening, she told me her boss wasn't washing dogs properly, and proceeded to explain how she did it better than the owner. Concern flared in my head. In all the years we had owned Arthur, Lindsey had not once given him a bath. I reminded my daughter of that and suggested she complete the tasks as her boss instructed. "Mom, you're not listening to me," Lindsey said, causing my shoulder muscles to tighten. I was sick of her saying that. Besides, catastrophe work left me mentally exhausted. I didn't want to continue the conversation and asked Lindsey to put Dad back on the phone.

I slid the rectangular dish of lasagna into the oven, then turned in Lindsey's direction, crossed my arms, and waited for her answer.

"I don't know," Lindsey said, shrugging her shoulders. "But I don't wanna work for people that steal Dr Peppers anyway."

"You need to work on being tactful and courteous." I glared at my daughter's face, explaining that some of the statements coming out of her mouth sounded inappropriate. "You're overreacting."

John pulled a box of Reynolds Wrap from the drawer. "Think before you speak," he said. "Because if you don't quit bossing people around, you aren't going to keep any job." He laid a large sheet of foil flat on the counter and set the sourdough on top. "And pull up your pants. I can see your underwear." Lindsey giggled at the word *underwear*. John wrapped the tinfoil around the bread and crimped the ends. "And nobody wants to see that."

I peered at my daughter's pants, then lifted the bottom of her sweatshirt so I could see better. The waistline gaped; the seat sagged. "Guess you've lost some weight," I said, momentarily forgetting about the second lost job in just a few months. Since Lindsey had been back home, she'd walked all over town, delivering resumes. Then, once she'd been employed, she'd walked to and from her jobs. Now she showered daily and her complexion had cleared up quite a bit. It was great to see her regaining her health. "Guess we'd better do some shopping."

The next morning, I drove her to Christopher & Banks. We picked out several armloads of tops and bottoms in a variety of sizes; then Lindsey went into the dressing room.

"Can you help me, Mom?" Lindsey pushed her striped T-shirt over her head. "Which one should I try on first?"

I closed the dressing room door and glimpsed a colorful cartoon character inked on my daughter's shoulder blade. *I would have noticed that earlier. Right?*

"What *is* that?" My eyes grew wide. "When did Emmett talk you into getting a tattoo?"

Lindsey smirked. "It's not Emmett's fault. I did this on my own. He said I couldn't have one."

I reached out and pressed my finger against a blue-and-red beach ball with a monkey balanced on top.

"It's Boots. From *Dora the Explorer*." Lindsey turned her naked midsection in my direction. "And I got my belly button pierced, too." A silver rod speared the flesh of her navel. Attached to the rod were three strands of purple, pink, and white beads dangling southward.

"When?"

"Last month. I used my paycheck."

I frowned. "Does Dad know?"

"No."

Is this what my daughter is doing while I'm out of town? Getting tattoos and piercings? What else is she doing when I'm on the road?

As my eyes locked on my daughter's belly, a gentle quiver rippled through my body. When I was a teenager, I had come close to fainting after a needle punctured my right earlobe. I had almost passed on having the left side done but had realized I couldn't leave Montgomery Ward's jewelry department with only one hole in my head. Since that day, I'd never amassed enough courage to add any additional piercings to my body.

I spun my girl around to examine her tattoo once more. John and I had never been fans of body art. We had been in Okinawa three days when our son showed us the designs tattooed on his back and chest, and our initial reaction had been disappointment. "You and Dad are so lame," he had told us. "Tattoos are cool and I'm getting more, so you better get used to them."

John and I were not naive. Piercing and tattooing were popular options for lots of young people. Heck, people of all ages were poking holes in their bodies and coloring them with ink. I just didn't realize Lindsey had the same fascination with these trends.

Maybe Michael was right, I thought, studying Boots and his beach ball. *Maybe we are lame.* Besides, our children were adults now. We really had no control over what they chose to do to their bodies. I ran my finger along Lindsey's tattoo. The design was small, less than the length of my thumb, and its placement ensured it would always be covered by a shirt.

"Well, I hope you don't get any more," I said, softening my stance. I expected this to be the end of the discussion.

Lindsey put her hands on her hips. "I already have more. I use my own money, so I can do what I want."

"You do? *Where?*"

Lindsey pointed to her Maidenform-covered breasts. I squinted. Faint outlines of two small hoops pressed against the fabric.

I could not imagine piercing that part of my body. Ever! Still, I did believe my daughter had the right to make different choices than her mother. Yes, her nipple-piercing announcement did catch me off guard, but for some weird reason, I found myself to be more amused than upset. Compared with some of the choices Lindsey had made in the past, this decision suddenly felt trivial.

"Ouch!" I said, pressing my hands against my nipples in a dramatic gesture—partly as a protective measure, partly to diffuse the situation. Lindsey giggled, and I moved on, handing her a flowered button-down top and a pair of black slacks. "Try these on first."

After that outfit, I helped her in and out of several others. When we finished, we walked out of Christopher & Banks carrying three bags of new, flattering clothes.

20

By the time Lindsey had lived with us for nine months, another contract period had ended with the Farmers catastrophe team and I'd rolled back into a claims position at the local office. John and I had watched our daughter secure two jobs, then lose them. We had watched her, surrounded by applauding family, blow out twenty-five candles on the chocolate cake she'd requested for her birthday. And we had watched in shock as she tried to seduce men.

Despite our girl's promise to wait for Emmett, Lindsey talked endlessly about getting a new boyfriend. When any youthful-looking male came to the house—a friend, a repairman, a solicitor—the first question out of her mouth was "Do you have a girlfriend?" Then she would giggle and flash her movie-star lashes. Instead of looking seductive, John and I thought her moves bordered on desperate. We tried to counsel her on more appropriate ways to strike up a conversation.

"Instead of asking if he has a girlfriend," I said, "why not ask what kinds of things he likes to do?"

"Or you could ask if he likes sports," John said, pointing out that she liked to go to high school football and basketball games with him. "Maybe someday you'll meet a guy who would like to take you, so you aren't always hanging out with your old man."

"Or you could ask what kind of television shows or movies he likes to watch," I added, knowing how much time my daughter spent in front of the TV. "All these questions would help determine if you have anything in common with him." I wasn't opposed to Lindsey's being in a relationship if she found the right guy. John and I were both leery of another man trying to take advantage of our daughter, but the small advancements she'd made in the independence arena filled us with hope she might now have higher standards and would expect a beau to treat her well.

Lindsey stood in the kitchen, blueberry eyes bouncing from one parent to the other, shaking her head. "You don't know what you're talkin' 'bout."

John and I looked at each other and raised our eyebrows. Maybe we didn't need to worry about the guys taking advantage of Lindsey. Maybe we needed to worry about Lindsey taking advantage of them.

One afternoon, late in the day, Lindsey came through the back door, carrying two bulging plastic bags.

"Gabe was at Roth's today," she said breathlessly, tossing the plastic bags on the counter. As far as I knew, my daughter hadn't seen Gabe since we'd called the family meeting at our house after their first sexual encounter. My ears perked up. "His shopping cart bumped into mine." Lindsey pulled a dozen or so Lean Cuisines from the two bags and stuck one box at a time into the freezer. "And guess what, Mom?" Lindsey's voice increased in volume. "He likes Lean Cuisines, too! His shopping cart was full of 'em. Just like mine! See, we have something in common!"

Eating prepackaged meals wasn't exactly what I'd meant when I'd told her to find something in common with a man, but I figured it was as good a place as any for her to start when rekindling a friendship.

"And he likes *Star Trek!*" Lindsey closed the freezer door. "And he likes Arctic Circle! He told me if I paid for the gas, he'd take me there." She picked up the plastic bags and tossed them in the trash. "He doesn't care so much for sports, like I do, but that's okay. We don't have to to like all the same things."

"That's nice."

"And he said he'd take me tomorrow."

"He's coming here to pick you up?"

Lindsey shook her head. "I'm gonna walk to his house. He lives right down the road, in a trailer."

"Maybe he could pick you up, come in, and talk to us before he takes you someplace."

"I don't think that's a good idea," she said.

"Why not?"

"He's afraid of you and Dad."

I didn't even have to ask why. "Whatever," I said, remembering the discussion we'd had on condoms and marriage in front of his parents. Gabe probably figured if we weren't uncomfortable talking about those two subjects in a group setting, we'd likely be okay discussing a slew of other intimate subjects, too.

"Gabe doesn't need to be afraid of us," I said, pulling a can of Diet Pepsi from the fridge. I filled a tumbler with ice, popped the can's tab, and poured the liquid over the cubes.

"Yeah, right, Mom," Lindsey said, marching off to watch TV.

<hr/>

"I got a full-time job working two hours a day." Lindsey's shaking hands darted around in the air. "I'll be filing papers in a back room," she said, explaining a State Farm Insurance agent had hired her. The hours were noon to two—perfect for a girl who hated mornings and took several hours to ready herself. "And, Mom," she said, "since I work for State Farm and you work for Farmers"—she paused, with a glint in her eye—"we'll be in direct competition."

"Yes, Lindsey," I said, a wide smile forming on my lips, "we certainly will." I doubted Lindsey would have come up with this conclusion all on her own—her new boss had likely planted the seed—but I was tickled that my girl was trying to tease me.

John gave her a high five; then I pulled her in for a hug. A whiff of lavender filled my nostrils, and my smile widened.

"That's great news." I said, giving her an extra tight squeeze, unsure whether I should proceed with my next statement. Lindsey had been doing so well, John and I had begun to talk about her taking the next step toward independence. "So, you've probably been thinking about moving." Lindsey pushed herself away from my embrace. "Into your own apartment," I clarified.

"I don't wanna move." Anxiety filled her voice. "I like it here."

I glanced at John. He shrugged and gave me an *are you sure you want to do this right now?* look. His leg started jiggling. My expression puzzled. I thought she'd be happy to have her own place again. Besides, I'd just discovered Lindsey could reapply for Section 8 housing. The penalty for breaking her lease after she'd run away with Emmett was a one-year wait. Lindsey had well exceeded that time frame.

"Why can't I stay here?" Her voice quivered. "Forever."

"*Forever?*" John and I said the word at the same time. We looked at each other nervously.

"Well . . ." I paused, shifting from foot to foot. "For one, you've been spending a lot of time with Gabe. Wouldn't you like a little more privacy?"

Lindsey cocked her head to one side. "I do like Gabe," she said. Her eyes darted right, then left. She held her tremoring hands against her stomach.

For this discussion to go the way I wanted, Lindsey needed to think moving was her idea.

I peered into my girl's face. "If you stay, we have a few more rules for you. One of the new rules is . . ." I paused for a moment to think. "You'll have to go to bed when we tell you."

John followed my lead. "And you'll have to get up when I do."

My face turned quizzical. *At six o'clock in the morning? What is John thinking?* But this wasn't the moment to divide as a couple. "Yeah, Linds. Is that what you want?"

Lindsey's blue eyes widened, and she frowned. "I'll have to go to bed when you say?"

"Yep. Our house, our rules." I placed my hands on my hips. John nodded.

"Then I'm moving." Lindsey spun on her heels as fast as Lindsey could, which wasn't all that fast. Then she stomped out of the kitchen, flailing her arms in all directions.

21

❧　❧

"M om, I don't want the pans in that cupboard." Agitation filled my daughter's voice, startling me. John and I had just moved Lindsey's limited furnishings into Silver Bridge Apartments. FoxCreek had been my first choice, but it had a one-year waiting list. I didn't think my husband and I could hold out that long.

My mother stepped out of Lindsey's new bedroom. "Can I help?"

"Are you finished hanging her clothes?"

"Not quite."

I shook my head, and Mom retreated out of sight. I heard what sounded like a hanger clicking onto a wooden rod.

"And I don't like the color of the towels," Lindsey ranted. "I told you I wanted blue. Why don't you ever listen?"

John looked up from the one-drawer file cabinet he was assembling and shook his head. "What's her problem?" he mumbled.

I ignored my husband's question. Hardware, cloth seats, and wrought-iron legs—the pieces of a partially unassembled Walmart table and four chairs—were scattered in front of me. I laid down a Phillips-head screwdriver and stared at Lindsey. Remembering some of the counselor's many recommendations, I counted to ten, then fifteen. I took a mental trip to St. Thomas but couldn't get past how unappreciative my daughter was acting.

We had used all the rent money we'd collected from her to buy towels; a mattress, box spring, and bed frame; a kitchen table and chairs; a small entertainment center; a garage-sale sofa and chair; and a one-drawer file cabinet that could double as an end table because Lindsey had insisted she needed it. Her demand didn't make sense to me, but I let her have the file cabinet anyway. Now we were working our tails off, trying to make things nice for her, yet her mood was foul.

"First of all, Lindsey, move the pans if you don't like where they're located. It's your place," I said. "You picked the towels. Remember? We shopped together. Maybe they look different in here because of the lighting." I snatched the screwdriver, lined up a leg with the seat, and twisted the screw into place. "You need to be nice."

Lindsey banged three pans, moving them from one spot to another. She stomped her feet, shaking the room when she marched out of the kitchen, down the five-stomp hall, and into the bathroom.

"There's a big, ugly stain in the sink!" she yelled from the next room. "I don't like it. I can't live here!"

I'd seen the stain. A piece of porcelain had chipped, leaving a black, rusty-looking spot the size of a nickel. Compared with some of the places Lindsey had lived in the past few years, the stain was nothing.

"Lindsey." My voice rose, matching her pitch. "I'll buy some porcelain paint and fix it. But you are living here." I held the fourth chair in my hands and concentrated on securing the last screw. Almost done!

"Grandma! You didn't make the bed right!"

"Your mother made the bed, and it looks perfect," Mom said. "Why are you in such a bad mood?" My mother's voice didn't contain the ruffled tone mine did as she picked up her purse and slid the strap over her shoulder. I wanted to scream, *She doesn't want to move, that's why! She's taking her anger out on me, like always!*

"Stop being a pill, Linds!" John used his teacher voice as he turned the wooden table with the wrought-iron legs upright and set the piece in the dining room. "Why don't you do something useful, like unloading your papers, pencils, and pens into the file cabinet?" John placed the three chairs around the table; I finished the last one and scooted the legs into the remaining opening. These new furnishings were not as nice as the ones she'd had in the cottage. Part of me still stood on that sidewalk outside the used-furniture store, longing for her old stuff. *That chapter in our life has closed,* I told myself silently. *It's just stuff. Let it go. At least she's home.*

Lindsey did what my husband asked, but she muttered, fumed, and stomped when she put away her treasures. John flattened two cardboard boxes, then held the compressed pieces under his arm, waiting to walk out to the recycling bin when my mother left.

"Thanks, Mom," I said, giving her a hug. She gave Lindsey a peck on the cheek, then followed John outside. I watched my guy walk toward the big blue bins and toss the cardboard inside as my mom got into her car, waved, and drove away.

My mother had always done her best to support me in my struggles with Lindsey, and I was grateful. After Lindsey had shouted out that she had head lice in that crowded gift shop, Mom had talked with her, distracting her for a few minutes, while I had walked in the other direction and blown off my anger. When the OHSU doctors had said, "Mildly mentally retarded," my visions of a superstar daughter who would go to college, get married, and have 2.3 kids had been dashed. And for a short period of time, I had sunk into a depression. Mom had given me a "Dear Abby" column about what it's like to learn you have a child diagnosed with a birth defect. In it, a couple planning a trip to Holland spends nine months reading travel books, watching movies, and taking notes.

"I want to see the windmills." The wife giggles with anticipation. "And to ride on a canal and visit a tulip field."

"We'll take walks," the husband promises. "And ride bikes. We'll see the Anne Frank House." They talk about the wine they'll drink, the gouda cheese they'll eat. "We'll buy a miniature windmill," they say, holding hands and snuggling.

Giddy, they purchase airfare and pack their bags. The night before their flight, they can't sleep. They get hardly any shut-eye as the jet barrels across the ocean. The trip seems like it takes days, instead of hours.

As they approach their destination, the couple peers out the window, searching the horizon for anything Dutch. "It's finally happening!" the husband says, patting his wife's hand. When they land, they immediately realize Holland doesn't look like the pictures.

"Something's different," she says.

They deplane and hear, "Welcome to Germany. Enjoy your stay."

They stare at each other. "What?" the wife says. "We didn't want to go to Germany."

"We packed for Holland," her husband says, shaking his head.

"We know nothing about Germany," they say in unison. The man wistfully fans a pile of Netherlands maps he studied on the flight, then dumps them in the first garbage bin he passes.

A local ambassador pumps their hands, giving them literature on Germany. They leaf through a few brochures. Disbelief washes over them. They sigh.

"Germany does have a lot to offer," the man tells his wife. "See." He points to a glossy photo in the pamphlet. "There are castles, tons of history, meandering rivers, lush countryside . . .

even Oktoberfest. It's not Holland, but there are some great things about Germany."

"I guess we can do this." She hugs her husband, and they walk hand in hand out of the airport, eager to find the joys of Germany.

My first reaction to this fable was to tear the newsprint into teeny-tiny pieces, open the woodstove, and throw the confetti inside to burn. I wanted to go to Holland. With time, though, I eventually saw some of the beauty of Germany and appreciated my mom's gesture.

Yet it sure was hard to find beauty amid constant arguing, and right then I envied my mom because she got to drive away. I twisted a strand of hair around my finger, trying to focus on the point of the Germany-Holland lesson: choice.

"Lindsey!" I snapped her name. "You have two choices," I said, snatching the handle on the red toolbox. "Either you can choose happy or you can choose mad. Which one is it going to be?" I didn't wait for an answer. I stomped over the threshold, slamming the door behind me. I was choosing frustrated.

My daughter's reaction to moving shouldn't have surprised me. For her, this was a huge change, and change always required extra adjustment time. After all those years away, I was glad to have her back, but most days I was the target of her angry daggers, and the mental toll of deflecting them got to be exhausting. My neck and shoulders ached. I felt the years of stress and underap-preciation coming to a head. My insides felt ready to explode.

I didn't speak when John and I stepped out of the truck and walked into the house. I didn't speak when I closed the back door and paced back and forth across the family room's oak floor.

"I'm. Going. To. Have. A. Meltdown," I told my husband, spacing the words out so each one had equal importance.

"What's that going to look like?" Worry spread across John's face.

"I'm going to sit on the couch, put a pillow over my face, and scream as loud and as long as I can. And I'm going to beat the cushions with my fist." I knew I sounded silly. It was senseless to allow myself to come undone. "I'd rather you not watch," I said.

"Okay." John frowned, then hurried from the room.

I screamed until my throat hurt. Stopped. And screamed some more. I pounded on the cushions and kicked the sofa with my heels.

During a pause, John returned. He sat next to me and patted my leg. "The pillow really isn't muffling your screams. Do you feel any better?"

"No. I. Don't. Maybe alcohol will help." I searched the liquor cabinet for a bottle of Baileys Irish Cream. I grabbed a tumbler, filled it with ice, gripped the lid of the Baileys, and turned. Nothing. I ran the lid under hot water, banged the bottle's neck on the counter, and tried again. Nothing. I marched out to the garage, seized a wrench, and sized the jaw just right. Nothing. I placed a wetted hand towel between the wrench and cap and twisted. The lid moved. I filled my glass with the creamy liquid and drank. Surprisingly, I felt better.

Two days ticked off the calendar before Lindsey called and said, "I love my 'partment. Last night I went to bed when I wanted, and I can walk to work really fast." She gulped oxygen. "And, Mom, I choose happy. I'm sorry for the way I acted."

My mouth formed a slow, wide smile. Maybe this would be a turning point in both our lives.

⟿

I contacted Resource Connections of Oregon (RCO), a state-funded program providing personal agents for disabled adults. The organization's primary goal was to develop individualized plans to assist clients with their employment issues, transportation, or anything that helped them to live independently within their communities. Depending on the client's needs, RCO supported the disabled adult and provided respite to family members.

We'd used RCO when Lindsey had moved into the cottage, and it had worked out great. Now, after living without their services for over five years, Lindsey resisted the idea of support. "I don't need it anymore," she said at first. But once she met the new RCO case manager and learned she got to help interview and hire her personal agent, my girl was all in.

The case manager asked for ideas about how to support Lindsey, explaining RCO liked to combine client requests with parent or caregiver needs.

When Lindsey first started her foray into independent living in the cottage, John or I took her on twice-a-month grocery-shopping trips, with little success. Whenever we suggested a healthier meal, a less expensive store brand, or an item on sale, we were met with a silent glare, before a loud argument ensued. By the end of the outing, we couldn't wait to take Lindsey home. We tossed the bags onto her kitchen table and escaped with a hasty good-bye. So I suggested assistance with grocery shopping, and Lindsey clapped her hands and said, "Yes, my parents don't do that well!"

The case manager asked about our daughter's ability to cook her own meals.

"I make really good scrambled eggs," Lindsey said. I rolled my eyes, remembering the time she decided to scramble a couple of eggs on her own. She couldn't remember which knob went with what burner on the stove and turned on the wrong one. A pan with leftover oil began bubbling and smoldering, and Lindsey didn't understand why—though at least she had enough sense to run to a neighbor's house for help. Then there was the time Lindsey put leftovers in the microwave without removing the aluminum foil. The foil started sparking and hissing and smoking. She jumped up and down, and John shouted, "Open the door!"

Surely she's gotten better over the years, I said to myself, but aloud I added, "Yes, an agent who teaches cooking classes would be very helpful." I explained how difficult it was for my daughter to follow a recipe and that her money would go further if she'd prepare home-cooked meals. "You could learn to make your favorites," I said, suggesting beef Stroganoff, lasagna, calzone, and tuna casserole. "Then divide them into individualized portions and freeze them for future meals."

"If I don't have to work with my mom, I'll think about it," Lindsey said. "We get along like oil and vinegar."

RCO and Lindsey agreed to the plan of assistance. A forty-something woman named Sandra was hired to assist my daughter. She had short, naturally curly brunette hair and wore lots of loud colors in bold prints. "I love her zebra dress," Lindsey told me. And after one trip to Walmart, she said, "I like the way she shops for groceries."

꙳

A week after our girl turned twenty-six, I was kneeling on the grass in our front yard, planting pink and white impatiens, when Gabe's sienna Oldsmobile pulled up to the curb and Lindsey climbed out. I waved a gloved hand in his direction. Gabe flopped his hand in return, dropped his gaze, then peeled out of our neighborhood. Based upon the information our daughter shared with us, they were seeing each other infrequently, mainly for sex, and mainly on the sly. In the seven months Lindsey had been living at Silver Bridge, we'd never once encountered Gabe there. And even though we'd told Lindsey that Gabe was welcome anytime, he still refused to set foot in our house.

Because Lindsey was doing two things at once, holding a can

of Dr Pepper and climbing the concrete steps, it took her a full minute to reach the top. As she ambled toward me, she hollered, "I just got in big trouble from Gabe." I looked up, and the sun blinded me. I raised a gloved hand to shade my eyes so I could see my daughter's face. "I called his house, but he didn't answer," she said. "So I left him a message on his answering machine. I told him to come over—I want sex."

My shoulders tensed. I wanted to cover my ears. I pulled off the garden gloves and sat down on the lush lawn. *Why do I need to know this?*

"Gabe told me, 'Don't call and leave that kind of message.' He said his parents listen to the answering machine and they don't wanna hear 'bout our sex life."

I sighed, knowing I wouldn't want such a message greeting me, either.

"Now we have a secret code." Lindsey grinned. "I call and say, 'ABC123' and hang up. Then Gabe comes over, and we have sex."

ABC123? I held in a chuckle. Yes, it shocked me that my daughter called and left graphic messages on the Posts' machine, but the practical solution she'd come up with was rather amusing to me. "Gabe should use condoms," I reminded her for the umpteenth time. Even though pregnancy wasn't a concern since she'd had the tubal, she still needed to protect herself from sexually transmitted diseases. I surveyed my daughter's face, hoping she would heed my advice. "And by the way, Gabe should be the only person you're having sex with."

Lindsey laughed like I was ridiculous. "I don't wanna have sex with anyone else."

I pulled the garden gloves back over my hands and picked up the trowel. "Gabe should also take you to the movies, out to dinner, or for a walk." I shoved the trowel into the soft dirt and dug a hole deep enough to hold the roots of an impatiens. "You could do other things, too, besides sex." My fingers and palms pressed the dirt around the stem and patted it down firmly. "How about a picnic?"

"Gabe doesn't like doing any of those things." She tee-heed. "He just likes sex. And so do I."

Lindsey tired of watching me garden and decided to walk the mile to her apartment, rather than wait for me to drive her. As I replayed her latest declaration, I wondered if she and Gabe would ever want to get married. From what Lindsey shared, it sounded as if they were spending a lot of time together. Before a serious commitment could happen, though, Gabe would have to forgive us for that embarrassing confrontation several years before and start warming up to us. But it didn't sound like marriage was a topic I needed to contemplate just yet. Lindsey told me the subject was off limits because Gabe had married once, then divorced, and now he had no interest in trying out matrimony a second time. Lindsey claimed she didn't want to marry, either, that she liked her independence, but I felt certain she'd reconsider if he asked.

On the other hand, was Gabe the right guy for my daughter? On one occasion, Lindsey had provided an expanded explanation of their Arctic Circle agreement. Not only did she have to put gas in his car, she also had to buy the burgers for both of them.

That night during dinner, I filled John in on Lindsey's latest shenanigans. When we climbed into bed that evening, my husband wrapped his arms around my waist and whispered in my ear, "ABC123. Will that code work for me, too?"

❧

At the end of my workday, I pulled my company vehicle into the Hi-School Pharmacy parking lot just as Gabe came out through the store's glass door. His mental challenges were different than Lindsey's. In many ways, he was higher-functioning, but I still thought he might appreciate a refresher course on how to treat a woman he was sleeping with.

Gabe must have seen me step out of my car, because his short legs moved toward his sienna Oldsmobile at a pretty brisk pace, but he wasn't quick enough to outrun me. When I caught up to him, we exchanged niceties; then I told him John and I thought it was sweet he was dating Lindsey.

"You're welcome to come by anytime," I said.

"Okay." Gabe shifted from one foot to the other and rattled the paper bag in his hand. I suggested how thoughtful it would be if he took Lindsey to the movies or out to dinner once in a while. Without the slightest hint of discomfort, Gabe said he didn't have much money and he used every extra penny to buy comic books. In a few short minutes, he told me all about *Star Trek* and Superman and Batman and how he didn't like to spend his money on anyone but himself. When I walked away, there was no confusion left in my mind: Gabe had no intention of spending *any* of his money on my daughter.

The next time Lindsey came by, I told her about my conversation with Gabe. Lindsey shrugged.

"But if you two are having sex, don't you think he should at least take you out for dinner once in a while?" I wanted Lindsey to demand a little respect for herself, to believe she was more than just a roll in the hay. I explained it was customary for couples in committed relationships to work together and to contribute equally to agreed-upon expenses and outings.

"But Gabe has no money. He spends everything on comic books and car expenses." I had not considered his auto-related costs. Besides gas, he had to pay for oil changes, tires, insurance, and any mechanical failure. The Oldsmobile was an older model and most likely required quite a bit of upkeep. My daughter did not have any such concerns. Maybe my girl was right. She should help with gas—that was only fair. Besides, I reminded myself, Gabe lived on limited Social Security income, too.

Although he continued to refuse to spend any money, even on a card for Lindsey's last birthday, Gabe had told my daughter, "Family is really, really important." And, unlike Emmett, Gabe meant it. He also told her, "They're all we have, so you need to try to get along with them." He encouraged Lindsey to go places with us and to visit us often. He even dropped her off at our house so she wouldn't have to walk up the steep hill to see us, and I sure liked that about him.

～❧

The yearlong lease at Silver Bridge Apartments ended at the same time a unit at FoxCreek became available. We moved Lindsey one mile northwest into a better one-bedroom unit with a spacious kitchen and living room. Everything looked clean, and the porcelain sink in the bathroom didn't have any chips.

FoxCreek had grassy common areas and trees and social activities, like potlucks. A community hall near Lindsey's unit held meetings and gave residents a place to meet. Two women were working on knitting projects, and another was creating a photo album. The on-site laundry facility pleased Lindsey; the on-site manager pleased me. Lindsey could live there forever!

We'd saved enough of her Social Security money for a new, lime-green sofa and a yellow rocker that resembled a flower garden. "I like these so much better than those garage-sale ones," Lindsey said. "It's like having lots of sunshine inside my 'part-ment." I couldn't have agreed more. Lindsey sat in the rocker and swiveled around and around.

Once we unpacked all the boxes and finished decorating the rooms, Lindsey asked, "Can I 'dopt a kitty?"

"Let me think about it," I said, hoping time would be on my side and Lindsey would forget this request.

Within a few days, Lindsey began socializing with some of the other FoxCreek tenants and talked to us about Dixie or Trudy or George. Then Trudy fell and broke her hip and moved into an assisted-living facility, Dixie died, and George went to live with his kids. New tenants moved into the apartments vacated by those senior citizens, and Lindsey got acquainted with more elderly folk.

But then she started talking about a new neighbor, a really, really tall guy named Forrest. At first, I didn't pay much attention. Her chitchat sounded similar to the verbiage she'd used to describe all her other so-called new friends, and I figured another senior resident had been brought into the fold.

"He's nice, and he's kind," she said a few days later, and a shiver ran up my spine. Those words reminded me of ones she'd used to describe Emmett after he'd taken a keen interest in her. John and I drove as fast as we could to our daughter's apartment.

Forrest stood on the sidewalk near Lindsey's unit, moving his hands as quickly as his mouth. His body was as thin as a two-by-four, and he appeared to be seven feet tall. Lindsey looked like a munchkin standing next to him. We interrupted their conversation and introduced ourselves. In less than a minute, we learned he was fifty, had just moved in, and used to live in the Portland area. Then he excused himself and walked off.

Lindsey turned and marched into her apartment. "He keeps invitin' me places." Her body shook as she explained he'd asked her to go for coffee, to McDonald's, and inside his place to watch movies. "Even when I say no, he keeps asking."

"Tell him 'no, thanks,' then walk away," John said.

"John, 'thanks' might be too nice," I said. "Tell him you're way too busy."

"Or tell him you're not interested in going anyplace with him," John said.

Lindsey's eyes bounced between John and me. Her arms and head tremored. "Mom, can you just go talk to him? Pleeeaaasse. JoAnne says he lives over there." She pointed at his unit. "He makes me feel un-com-ter-ble."

I felt torn. Should we insist our daughter handle this? If she resolved the situation on her own, surely she'd feel more confident in any future, similar scenario. For several minutes, John and I discussed the pros and cons of our handling it, versus Lindsey.

"We don't want another Emmett situation," John said. "I'll go talk to him."

"I think it should be me," I said, explaining that this Forrest guy might feel less intimidated if I talked to him first. "But if that doesn't work, you'll have to."

"You could be right," John said, nodding reluctantly. "But if you're not back in a couple minutes, I'm coming after you."

I walked through the grassy commons, past four other buildings, to Forrest's apartment and rang the bell. He cracked the door open a few inches and peered at me. His face was blank, like he didn't remember meeting a few minutes ago. I reintroduced myself and told him Lindsey didn't appreciate his invitations.

"It's okay to say hello when you see her, but please don't invite her places anymore." I trembled some myself.

Forrest's eyes narrowed. "Okay." He grunted and shut the door hard.

The next day when Lindsey left for work, Forrest stood on the sidewalk near her unit and stared. When she walked home, he sat on a bench along her route. He offered his assistance when Lindsey carried a bag of dirty clothes into the laundry room. We weren't sure if Forrest was stalking our daughter, but we weren't taking any chances.

John and I drove Lindsey to the Silverton Police Department so we could check him out.

"He's a registered sex offender," the officer said, encouraging my daughter to file a report if the subtle harassment continued.

"Why is he living with the elderly and disabled?" I wrung my hands.

"These guys have to live somewhere," he said.

"But there's a school across the street," John said, grumbling that Forrest was way too close to a place kids studied and played. "I wouldn't want him that close to *my* school."

"We'll be watching him," the officer said, promising to stop by Forrest's apartment to request he keep his distance from our daughter.

We didn't want Lindsey staying at her place for the time being, so John and I drove Lindsey to our house, dropped her off, and headed to the FoxCreek manager's office.

"Why has Forrest, a sex offender, been allowed to live in this complex?" John asked, jiggling his leg.

I crossed my arms and glared at the manager's freckled face. "The residents who live here are vulnerable. This isn't right."

"Now that he's here, we can't make him leave," the manager said, "unless he violates one of the rules."

John shook his head. "But he could be a danger to the residents."

"In the past, we did random background checks," the manager said, moving a stack of papers from one side of her desk to the other. "Now we're doing them on every applicant." She got up from her chair and escorted us to the door. "Right now, there's nothing further I can do."

John and I looked at each other, eyebrows raised. The one recourse we had was talking. So we warned our neighbors, our friends, anyone with children to keep an eye out for this incredibly tall man. And because of his height, Forrest got noticed. He wore skimpy running shorts, and his long, long legs looked like skinny tree trunks striding toward Silver Creek Lanes or Safeway or Roth's.

"The po-lice are at the 'partments a lot more than before," Lindsey said. We felt some relief knowing law enforcement was visible, but we insisted she stay at our house off and on so her schedule couldn't be predicted.

One late-summer afternoon, I picked up the local newspaper and saw that a Silverton man had been arrested for rape. I instantly recognized the person in the mug shot. It was Forrest. My first thought was to move Lindsey out of FoxCreek and return her to the safety of our home. But moving wasn't the answer. Crime could happen anywhere. Even in our idyllic small town. Lindsey had listened to her inner voice when it whispered, *Stranger danger.*

"Always trust your gut," I said the next time I saw her. I wrapped my arms around her and hugged her tightly. "Dad and I are proud of you, girl!"

After Forrest was arrested, Lindsey focused all her attentions on getting a kitten once again. For several days in a row, she called two or three times each day, telling me how much she wanted one.

"A pet is a lot of work. You have to buy him food, clean his litter box, and take him to the vet when he needs to go," I said.

"I know I can do it. I help with Arthur when you and Dad go away, and I take good care of my 'dopted daughter in the Philippines. So I know I could take good care of a cat."

As far as the daughter in the Philippines went, Lindsey just sent money, but she'd done it for so many years, I'd lost count. Overall, she presented a decent case, and it made me smile. It was a great improvement over arguing ad nauseam. Besides, she'd handled the move from Silver Bridge apartments to FoxCreek like a pro; then she'd handled Forrest far better than we could ever have expected. Maybe a cat should be the reward for two jobs well done.

I drove Lindsey into Salem Friends of Felines. She picked out an eight-week-old tabby that was purring as loudly as a jackhammer. Lindsey named her Cuddles. "I've had that name picked out for a long time, Mom."

The volunteer completed the paperwork, and Lindsey signed the form. We purchased all the necessary supplies: a litter box, food, toys, and a scratching post. But before we'd walked out the door, a second nonprofit volunteer blocked our exit.

"Don't you think Cuddles would like a companion?" the woman asked, shoving a tiny snowball with ceramic blue eyes into Lindsey's face. "They're sisters." The pure white fluff looked nothing like its marbled sibling.

Lindsey and I eyed the second kitten suspiciously. With a shaking hand, Lindsey reached out and scratched her cotton-colored head. "Well, if they're sisters," she said, "I can't leave one behind." The white kitten pushed her head against Lindsey's fingers. "I'm gonna name her Sally."

We walked out of the agency with the provisions divided between the two of us. One of my hands clutched the carrier containing two kitties. I glanced in my daughter's direction. Lindsey's face glowed; she looked as if she had just won the lottery.

22

Whenever Lindsey was with me and I introduced her to someone new, my daughter grinned from ear to ear, sharing that she was a mama to two frisky sister kittens and her third sponsor child from the Philippines.

"My first two kids graduated from the program," she'd say, explaining how Children International worked. "And I work full-time, two hours a day." She'd tell my friend more about her State Farm job. "And I haven't got fired yet," she'd add with a giggle. I wasn't sure what the giggle meant, but the delight in her voice was endearing. As long as the person stood there and listened, Lindsey kept talking. "And I have my own 'partment, too. I'm soooo in-de-pen-dent!"

Sometimes the conversation would go on for too long and I'd tactfully direct my girl away from her new acquaintance, but Lindsey was doing well in general. In fact, it was rare for her to mention Emmett's name anymore. And that young woman, that completely different young woman who had come back to us three years earlier, was becoming a distant memory.

Lindsey's flirtations now focused entirely on Gabe. After several dinner invitations, he agreed to go to Home Place for pepperoni pizza with Lindsey, John, and me.

He and Lindsey were awkward at first, one stealing a glance at the other, then nervously looking away. They acted more like two kids at a junior high dance than two people who had sex on a regular basis.

The server slid the silver tray onto the wooden table in front of us, and Gabe dragged four slices over to his plate. Lindsey used both hands to pick up a triangle, took a big bite, and smiled. Between munches, Gabe found his voice. He talked about Captain Kirk and Spock and Dr. McCoy. I was surprised anyone could outtalk my girl, but he was definitely in the running. John and I tossed in a question or two, but Gabe was on his very own *Star Trek* voyage. A half hour, forty minutes, then seventy-seven minutes passed. We nodded, listening to so much USS *Enterprise* minutiae, our eyes glazed over.

John started jiggling his leg. "I think we should get going." I jumped up and guided Lindsey out of the booth, through the restaurant, down the front steps, and into the car. Gabe followed, chatting about space missions and aliens. After Home Place, he accompanied Lindsey to our house on a regular basis, acting as if he'd been coming over for years, and telling us more *Star Trek* intricacies than we ever wanted to know.

⤸

Despite Lindsey's progress, on occasion she acted out in unacceptable ways, and usually at my expense. She had also proven she didn't need me around as much, so I decided to go back to the work I enjoyed most, and in March, I rejoined the Farmers catastrophe team for another contract period. Since my last stint, significant technology changes had occurred and I was scheduled for three weeks of training before I headed back out to the field to handle more weather-related claims.

Farmers flew me into the Kansas City airport, then booked me a room at a Residence Inn in Olathe. The next evening, after my first day of class, I scooted the chair in closer to the desk, turned on my computer, and was waiting for the password prompt, when the phone rang.

"Dad died," my sister's voice said. I pulled the cell phone away from my ear to look at the caller ID. Maybe it wasn't Kandi. Maybe it was someone else's sister on the line and she'd dialed the wrong number. *We must have a bad connection.* I pressed the phone back against my ear.

"*What?*" My insides turned numb. "Dad died?" Call waiting beeped. Mom's number flashed on the screen. Then the hotel phone rang, too.

"I'll let Mom tell you." Kandi hung up, freeing up the line.

They'd been in Arizona and were on their way home. It happened in Bishop, California. Dad was driving; Mom was sitting in the passenger seat, reading. The vehicle began to move more and more slowly. Mom looked over. Dad was slumped over the wheel. There was no plea for help, no "ow, this hurts." Nothing. One minute, Dad was there. The next, he was gone.

We were lucky. His heart could have exploded when Dad was driving sixty miles an hour down a desert road, but somehow he'd slowed the car enough that Mom was able to grab the wheel. She steered the Chrysler toward the curb, put it in park, jumped out, and called for help. The paramedics arrived within minutes, but they couldn't save my dad.

"But they tried for a very long time," Mom said, her voice full of shock.

In less than twenty-two hours, I was back in Portland and John was picking me up at PDX. He wrapped his arms around me and held me while I cried.

"I never got to say good-bye." I choked out the words. "That's the hardest part." I felt as if I were living in a dream and any minute now Mom would call and say it had all been a mistake. "How'd Lindsey do?" My voice cracked. I cleared my throat and quickly composed myself. "When you told her?"

"She acted brave at first, so I wasn't sure she understood," John said. He told me how Lindsey's lips had quivered; then she'd covered her face with her hands. "I gave her a hug and told her Grandpa loved her. I said, 'He wouldn't want you sad, Linds.'" John scratched his temple. "But then she asked me, 'Who will I share my birthday with now?'"

Her question broke my heart. She would no longer share a birthday with anyone. It would be her birthday alone to celebrate.

⌣

"Grandma says Grandpa is in a better place." Lindsey sniffed loudly. She'd been waiting for me to walk into the house. I nodded and pulled her close to my chest. "Heaven," she added, in case I might not know. I nodded again and told her I was sorry and that I hoped she'd stay with us until after Grandpa's funeral.

Michael was now stationed at Nellis Air Force Base near Las Vegas; he called an hour before we were scheduled to pick him up at Portland's airport. "Memories of Grandpa kept flashing through my head," he said, explaining why he'd missed his first scheduled flight out of Vegas. "I didn't sleep all night." He paused, and I wasn't sure if he was choking back tears. "When I got to the airport, I sat down and fell asleep on the seat. I never heard anyone announce my flight."

Several hours later than planned, Michael arrived home. More hugs, more stories, more tears passed between us all. After Michael's initial reaction, he held his grief inside; Lindsey openly displayed hers whenever Grandpa's name was mentioned.

"My birthday just won't be the same." She rubbed her eyes and sniffed. I nodded and patted her shoulder, knowing it never would.

During the next seven days, we had to get Dad's body home from California, pick out a casket, prepare him for a viewing, notify a plethora of organizations that he had died, plan a service, and buy burial plots. My siblings and I all stepped up and helped Mom do everything she needed, consoling each other with Dad stories. The most important one? He'd always said he wanted to go quickly and without pain. He certainly seemed to have gotten his wish. Knowing that gave us a lot of comfort.

After the memorial, Lindsey came to our house and stayed one more night. She still didn't want to be alone, and I didn't blame her. It had soothed me to have both of my children back home for the past week, eating meals with us, walking our halls, and sleeping under the same roof. Lindsey hugged Michael and John and me often, asking each of us how we were doing. I patted her back, said "fine," then asked her the same question. She said "fine," too. But sometimes I walked into the family room and found Lindsey sitting on the sofa with Arthur, staring at the television when it wasn't on. "I miss Grandpa," she'd say over and over, petting the dog. I'd hug her again and say, "So do I, Linds. So do I."

Lindsey had been by her apartment daily to feed and water Cuddles and Sally, but now she was going back there for good. Michael had to fly back to Nellis, and I to Olathe.

"Life goes on," Lindsey said, as we walked out the back door. Her tremors had intensified since Dad's death, so Michael and I helped her down the wooden garage steps. I hoped her grandpa's passing wouldn't add more anxiety to her world. "Gabe told me that," she added, moving a single foot to the tread below. When both feet were on the tread, Lindsey paused, then lifted one foot to the next step. She paused again, moving more like a toddler than like a twenty-seven-year-old.

"Gabe's right," I said. "Life does go on."

❧

Lindsey's twenty-eighth birthday, only two months after Dad's death, was anything but joyful. I ordered a devil's food cake at Roth's and had it decorated with a *Dora the Explorer* theme. "Happy birthday, Lindsey" was written on it in block letters, because cursive was difficult for Lindsey to read. When I picked it up, the memory of my daughter's yellow Big Bird cake came rushing back. I didn't need to add my dad's name as an afterthought this year. Before I drove home, I put the cake on the backseat, then sat in the car and cried. Later, after Lindsey opened her presents and it was time to light the candles, the sparkle in her eyes disappeared.

"I wish Grandpa was here to help me blow them out," she said. Everyone in the room froze in place, staring in my mother's direction.

"Grandpa would want you to have a happy birthday, Lindsey," she said. Then someone started singing loudly. We all joined in, but we were so off-key, instead of sounding celebratory, the lyrics sounded like wounded animals crying out in pain. The afternoon fell flat, and Lindsey sulked around the remainder of the day.

Christmas that year didn't go much better. Even though it wouldn't be the same without my father, I decorated the house with cedar garlands and red poinsettias. A noble fir held the hundreds of ornaments I'd collected over the past thirty years. White lights twinkled on the boughs. A nativity cross-stitch hung on the wall, and my Santa collection filled an entire shelf. Everywhere I turned, a holiday memento graced a wall or cubby.

"Dad would've loved this," I said aloud, stepping backward to take in the entire room. *Now for the finishing touch.* I positioned a photograph of Dad in the center of the table.

Mom, my siblings, and their families arrived to Jewel's "Silent

Night." Michael had finished his stint in the air force and been honorably discharged with coveted high-security clearance. But instead of returning to Silverton, he had moved to Texas, married, and accepted a lucrative one-year civilian contract in Saudi Arabia, so he wouldn't be coming home.

Even though the dynamics of Christmas had changed, after the food and chitchat, we kept to tradition and told Lindsey, "Time to open presents."

I expected her to be giddy, as usual, but on this eve, my twenty-eight-year-old didn't appear anxious to get the present party started. "Is it wrong to open my gifts tonight if I told everyone at State Farm I'd open them on Christmas?"

"It'll be okay." John handed her a red-wrapped box.

"No one will mind," Aunt Kandi's husband, Verlyn, said.

Lindsey nodded, studying her uncle, considering his words. Her eyes darted right. She held the rectangular box with trembling hands. Lindsey understood fibbing was against God's rules. Verlyn pastored a small church. Besides being honest and a lot of fun, he gave great hugs, just like Grandpa used to, and Lindsey trusted him.

"But isn't that lying?" Lindsey said.

"No, Lindsey, it's not," Uncle Verlyn said, rubbing her shoulder.

"But don't you think my workers at State Farm will think so?"

Thirteen voices interrupted the discussion, giving advice, agreeing she'd have been lying only if she'd told them she'd open the gifts on Christmas but had planned, intended to open them on another day, like New Year's.

"No one cares if you open your presents on Christmas or Christmas Eve." My arms moved around in the air as I spoke. I suddenly felt impatient and tired.

"I'll wait till Christmas Day, since that's what I told them."

Lindsey slid the red box back under the tree. "I don't wanna lie." I rolled my eyes.

Anytime Lindsey used strong language, it threw me back to the years she'd spent with Emmett. *At least she used a kinder, gentler way to get her point across this time,* I mentally argued, refusing to allow that man's influence on my daughter's life to ruin another moment in ours. *At least we have that improvement.*

At the end of the evening, our guests put on their winter coats and said their good-byes. Mom, Lindsey, John, and I stood on the front porch, waving, until all the headlights disappeared into the fog. Mom headed upstairs to the guest room. I walked toward my bedroom while Lindsey shadowed behind me, tremoring.

"Mom, I only meant I shouldn't open the presents from work." Her little-girl voice filled with frustration.

"You didn't say that." My hand reached for the doorknob. "Everyone's left. Dad's in bed, Grandma's upstairs. We'll wait till morning."

"Mom, you aren't listening to me." Lindsey's volume increased. "I only meant the gifts from work. I didn't mean gifts from you and Dad. I wanna open those now."

"You never said anything about our gifts versus work gifts. It's too late. I'm not gathering everyone back. Sorry."

Lindsey repeated her words again while I stood in the hall, nodding, listening, tapping my foot.

"You said you were talking only about not opening the work gifts. You're okay opening the ones we gave you. Is that correct?"

"Yes." Lindsey locked her arms across her chest.

"I'm sorry we misunderstood, but this year, everything will be opened on Christmas Day." I twisted the knob. "I know you're disappointed, but I'm going to bed. Good night. I love you." I reached out for a hug, but she jerked backward and tripped over her feet. I closed the bedroom door, and Lindsey stomped away, her tennis-shoed feet smacking against the hardwood floors.

On Christmas morning, Mom and John and I gathered in front of the Christmas tree and waited for Lindsey to wake. At ten thirty, I tiptoed into the den and shook her. "Santa's come."

A smile crossed her lips. Lindsey slipped a robe over her bright pink stretchy pajamas, covered in penguins, and stumbled into the family room.

She had told us she wanted a bike but had added, "Oh, just surprise me! I love surprises!" She'd taken the three-speed we'd given her when she'd left with Emmett, but it hadn't returned when she did. Initially she had told us she'd given it to him, but then she'd confessed she couldn't remember whether they'd sold it or lost it or. . . We had spent a lot of money replacing the items she sold or lost, but the bike hadn't made the "need to be replaced" list yet. Besides, Lindsey's tremors seemed to be getting worse, and we weren't convinced a bike would be the safest gift.

In the months leading up to Christmas, Lindsey had called several times to report that her wooden bed frame had broken. "I'm afraid it will fall on my kittens and they'll get crushed." She had asked if she could use her Social Security money to buy a new one, but we'd decided to surprise her with an ornate wrought-iron frame instead.

I placed a picture of the bed frame in a shoebox, wrapped the box in snowman paper, and tied the package with lots of red curling ribbon. When Lindsey opened the gift, her face fell. John dragged in the oversize box, presenting the bed frame in Vanna White fashion, but his performance didn't elicit any excitement from our daughter.

"Thank you." Her tone was gracious, but disappointment grayed her eyes. She had expected a bike. Now that she was in her late twenties, we weren't buying tons of little gifts like we used to. We bought one large item and a few smaller stocking stuffers and called it good. *She's not a child any longer*, I thought, looking across the room, seeing a large carrying case filled with crayons, markers, and coloring and sticker books that Michael and his new bride had sent.

Lindsey feigned happiness until she gathered all her gifts.

"I. Need. A. Mother." Lindsey pushed out each word.

My mom's mouth dropped open.

"Same old, same old," John mumbled, escaping to the den to watch football.

"You're never here for me. You always make me talk to Dad." She gasped for air, then revved her vocal engines. "I'm trying to be a better daughter, but you're not trying to be a better mother."

"*What?*" I asked.

"You always make me talk to Dad. I need you. What if I have a im-por-tant mother question?"

I knew John helped out a lot. Especially when I was on the road.

"If you have an important mother question," I said, "I'll listen. Just like I listen to the five messages you leave on our answering machine every single day." My voice got quieter. "But after I listen, I call you back and give advice you don't like, so I figure you should talk to Dad."

"You should listen to me no matter how long I wanna talk."

I reminded her that the day before, she'd complained that the post office had returned two of the Christmas cards she had mailed, with "undeliverable" stamped on their envelopes. Darn good odds, considering her handwriting. I'd proposed she input the addresses into her computer and print off labels, which I would help her with. "But you didn't like that idea and pooh-poohed it." Then I'd overheard a conversation between Lindsey and her cousin. Karley had recommended computer labels, too.

"You agreed. Excitedly!" I hit my hand along the side of my head, like the guy in the commercial who should have had a V8. "You didn't like my idea, but you liked hers. Why is that?" I waited for her response.

"I had to answer that way. To be polite."

I wanted to mention the presents, Christmas Day versus Christmas Eve, but knew that would extend the conversation.

"Mom, I want you to listen to me. Whenever I talk, you should listen."

Lindsey lectured me for forty-seven minutes, shadowing me into the kitchen, outside the bathroom, and back into the family room, like she'd done since she was two. Mom sat in a chair, mouth gaping, shocked with Lindsey's volume, the acceleration of her sentences, their velocity. I felt like I was being pelted with stones, instead of words. Pound, pound, pound. The longer Lindsey lectured, the more her voice turned ear-piercingly loud.

"I'm done talking, Lindsey," I said. It had been a while since I'd felt the need to protect my heart from harm. I could've sworn some of the mortar had softened and a few bricks had tumbled away. But at that moment, the brick wall expanded and strengthened tenfold. I stomped into the kitchen to heat up some ham and rolls. Lindsey stomped to the bonus room to watch a movie, *The Little Mermaid* or *Beauty and the Beast* or *The Lion King*. I didn't care.

"I thought Lindsey had gotten better." Mom followed me into the kitchen to pour a cup of coffee. "That's draining. I wonder why she acts that way."

"Because she didn't get a bike, because we didn't open presents last night, because she didn't like my Christmas card mailing suggestion—all of the above and more."

I avoided Lindsey until dinnertime, and she avoided me. The family room turned silent. Mom and I read books while the prime rib roasted to medium rare. The aroma of salt, rosemary, and pepper drifted from the kitchen to the family room, and my stomach growled.

After dinner, I asked my tremoring daughter for a meeting. I sat on the sofa. Lindsey claimed the new tweed wingback recliner. Her back stiffened; her eyes darted right and left.

"Lindsey, I'm sorry I'm not the mother you wanted, but I'm the one you got." I told her I was tired of the confrontations, outbursts, and bullying. "When children are little, they need their mothers all the time. But as they grow, they need them less and less. We only talk to Michael a couple of times a month, if that." I paused, letting that information sink in. "You don't lecture Dad. You don't lecture Grandma. You take out all your anger on me. And I'm tired of it."

"You're my mother. I get to treat you that way."

"No, Lindsey, you don't. I wouldn't allow my friends, my relatives, anyone else to talk to me the way you do. And after today, I'm not allowing it from you. You're not a child anymore. You're twenty-eight. Old enough to know better." Lindsey sat in the chair. Her body shook. She tilted her head to one side, and her eyes darted right, then left. "I think you're disappointed you didn't get a bike."

"I wanted a bike." Lindsey's mouth twitched when she spoke.

"I know you did. But sometimes parents decide to get something else. You also said we could surprise you. That's what we did."

"I wanted a bike."

"That's too bad. We don't always get what we want." I paused. Another thought rushed into my head, and I inhaled sharply. "I also think you're angry about Grandpa. I think you miss him. It wasn't the same on your birthday, and it wasn't the same at Christmas."

Lindsey's eyes watered. Her face fell. She nodded slowly.

"I'm so sorry, Lindsey." I got up, walked toward my girl, reached out, and put my hand lightly on her shoulder. She stood, allowing me to wrap my arms around her. "I wish Grandpa was here, too. But being angry isn't going to bring him back." I squeezed tight. "And what do you think Grandpa would say if he saw you acting this way?"

"He'd say, 'Do you want Grandpa to get mad?'" Lindsey said.

I chuckled. It was exactly what Grandpa would have said. It was what my grandmother had said to me, and my dad had carried on his mother's tradition. None of us knew what either of them getting mad would look like, but we sure didn't want to find out.

"You're so right. But Linds, I'm no longer going to be your punching bag. You can see a counselor and talk about your feelings, but you can't take out all your anger on me."

"But you have to listen to me. You're my mother." Lindsey said, but her voice had weakened; the fight had vanished from her tone. I knew she would think about what I'd said and, in her own time, in her own way, she'd come around.

"Dad's taking you back to your apartment now. I love you, but, as a reminder, if you take out your anger on me again, I'm going to say, 'Pow, pow, pow.'" I grinned at her, hoping she liked the signal. "I hope I'll never need to use it, but that will be my way of telling you I feel verbally punched. If you don't stop, I'll end the call. If you're here, you'll need to go home."

Lindsey forced a half smile. "Okay, Mom." She gave me one more hug. "I sure miss Grandpa." Her body trembled. I reached for her fingers. She wrapped hers around mine, and we walked through the family room.

"Tomorrow, Dad and your uncle will come over and put your new bed together." I kissed my daughter on the cheek.

"That sounds great." Lindsey slipped her arms through the Hello Kitty backpack straps, then followed John toward the garage.

"Love you, Linds."

"Love you, too, Mom."

23

~~~

fter the holidays, Lindsey carried on as if her Christmas Day outburst had never happened, but my emotions remained guarded. *It's just a matter of time*, I thought, *until she takes her frustrations out on me once again.* I so wanted to love my girl without the brick wall being in the way. There were a few times when I felt hopeful that my shield of protection was no longer necessary. *Could the mortar be softening?* I wondered, right before another over-the-top-frustrating situation in which I could not reason with my daughter. By now, I figured, only something major—like an earthquake—had the power to take down the fortress.

Maybe a vacation would help, I thought. In the past, getting away and not worrying about "Lindsey stuff" for a while had been the perfect medicine for my mental health. I planned to come back relaxed, my internal well recharged, ready to handle whatever new Lindsey issue came my way.

In January, John and I flew to Mexico with two other couples from our cruise group—a group of friends we'd been traveling with for years.

"Welcome to Mazatlán," the driver said, loading six suitcases into the back of his van. As he drove toward our resort, I held my backpack on my lap. My eyes searched both sides of the road, taking in our surroundings: roosters strutted through front yards;

hungry, scrappy dogs ran free; and metal bars covered windows on vacant-looking houses. The last time John and I had been to this city was on a cruise to the Mexican Riviera with our kids. Back then, we had witnessed poverty, but the inland neighborhoods we passed through now unnerved me. When the driver stopped at a red light, it seemed to take forever to change, and I tightened my grip on my backpack.

"There's your place." The driver pointed in the direction of the marina. The light flashed to green, and he turned the van toward Golden Isla Resort, slowing as he crossed over an old stone bridge. The security guard waved us through, and the wrought-iron gate rolled closed behind us. Left outside was a one-legged old woman lying on the walkway, rattling her tin cup, and three barefoot children selling bright-colored boxes of Chiclets. I turned my gaze away. *Sure makes my problems seem small.*

For the next ten days, our friends, my husband, and I could do whatever we wanted, and we wanted to stay in the touristy sections of town. We sat on benches and listened to a mariachi band in Old Town Mazatlán; we stepped inside the golden-yellow cathedral and snapped a photo; and we visited the open-air market, where the mixture of raw fish, chicken, and pork created a stench unpleasant enough that I sucked in my breath and held it until we passed by. No matter what we did or where we went, I felt Lindsey and Michael's footprints on the sidewalk, in the square, and in the market—and my mind tumbled back to that spring-break trip.

"What are those?" ten-year-old Michael asked, pointing to pig heads and feet and intestines, the parts of an animal we'd never seen displayed at our grocery store.

"This doesn't smell like Safeway." Lindsey scrunched her face and plugged her nose. "I wouldn't wanna eat that." She used her free hand to point to a chicken breast covered in pesky flies.

"They don't have the same food-handling rules." I seized the opportunity to educate Lindsey and Michael on differences between the United States and Mexico and pointed to a thin layer of ice under the meat. "Or the same refrigeration methods."

As John and I strolled along the Malecón with our friends, my mind drifted back to the day we'd walked the same ocean-front stretch with our kids. Warmth filled my insides. *Now, that was a fun vacation.* I smiled. Well, if you didn't count how much Lindsey struggled with the constant change of schedule between the days at sea and the port stops. Change was incredibly discombobulating for a girl who required—no, *demanded*—structure. We tried over and over to teach her the wonders of traveling, but it never worked.

The trip that broke our travel back was the one to Canada. John ended it early when Lindsey wouldn't change out of her Strawberry Shortcake baby dolls, and after that, she didn't ever want to travel again. I was so angry about my daughter's poor attitude, I didn't want her to travel anymore, either—until she told us, "I prefer to stay with Grandma and Grandpa." As soon as my girl spoke those words, disappointment stung my heart. Ever since I could remember, one of my main goals had been to show my kids the world. Now one of my offspring didn't want to explore anywhere anymore.

In the end, we didn't fight Lindsey on that decision—some battles just weren't worth fighting. She had marvelous one-on-one times with Grandma and Grandpa or her aunt. John, Michael, and I continued traveling, enjoying a couple of trips per year until our son graduated from high school.

Years later, when Michael married his bride in Calgary, I assumed Lindsey would agree to fly to Canada, but the day we told her about the flight and hotel stay, her eyes widened with alarm and her face twisted into fear. "I don't travel so well," she said, just as she'd said all those other times. John and I reluctantly attended our son's wedding without our daughter.

For as long as I could remember, vacationing had been a natural part of our life. We'd traveled as a couple, as a family, and with friends. The only person missing from my mental travel flick was Lindsey. I shook my head back and forth. *For someone who planned to use this vacation to get away and not think about parenting, I'm not doing a very good job!*

We found a bar on the beach, and everyone ordered a Corona. "To friendship!" we toasted, clinking six bottles together. The sky turned orange and red and purple, and the sun disappeared into the ocean.

I squeezed a lime through the neck of my beer bottle. "We're flying home in seventy-two hours," I said. Everyone groaned.

John shook his head, put his lips against his drink, and tipped the bottle.

"Don't remind us," Sara said, glancing at her husband.

Chuck nodded. "Yep. Not ready."

"Maybe tomorrow should be a pool day," I said.

The next morning, we donned bathing suits. All six amigos strode past the sailboats, catamarans, and small yachts moored in the marina, toward the mosaic-tiled pool. Spirited Mexican songs blasted from a portable CD player. Adán, the dark-haired, brown-eyed pool attendant, reminded me of a rail-thin Ritchie Valens. He noticed our English conversations and changed the music to Elvis. We explained in animated, broken Spanish that we preferred the authentic tunes, but Adán laughed nervously, mixing another tropical drink concoction of mango, coconut, and pineapple.

"You did an awesome job raising Lindsey," our friend Jim said. The lyrics to "Hound Dog" blared. I closed my eyes. Pleasant and not-so-pleasant images of my daughter's last twenty-some years swept through my mind.

"Well, thanks," I said, certain he was just being nice. My skin warmed from the sun's heat. I visualized the cool water and imagined moving from the chaise to the bright yellow floating raft we'd nicknamed the *Titanic*.

Jim set the cribbage board on the table and stuck red and blue spillikins into the starting positions. "She lives on her own, in her own apartment," he said, waiting for my husband to deal the first round. "She walks everywhere. I see her around town all the time. Not all kids like Lindsey are able to do that."

Hmm, I thought. *Jim should know*. He was a retired school administrator and special education instructor. An expert.

"I love Lindsey stories." Sara put down her book and laughed. "My favorite was when she came to school and told the counselor she had to pay ten cents a minute to talk to you. Now, *that* was funny. Remember?"

"Yeah, I remember." A chuckle erupted from my mouth. *My daughter sure does give me plenty of stories*. Not only had Lindsey visited the counselor at Silverton High after the Arthur "leash" incident, she also went to see him after this situation, too. And then, of course, we received another concerned call from the school.

"I agree with Jim," Sara said. "Lindsey's turned out great." My ego swelled, inflating like the helium balloon we'd filled at the Hi-School Pharmacy on Lindsey's last birthday. It was hard to believe she was so grown-up.

Because her challenges often overwhelmed me, I seldom took time to acknowledge all her successes or how well she was doing. It was news to me that other people thought we'd done a good job with our daughter. My balloon grew bigger.

I moved from the lounge chair to the water, stepping into the pool. My body froze. I grabbed the *Titanic*, inched deeper into the water, and lay on the raft, letting the chilly liquid splash over my legs, arms, and abdomen.

"I'm not sure we could've handled the Emmett incident," Jim's wife said. "Lindsey is definitely a survivor."

I winced, and my body stiffened. Emmett's name still aroused fury in me. If only Lindsey had shared what had happened to her during that time, maybe my mind wouldn't hold on to the distressing images it had fabricated. *It's over now*, I reminded myself, for the thousandth time since she'd been back. *But I still wish she would talk to a professional.*

Even though I wanted her to stop using inflammatory language and to learn to control her anger better, my greatest wish was for Lindsey to recognize her value, her importance. I wanted her to realize she deserved to be treated well in all of her personal relationships, and to expect, even demand, in a socially acceptable manner, respect from the men in her life. I'd spent hours going over what I hoped Lindsey would gain from counseling, but as I sat around the pool, listening to my friends share Lindsey stories, I realized it wasn't enough for me to want these things for my daughter—she had to want them for herself.

Sara's hearty laughter brought me back to the conversation. As John and Jim played cribbage, our friends offered many verbal pats on our backs, dimming the Emmett fiasco.

I stepped out of the pool and laid the *Titanic* on the deck, thinking how spectacular it felt to be on a relaxing vacation with my husband and dear friends. For a moment, I believed we really had done a remarkable job with our beautiful, challenging child, and my head swelled further. My girl seemed incredible, we seemed incredible, and I suddenly had an urge to call Lindsey.

After dinner, John and I held hands as we strolled across the stone bridge to the pay phone on the marina. By this time, my ego had bloated to the size of Woody Woodpecker's in the Macy's Thanksgiving Day Parade. My steps felt light; my feet scarcely touched the walkway.

I lifted the receiver and dialed my daughter's number. "Hello, Linds, this is Mom." So much joy filled my voice, Lindsey probably didn't recognize me.

"Mom, isthatyou?" My daughter shouted into the phone, hurrying her words once again.

"Yes," I said, mimicking her pitch. "We're still in Mexico."

"I don't wanna ruin your vacation," she said, gasping for air. Lindsey had used that warning when we were in Vegas—right before declaring she'd had sex for the very first time. *Nothing could be that bad. Could it?* I clutched the phone, preparing myself for the worst.

"I had to call the police," she said. My Woody Woodpecker balloon darted across the sky like an out-of-control firework, releasing every ounce of helium. The shriveled remnants landed on the cobblestones near my feet, looking like the leftover elongated inflatables clowns use to create wiener-dog sculptures at fairs. "They came to my 'partment," she continued. "Sandra will tell you everything when you get home. Areyouhavingfun?"

I sighed, then frowned. "Why did you call the police?" *Stay calm.* "Are you okay?" I asked, wondering what could possibly have happened that required police intervention. Lindsey usually took care of Arthur at our house, but this time she had wanted to dog-sit at her apartment. Had that been a mistake?

"Yeah, I'm okay, Mom. Terry moved us. Now I'm dog-sitting at your house. I don't wanna ruin your vacation."

I wanted to finish the call with my daughter and dial Terry, our longtime family friend, who was always willing to help out whenever we needed him. Or Sandra. Maybe Lindsey's provider could explain things better. Yet I was pretty certain her agent would not appreciate being disturbed this late in the evening, especially when Lindsey seemed fine.

"You're not going to ruin my vacation." My voice turned flat. *Was there a fire? Did someone break in?* "What happened?"

"Well, Mom, I don't wanna ruin your vacation."

I wish she'd quit saying that! My whole body was tense.

Without taking a breath, Lindsey said, "There were some cats and the neighbors knocked on my door and they aren't supposed to let their cats out. Arthur barked and I called the office and the manager said she couldn't do anything and . . . there might be *a knife*. . ." Lindsey gasped. "Sandra will explain and—"

"A *knife?*" I interrupted, hearing the shrillness in my voice. "Are you sure you're okay?" This conversation was going nowhere. Moreover, Lindsey never made sense when she was nervous, and, worse than that, she tended to exaggerate. I pictured her standing in our kitchen, wisps of brown hair escaping a stretchy pink or green headband, her blue eyes darting right, then left, searching for the correct words: *police, cats, neighbors, Arthur, knife.* Most of the time, even with minimal facts, I could decode Lindsey's spastic explanations, but tonight she wasn't giving me enough information, so I told myself, *She is safe. We'll have to wait to learn more.*

"I already told you, Mom, I'm fine."

"I love you, Lindsey." I cut the conversation short. "We'll talk about this when we get home."

"I love you, too. But I don't wanna ruin your vacation." *Gasp.* "I'll see you soon. Tell Dad hi." *Click.*

John shook his head. "Another crisis?" He reached out to touch my arm, but I jerked away. We made a quick call to Terry and confirmed things were stable at home—at least for the time being.

My feet felt like lead as they clomped over the stone bridge and toward the resort, dragging that heavy, shriveled-up, make-believe balloon along the solar-lit path. It was going to be a long two days.

✧

Spent. It means completely exhausted, depleted of energy or force or strength, drained of effectiveness. *Spent* was the only word that accurately described how I felt after we arrived home from our ten-day Mexico vacation. I should have felt rested, peaceful, relaxed, but I'd just devoted the last two days, and a long plane ride home to Oregon, mulling over my daughter's latest announcement.

When we opened the back door, the clock hands pointed to 12:30 a.m. Lindsey and Arthur raced to greet us. Chaos ensued. Arthur yapped. Lindsey shouted over the barks. The eighteen-pound shih tzu scrambled up my leg, scratching at my khaki pants. I lifted him to my chest and petted his black-and-white fur. He licked my neck. I put him down and turned to Lindsey. She smiled naturally, not one of those forced smiles she did for photos. Her whole face brightened. Her once-brushed hair was sporting an elastic lime-green headband. Dark brown wisps stuck straight up and jutted out like she'd been slightly electrocuted.

"Did we wake you?" I asked. From the looks of her hair, she must have fallen asleep on the sofa. Her pale green pajamas were nowhere near the color of the headband, but they were both green. "So they match," she'd say if I asked.

Lindsey ignored my question and asked one of her own. "Did you have a good trip?" Her voice sounded scratchy, groggy.

"Yes, wonderful," John and I said in unison, taking turns wrapping our arms around Lindsey. Her shoulders, arms, and torso shook.

"Thanks for taking care of Arthur," I said. "And the house, too. We love you."

"I'm the only person who watches Arthur pro-per-ly." Lindsey's voice snagged on the last word.

John busied himself unloading the car. As I moved through the house, my Keds met the hardwood floors and squeaked. I walked along the hall, past the den, and into the master bedroom.

Squeak, squeak, squeak. Lindsey followed, her mouth in constant motion. Arthur fell in line behind Lindsey, trotting from room to room, keeping me in sight. I put my red leather handbag on an upholstered chair by our bed. I'd been home three minutes. Lindsey was like a shadow—it was hard to tell where I ended and she began. I pulled my cosmetic bag out of my carry-on and headed to the master bath. Like a parade, Lindsey and Arthur followed. I placed my toothbrush and a tube of Colgate on the white tile counter.

It was after midnight, but neither Lindsey nor Arthur showed any intention of being left behind. I stepped, Lindsey shuffled, and Arthur trotted. Lindsey's arms flung about. She pulled them close to her chest, and her tremors calmed. She trailed me back to the den. I switched off the lights. Lindsey shadowed me, sharing in one long breath how glad she was that we were home how much she missed us that Arthur was good and how she had to call the police but the police said her call wasn't an emergency and they threatened to give her a ticket. She gasped.

I wasn't ready to discuss this yet. I'd replayed the Mazatlán call over and over in my head, anticipating what awaited us. Distressing words had littered her explanation. I hoped to be rested when we discussed everything. At 12:36 a.m., I didn't have enough energy.

I walked into the half bath. Arthur scampered inside before I closed the door. Lindsey stood outside. "Arthur only had one accident, but I cleaned it up. I took him for a walk every day. My neighbors helped me when I had a problem."

I flushed the toilet and turned on the faucet to wash my hands. Lindsey continued sharing, but I no longer heard her words. Only white noise. I'd been home twelve minutes.

John finished unloading the luggage and rolled two suitcases into our bedroom. I headed back to the master suite to see what items had to be unpacked tonight and what could wait. *Squeak, squeak, squeak.*

Lindsey tagged behind me, chatting. She gulped for air and continued her nonsensical explanation.

Finally, I asked, "So, exactly why did you call the police?"

"Sandra will explain. Call her tomorrow."

I sighed, rushing through the hall, past the half bath, and into the kitchen. *Squeak, squeak, squeak.* Lindsey traipsed behind me, shaking. I was accustomed to the parade, the following and talking, the never letting me out of her sight as we moved from room to room. I'd hoped Lindsey would outgrow this mode, but she never had.

Lindsey had stacked her bills in a neat pile on the counter for me to pay.

"You did a good job." I leafed through the mail. Lindsey didn't acknowledge the compliment. She fixated on her agenda, staying close, excited to tell her tale but never really telling me anything.

I hurried down the hall, past the den, and back to the bedroom. Lindsey's warm breath landed on the back of my neck as she told me Gabe had introduced her to a new friend.

Hmm. That's odd. Gabe never took Lindsey anywhere, unless, of course, she paid for the gas.

I'd been home sixteen minutes.

"His friend lives in Mount Angel," she said. I nodded, visualizing the little German town near Silverton. "Gabe likes me to visit his friend. I like the friend."

My body stiffened. I held my breath, bracing for more.

"The friend's a girl. She can't drive." I released the air, and my body relaxed. I stepped into the master bath and grabbed the toothpaste. Lindsey followed.

I asked my daughter if this girl, the one who was a friend of Gabe's, was "a friend with benefits," too.

"No," she said, but I was not convinced. Lindsey talked like she'd been to her apartment, like she was way too familiar with this girl.

A shiver ran down my spine. I recognized the sensation immediately—a foreboding of sorts, reminding me of when Emmett had been in Lindsey's life. I paused and glared into my daughter's baby blues. "Is Gabe pressuring you to have a threesome?"

Lindsey stopped, took two steps back, placed a hand on her hip, and looked me straight in the eyes.

"No." She tilted her head. A smirk dashed across her face. "But I've dreamt about it."

"You've dreamt about it?" My mouth dropped open, closing and opening again, like a fish gasping for water. I couldn't believe she knew what a threesome was, let alone considered one. I stared at my daughter. "Are you sure Gabe isn't suggesting a threesome?"

"No." Her smirk grew wider. *Could* Lindsey *be doing the suggesting?*

Spent. I felt spent. I'd been home twenty-three minutes.

"Lindsey, we'll continue this conversation in the morning." I ushered my daughter out of the room. "I'm tired of talking. Good night."

"I need a vacation," I told John when he strode into the room and closed the door.

"We just got back from Mexico." John flicked off the light switch, and the room turned dark.

"I know, but I need to go again." I climbed into bed, trying to quiet my mind. Lindsey's announcement swirled around in my head. *Threesome . . . threesome . . . threesome.* Morning would come soon enough. I'd get to the bottom of this then.

⤳

The next morning, I positioned myself on the family room sofa with the phone and my dog. I needed emotional support. Sandra answered on the second ring. When she heard my voice, words spilled from her mouth as if a faucet had been turned on full blast.

"Lindsey sure was stressed out," she said. My stomach twisted, and I dug my fingers into Arthur's fur. Before flying to Mexico, we had shared our itinerary with my mom, Terry and several other friends, as well as Sandra. We wanted Lindsey to operate on as independent a level as possible, but if a situation requiring additional assistance arose, Lindsey needed to be prepared, so we had given her an emergency phone list.

Sandra explained that the manager of Lindsey's apartment complex had listened to seven messages from my daughter about animal abuse before she could call her back and tell Lindsey she didn't need to worry about the neighbor's cat being outside.

My stomach churned, as if one thousand Mexican jumping beans were having a rumble. I scratched Arthur behind the ears.

"Oh, and by the way, the manager told Lindsey, 'Don't leave multiple messages about the same incident ever again.'" Sandra went on and described Lindsey's concern about the cat outside. "Apparently that, and the fact that the neighbor owned knives, led her to escalate the issue with a 911 call," she said, explaining the police weren't too happy. "They told Lindsey an outdoor cat was not considered an emergency, and then they warned her that if she called again when it wasn't an emergency, they'd issue her a ticket."

I shook my head, wildly rubbing my dog's soft coat. Arthur wagged his tail.

"It turns out the Silverton Police Department is very familiar with your daughter," Sandra said. "She visits the station several times a week, reporting 'almost hit-and-runs.' When the dispatcher asks for the perpetrator's license plate number, Lindsey never has one. But she always tells them, 'It was a blue car or a green car or a brown car—I'm not sure which.'"

I understood Sandra completely. A week before we left for Mexico, I was downtown, entering the Silverton Pill Box, when I noticed Lindsey. A pink Hello Kitty backpack was strapped to her twenty-eight-year-old shoulders. She stood on a corner, two blocks away, looking like she wanted to cross the street. The task should have been easy. Most of our downtown streets intersected at four-way stops. A tan Buick pulled up to the intersection and rolled to a halt. Behind the wheel was a serious old guy, his hair shaved in a flattop, his face thick with wrinkles. His eyes fixated on my daughter. Lindsey stared at him. The old man motioned with his hand, his mouth locked tight, as he waved permission for her to cross the street. Lindsey shook her head with such vigor I was afraid she'd get dizzy and fall over. The driver didn't move. Lindsey used both her hands to make short scooting flicks, indicating he should go.

The old guy shook his head as feverishly as my daughter. His dramatic hand motions reminded me of a grade-school crossing guard. But Lindsey didn't budge. She stood there, staring, tremoring, her Hello Kitty decal looking cheerful.

The ritual of shaking and motioning between the old guy and Lindsey continued for fifty long seconds, turning into a contest of wills. Lindsey braved up, put one foot in the crosswalk, and took one step. The driver, tired of the "you go first" game, accelerated at the same time, and his Buick moved forward. The old guy slammed on his brakes. Lindsey jumped back to the curb, muttering to herself. Then the old guy sped off.

Later that day, I asked Lindsey about the incident.

"They always try to hit me. He was gonna run me over."

"Quit dilly-dallying, Lindsey!" I reminded her that once she made eye contact with a driver and he granted her permission, she should cross the street!

"Sandra," I said, returning to this moment, "Lindsey's probably told you she doesn't like to cross unless no cars are in sight." I held the phone even more tightly. My shoulders ached. A shooting pain pierced my temple. "But she stands there like she wants to cross, and it confuses the drivers."

"I completely understand." Sandra laughed. "I've seen her, too." I held one of Arthur's paws in my hand and stroked it. He cocked his head, then set it back down on my thigh. "After she called the police, Lindsey dialed me, but her call went to voice mail. I think it was the culmination of everything that sent her over the edge." Sandra took a breath. "She had an anxiety attack. I'd never seen her so upset. By the time I returned her call, she'd already phoned your friend."

I nodded, said, "Yes." I knew the rest of the story. Terry had moved Lindsey and Arthur to our house, and all had stayed well until we'd returned home.

"I want to give Lindsey some credit," Sandra said. "She found a realistic solution to this problem. Moving from her apartment to your house worked out fine."

I should have been happy with the outcome, but I was disappointed and embarrassed. I didn't want Terry to have to rescue Lindsey whenever we were out of town. I wanted my daughter to advocate for herself, not be a pest. Overall, I wanted to believe Lindsey was doing better, yet she obviously still struggled. As long as life went her way, on her schedule, she was fine. Throw in something new or out of the ordinary, and confusion set in.

Then I remembered Lindsey's late-night admission and the Mexican jumping beans started up again.

"I have one more question for you," I said, digging my fingers into Arthur's tufts and scratching him. He leaned in to my touch. I knew Lindsey had given Sandra permission to talk to me about specific incidents, but I also knew Sandra had no obligation to divulge private conversations. It was one of her duties as a personal agent.

"Is Gabe pressuring Lindsey to do some, um, sexual things?"

"Funny you should ask," Sandra said. "Lindsey's been dropping hints. I've been concerned, too. But I really can't comment further without talking to Lindsey first."

"I understand." I told Sandra I still hoped Lindsey would go to counseling. "It would be great if she could work on decision-making and conflict-resolution skills."

"Mmm," Sandra said. "She could use some coping ones, too, particularly when things don't go her way."

"Thank you, thank you." I pressed END and tossed my phone on a sofa cushion. My hand continued to stroke Arthur's fur as I thought about how Lindsey's stress level crescendoed when we weren't near. I visualized her verbal rampage to the apartment manager and the police. My stomach knotted, and my face felt hotter than the concrete in Mexico. I took a deep breath, held it for a second, then let it go. *We have work to do.* "One issue at a time," I said to Arthur. He lifted his head and licked my fingers.

When I talked with Lindsey, her posture was straight and stiff. She folded her hands and rested them on her lap, looking as if she expected a firing squad.

We talked about the cat incident and her call to the police, but I transitioned to what I believed was even more important. "I'm concerned you may feel pressure to do some things . . ." I paused, taking a long, deep breath. "Some sexual things, like a threesome, that you're not emotionally equipped to handle. Or should even consider handling." Personally, I couldn't imagine being a participant. And I told her so. "I really think you need some counseling, Lindsey." I tried to sound casual, as if I were asking my daughter to come for dinner. "Will you go? Please?"

My mind flashed back to all the conversations we'd had

about sex: sexually transmitted diseases, risky behaviors, and the importance of protection. I'd answered all of Lindsey's questions in detail, even the embarrassing ones. I told her, "It's your body. You get to decide what's pleasurable and comfortable for you."

"I'm not sure about counseling." Her words came out slowly, bringing me back to the moment. Her palms flew open, and her slender fingers parted. "Gabe says counseling is when they try to get you to tell all your pry-vit thoughts. I don't wanna talk about sex." Lindsey moved her hands around in the air, blocking my view of her face.

My mouth formed a wry smile. A bit of my anxiety eased. She'd never had any filters when it came to the subject of sex.

"You went to counseling in junior high and high school," I said. "You chose the problems or feelings you wanted to discuss. And afterward, you told us it had been nice to talk to someone other than us. You said it gave you a different perspective. Remember?"

"Mom. You know I can't remember that far back." Her blue eyes widened. Her long lashes blinked. "What you say just goes out one ear and through the other."

"Don't you mean 'in one ear and out the other'?" I playfully challenged her.

Lindsey's eyes darted back and forth. She didn't say anything for several seconds. "Mom, you have your way. I have mine," she said. "And I prefer my way."

John walked into the family room then, dressed in Levi's and a long-sleeved gray sweatshirt. He leaned against the sage wall and crossed his arms. "Lindsey, I think you should talk to someone." I wondered if he'd been listening from the kitchen. "You can discuss what you want, the areas you'd like some help with." His deep, steady voice was a nice diversion from ours. "I just had my birthday. I don't want a present. Will you go for counseling instead of buying me something? How would that be?"

Lindsey sat without speaking, placing her hands back on her lap. Her eyes darted upward, processing, thinking . . . thinking . . . thinking.

"Yeah, Dad." She smiled and leaned forward. "I'll go once. For your birthday. Will that make you happy?"

"Yes." John winked at me. Often his birthday present from her was a bag of miniature Reese's Peanut Butter Cups delivered in the plastic bag she got from the store. Sometimes the receipt was still stuck to the inside of the sack.

I mouthed, "Thank you," but John's attention was already focused back on Lindsey. "I've loaded your stuff in the truck. Let's get you home." Lindsey stood, gave me a hug, then followed John through the dining room, down the hall, and out the garage door.

I leaned back against the sofa, crossed my arms, and closed my eyes.

Welcome home, Linda.

24

ithin a week of our return from Mexico, Lindsey's focus changed from police, cats, neighbors, Arthur, and knives to her upcoming May birthday—still four months away.

"I wanna bike," she said, handing me a folded, blue-lined sheet of loose-leaf paper. "I've made a list." I took the paper from my daughter's shaking hands, unfolded it several times, flattened the sheet against the tile on the kitchen counter, and studied the so-called list. "Bike" was the only item written on the page.

The timer's buzzer rang. I grabbed potholders from the drawer, opened the oven door, and pulled out two tins of banana bread. Steam rose from the surface as ripe fruit, vanilla, and spices filled the air. "Don't you want anything else?"

"Well," she said. "Since I'm gonna be twenty-nine, you could surprise me." Lindsey waved her hands in the space in front of her face. "But I really wanna bike."

My daughter sounded like a prerecorded message set on repeat. We'd tried doing the "surprise thing" at Christmas, but that had been a complete failure. It was still hard for me to want to buy her a new bicycle when the previous three-speed hadn't been important enough for her to bring back home. That realization irritated me more than I cared to admit. Furthermore,

Lindsey's tremors seemed to be getting progressively worse. And John and I weren't the only ones who were noticing them.

The day before, Lindsey had left an incoherent message on our machine. She sounded so upset, John picked up the phone and returned the call before the message finished playing.

"I got pulled over today by the Silvaton Police," Lindsey said, slurring her pronunciation.

"I didn't know you could drive," John teased, trying to lighten the intensity in our daughter's voice.

"Dad. I don't drive," she said, serious as a stone. "I was walking."

"Were you walking too fast?" John tried to maintain a straight face. "Maybe you'd better slow down."

"The policeman said I was walking funny. But I told him about my disability and he let me go."

When John relayed his conversation, I figured the officer had to be new to the force because most of the police in town were familiar with our daughter's unstable gait. Any officer who tangled with our girl had his hands full—that was for sure. I was proud Lindsey had advocated for herself, but why had she been mistaken for a drunk?

Well, she seems fine now. I dumped the hot loaves onto a cooling rack and licked my lips. "Do you want some banana bread?" I plucked a knife from the drawer, heaped butter on a couple of warm slices, and handed one to Lindsey. "We already bought you a bike, Linds. But you gave it to Emmett. If you wanted one so badly, you should've kept the one you had."

"You're not listening to me, Mom!" Lindsey's voice was piercing. Her hands awkwardly played hot potato with the bread. "He had to use it for business!"

"Dad and I will think about it," I said, not planning to spend another second considering her request. "But you should come up with a few more things, just in case."

My decision never to buy Lindsey a bike again was solidi-fied shortly after that conversation. I was driving to Hi-School Pharmacy; John was sitting in the passenger seat. It was unusual for there to be much traffic in our town, but as I approached the four-way stop on Main Street, I saw at least five vehicles stopped in front of us. No cars were moving through the intersection in any direction, either. John and I strained to see around the Les Schwab truck idling two cars ahead. Then Les Schwab's cab door opened and the driver jumped out and sprinted toward the crosswalk. The next thing we saw was this Good Samaritan bending over. In our obscured line of sight, we saw someone trembling horribly.

"It's Lindsey," I shrieked. My body started shaking too, but I couldn't move. The Good Samaritan supported Lindsey's body against his as she stepped slowly, clumsily, through the crosswalk. "Was she hit?"

John jumped out of our car and dashed to Lindsey's side, grabbing her elbow. I put the car in park and jumped out, too, reaching the corner at the same time as the Good Samaritan, John, and Lindsey.

"Thank you! Thank you! Thank you!" Lindsey and John and I said, all at the same time, over and over.

"She was crawling through the crosswalk," the Good Samaritan said, rushing back to his vehicle. Over his shoulder, he yelled, "Good luck!"

What in the world is going on? We helped Lindsey to our car. "Why were you crawling?" Adrenaline raced through my veins as fast as thoughts ricocheted through my head. *Does she have Par-kinson's? Cerebral palsy? Muscular dystrophy? Something even worse?*

"The sidewalk moves when I walk." Lindsey demonstrated, moving her hands like rolling hills. Lindsey's description made it sound as if she had been trying to walk during an 8.0 earthquake.

"Are you dizzy?" I asked, wondering if, instead of some incurable disease, she had an inner-ear issue, like vertigo. I waited for Lindsey to respond. In all my daughter's life, I'd never heard her use the word *dizzy* to describe any of her symptoms; I wasn't sure she was even familiar with the term. "Does it feel like you're spinning?" I clarified.

"No."

"Do you feel like you're going to throw up?"

"No. The sidewalk just moves when I walk."

We took Lindsey to her apartment, and once she stepped inside, she hung up her coat, unloaded her backpack, and looked under the bed for her kittens, moving like she was in a horse race. The girl we watched now was an entirely different person from the one we had seen ten minutes earlier. John raised his eyebrows. I crossed my arms. Was Lindsey doing this for attention? My daughter had been a hypochondriac for some time, and she had lots of aches and pains we (and doctors) had never been able to identify, but I really didn't believe she would crawl through a downtown crosswalk for attention.

"We need to schedule an appointment with Dr. Blount," I said, worry worming its way into my head. "And I want to come along."

There was a small problem, though. In two days I was being sent to Wichita, Kansas, to handle hail claims and would be gone for three weeks. John was teaching and coaching, and his day didn't finish until after the doctor's hours ended. Even if my husband could have worked this appointment into his schedule, I really wanted to be the parent to accompany Lindsey. John is excellent in many situations, but he doesn't pay as much attention to detail as I would like, nor does he use precise language to explain things. I was afraid he'd gloss over some of Lindsey's symptoms, even if I wrote them down.

When I called to schedule the appointment, the first open-ing available coincided with my next stretch at home. It seemed like a long time to wait, and while I was gone, I didn't want to fret about Lindsey's getting around town safely. Then I came up with an idea. *European walking sticks!* Hikers in the Alps, even some everyday walkers, use trekking poles to stabilize themselves. Maybe they'd work for Lindsey, too.

"I'll give 'em a try," she said. She looked skeptical, but as soon as she grasped them in her hands, her tremors eased and she walked fearlessly around her apartment. We went outside, and her mouth tightened in concentration. Her gait slowed as she coordinated her hand movements with her legs. "I'm more com-ter-ble with 'em," she finally said. "I'll use 'em."

〜✧

The nurse escorted Lindsey and me into an exam room. I helped my daughter climb up on the examination table, and we waited for Dr. Blount.

"Mom, I know I told you I wanted a bike for my birthday," she said, her solemn tone matching the expression on her face. I couldn't believe my daughter still wanted a bike after she'd crawled through a crosswalk. She definitely had equilibrium issues, and a person needed decent balance to ride a bike. Besides, she was using trekking poles to help her get around now, and no one, especially not Lindsey, could use poles and ride a bike at the same time. My daughter wasn't making any sense.

I was preparing a firm, "no fricking way" answer when she said, "But now I wanna walker." And without thinking, I started laughing. Long. Hard. I hoped the medical personnel couldn't hear me out in the hall. "Mom. I'm serious. I wanna walker."

I tried to stifle my chuckles. "There's no way I'm buying my daughter a walker for her twenty-ninth birthday," I said, staring at my girl. Lindsey's eyes darted right, then left. Her tremors increased dramatically. I reached out to touch her shoulder, but she jerked away, causing her body to almost topple off the exam table.

When Dr. Blount walked into the exam room and closed the door, Lindsey didn't give her a chance to offer any greeting.

"The sidewalk moves when I walk," Lindsey said, using her hands to demonstrate, just as she'd done with John and me. Dr. Blount nodded, scribbling notes in my daughter's chart. "I'm afraid I'm gonna fall again."

Lindsey had never mentioned that concern to me. She *had* fallen once—the time she gashed her forehead and was taken to the hospital in an ambulance—but that was a while ago. I didn't know she worried about falling again.

I offered the 8.0-earthquake analogy I'd come up with. "Her symptoms increase significantly when she's outside," I said. "And when she's in a building, they decrease."

Lindsey nodded in agreement.

"Could she have vertigo?" I asked.

"I don't think so." Dr. Blount picked up an otoscope and peered into Lindsey's right ear canal, then her left one. "Most people experience severe dizziness, and Lindsey hasn't complained of that." She placed a stethoscope against Lindsey's chest and asked her to take several deep breaths. "But her depiction certainly indicates some sort of spatial equilibrium issue."

"Spatial?" I said, unfamiliar with this usage of the word.

"Her position in the world. The bigger the space, the harder it is for her to ground herself. It's probably why it isn't as bad when she's inside."

Dr. Blount requested that Lindsey walk across the examination room. My daughter stepped quickly—nothing like her movements on the street. "I've seen Lindsey walking downtown," she said. "Her anxiety level has definitely increased recently."

Lindsey nodded again.

"We got her some walking sticks." I pointed to the corner of the room, where she'd leaned them against the wall. "They seem to be helping some."

"I want Lindsey walking as much as possible. It's good for her. So if they work, she should use them." Dr. Blount pulled a prescription pad from the pocket of her white lab coat. "I'd like to increase Lindsey's anxiety medication and see if a higher dose will help any. And I'm making a referral to OHSU's Movement Disorder Program. I'd like to make sure there aren't any new neurological issues going on."

I sighed. Dr. Blount had validated my concerns by making a referral, but another part of me was scared to death. *What if something has changed in her system and these new issues are a precursor to something worse?* I couldn't allow myself to think about that now. The best way to help Lindsey was to know, for sure, what was or wasn't happening.

When we left Dr. Blount's office, I carried Lindsey's trekking poles. My daughter walked fine until she stepped outside; then she gripped my arm like it was a lifeline, all the way to the car.

Lindsey was earnest in her request for a walker, but I couldn't imagine buying her one anytime in the near future. For me, the trekking poles were different. Active people used them, and I didn't think the sticks would slow her down or make her look as vulnerable as a walker might. I didn't want her to become dependent on a product she didn't need quite yet. The only way I'd give in to this request was if one of her doctors ordered it, and I told Lindsey that. But that evening, feeling glum, I posted Lindsey's walker request on Facebook. When I checked back, there were thirty-eight comments from friends and relatives. "Rhinestone it!" "Put a horn on it." "Let her beep-beep her way through town." "She needs a scooter, an adult tricycle." "Decorate it with streamers and balloons." By the time I finished reading, I didn't feel so blue.

Over the next two months, a fresh team of OHSU neurologists examined our daughter three times. In the end, the specialists ruled out Lindsey's having Parkinson's, MS, or any other progressive disease. They found absolutely nothing neurologically wrong—except Lindsey had a predisposition toward anxiety.

"So it's all in my head," Lindsey said, pointing a shaking finger to her temple. I looked at John. John looked at me. The doctor searched both our faces nervously, then nodded.

"Pretty much," John said, patting Lindsey on the back.

"So I can't have a walker?"

"I don't think you need one," the doctor said. "Once you start walking more, you'll get your confidence back."

"Okay," Lindsey said, standing. "I'll work on it."

~⋆

When May 10 came, John and I bought Lindsey two pairs of Nike tennis shoes, one bright pink, one purple, for her twenty-ninth birthday. "For all the walking you're going to do," we said. And, in typical, Lindsey-gift-recipient fashion, she clapped her hands and jumped up and down as if they were the best gifts she'd ever received.

25

I t was late summer and the last chance for John to barbecue before he headed back to teaching, and I drove my logo-plastered vehicle to Hobbs, New Mexico, to estimate hail claims. John dumped half a bag of hickory-wood pellets into the hopper and heated up the Traeger.

Forty-five minutes later, Lindsey and Gabe arrived. Lindsey had cut her dark locks shorter than ever. The funny thing was, as my daughter's hair was getting shorter, Gabe's was growing longer. The thin blond strands hung to the middle of his shoulder blades in a ponytail.

Gabe carried Lindsey's walking sticks into the house and out to the patio. I noticed Lindsey had on her purple birthday Nikes. She'd paired them with a purple-and-white-striped knit top and khaki shorts. A stretchy white headband pulled back her bangs, but a few delicate brunette curls escaped, gently swirling against her forehead.

After we exchanged greetings, John asked, "Who wants cheese?" We all raised our hands, and he added cheddar slices to all the burgers. When the cheese had melted just right, he pulled the patties off the grill. We slid the burgers onto toasted buns, loaded up our plates with chips and salads, and made our way to the wrought-iron patio table. Lindsey and Gabe picked up their cheeseburgers at the same time and started munching.

"Not even a little bit of ketchup?" I said, passing the bottle of Heinz. Lindsey and Gabe shook their heads in unison. I set the bottle down in front of John.

"We just like plain ones," Gabe said.

"I love my counselor," Lindsey said, her voice filled with excitement. "And I have lots more 'pointments scheduled."

John and I glanced at each other and winked. Lindsey had insisted she would go only once, and only for John's birthday present. But it hadn't been so easy to get her an appointment. After researching the Oregon Health Plan, I learned few therapists accepted Lindsey's program, and those who did had no immediate openings, so it took several months before she could get in. Now, she visited with a counselor every other week. I told her she didn't have to tell me what she discussed, but she often told me anyway. "I talk about you, Mom," she said, "and how we don't get along." I cringed. I thought we were getting along better. *Shouldn't she be using these sessions to discuss the things that happened to her during those years with Emmett?*

"She likes to talk," Gabe said. "That's for sure."

Gabe was right. Lindsey did like to chat, and I wondered if that trait bothered him because he liked to talk, too. Lately he'd shifted his conversations away from *Star Trek* and toward some of his medical issues. He had more health problems than Lindsey now. Ever since Dr. Blount had increased my daughter's anxiety medication, Lindsey hadn't been quite so argumentative, nor did she have as many unexplained angry outbursts, and she had never again brought up the idea of a threesome. That alone was comforting. Maybe the combination of counseling and medication was Lindsey's answer to handling future life challenges with success. I could only hope.

"I'm going to write a book about you," I said, changing the subject. "You give me lots of stories," I said, chuckling. I'd been thinking about this idea for a while. When OHSU first told me Lindsey would be able to live only in a group home, I was devastated. I didn't want to believe them, and now, as I looked across the patio table at my girl, I was happy for her, for me, for us. She was living the way I'd always dreamed she would: independently. But for how long? I didn't know the answer. Maybe a year. Maybe forever. "Is that okay?"

Lindsey cocked her head and eyed me suspiciously. "Are you gonna tell the good, the bad, and the ugly?"

My smile took over my face. *Where in the world does she come up with some of her lingo?* "Yes, I am."

"Well, I do make people laugh," Lindsey said, her face deadpan. "As long as it's the truth, I guess it would be okay."

26

❧ ❧

I clutched a crude map inked into the fibers of a paper napkin and hurried down the dirt road toward the village of San Marcos. With every footstep, my tennis shoes stirred a whirlwind of earth that instantly stuck to my damp ankles and shins. The dirt was so thick, I could have etched a temporary tattoo on my leg.

The scent of banana leaves and wood smoke mixed together in the air, and I inhaled deeply. I peered across Lake Atitlán at the extinct volcano. *Would I really do a cacao ceremony? With a Guatemalan chocolate shaman?*

A low rumble disturbed the jungle's quiet. I glanced at the map before looking over my shoulder. I stepped closer to the tangled vegetation, then stopped and waited. A corroded pickup rounded the bend, hurtling over the road's ruts. Six bodies bounced up and down in the truck's bed. I slapped at the air to clear the dust. Everyone in the pickup smiled and waved.

The village of San Marcos is known for massage, spiritual teachings, healing therapies, and yoga. The last thing I expected to do during a weeklong writing workshop was drink ancient Mayan cacao with a man named Keith, but it was one of the extra activities the hosting author offered. And even though I hadn't practiced any religion for close to forty years, whenever I planned to do something bordering on unconventional, childhood Sunday-school lessons assaulted my thoughts. *Thou shalt not spend time with chocolate shamans*. Or tarot card readers or psychics or . . . Still, I'd gone ahead and allowed a fortune-teller to read my cards on Venice Beach. Once. Then there was my good friend, the one with clairvoyant powers, who sometimes shared her predictions about my future.

To me, though, participating in a chocolate ceremony with a shaman screamed, *Huge sin*. And even though that particular lesson wasn't preached at the conservative Southern Baptist church I'd attended, it certainly seemed like anything alternative was touted as evil, satanic.

I stood in front of Keith's wooden gate, facing slats that had faded to pale gray. I blotted my forehead with a red kerchief. Below me, the sun's rays shimmered against Lake Atitlán's surface. I took a deep breath and rapped my knuckles against the wood.

"Keith?" I peered between the slat's cracks. Palms and ferns filled my line of sight. Red, yellow, and orange orchids burst from the greenery. A bird of paradise jutted its pointy, beak-like flowers in multiple directions. "I'm from the writers' workshop," I hollered. "Joyce sent me."

"Yes, of course," a gravelly voice said. "Pull the rope. It'll release the latch. I'm on the patio."

The pebbled path meandered through Keith's lush garden and ended at a space covered with a tin roof. Tapestries hung down the sides, protecting the ceremonial area from the sun of Central America. A woven Aztec rug partially covered the clay tiles. Random seats—beanbags, soft-backed chairs, a worn sofa, and comfy, cushion-size pillows—were placed in a chaotic circle.

A tall man stepped into view. Plaid drawstring pants hung on his slim hips. A wrinkled tied-dyed T-shirt covered his chest.

"Welcome," he said, stopping in the middle of the patio. "I'm Keith."

"Glad to meet you," I said, shaking his hand, not sure I believed that nicety quite yet. When our palms parted, Keith used his fingers to tuck strands of blond-gray hair behind his ears. He pushed his wire-framed glasses farther up his nose. As soon as he let go, they slid forward again. His beard matched his hair color but was scraggly, like his appearance. He resembled guys back home on the side of the road who held signs that said ANY-THING HELPS.

"This is Brenda," Keith said, "my assistant." A blond woman glided out of a makeshift kitchen and waved. The fabrics in her skirt didn't stop when she did. They floated around her legs like gentle ripples in a pond. The movements mesmerized me. I decided I must get a skirt just like hers. In the same instant, I knew it would never look the same on me. I was short and curvy. Brenda was tall and wispy. Like Keith.

"Take a seat." Keith swept an arm through the air. "Wherever looks comfortable."

I considered the colorful, mismatched space and decided on the worn sofa. The patio was so vibrant and interesting to the senses, I doubted any negative energy could exist there. Still, I grabbed one of the decorative silk pillows, held it on my lap, and sat rigid as a plank, mentally preparing for whatever came next.

"How do you like your chocolate?" Brenda said. I cocked my head, not sure I understood the question. *Like Hershey's?* She picked up a spoon and scooped teaspoons of cacao shavings into three faded Tupperware tumblers. They were the same style my favorite grandmother used for iced tea when I was a child. The cups didn't look as clean as Grandma's, though, and I wondered if they'd been sanitized after the last use. *Don't be silly*, I told myself. *Everything's primitive here. And you haven't gotten sick yet, have you?*

"We use Guatemalan cacao," the assistant said. "In its purest form." Every time Brenda moved, so did her skirt. "It's bitter, unless we add sweetener. Would you like honey or raw sugar?" she asked, adding a pinch of cayenne pepper into each cup.

"Raw sugar," I said.

She heaped a spoonful of brown granules into mine, then poured lukewarm water over the ingredients, and stirred vigorously.

One of Keith's long legs suddenly disappeared underneath him as he curled his body into a rattan chair that hung from a massive piece of steel. He was definitely limber. He probably did yoga at one of the facilities in town. His other leg dangled, and his bare toes touched the clay tiles, allowing him to rock his chair gently back and forth.

For the past three days, my feet had taken me all over the village of San Marcos. As I walked the narrow jungle paths from one edge of town to the other, I glimpsed, in open doorways and primitively enclosed gardens, locals lounging just like Keith. As he sat there in his hanging chair, the shaman's aura was tranquil, as if he'd been a part of the San Marcos culture ever since the Mayans. Maybe even before them.

"Several years ago, I was visited by a chocolate spirit," he said. "Now I'm an energy healer. I help people with inner work."

I thought about the ruckus late the night before as I'd tried to sleep: villagers banging tambourines, pounding drums, dancing, and howling—all to welcome the full moon. I wondered if Keith had helped any of those folks improve their inner work.

Brenda handed me a pale pink tumbler. I didn't do mind-altering substances. Ever. But Keith assured me cacao didn't alter the mind.

"It alters the heart," he said, encouraging me to enjoy the experience. "You might feel your heart rate increase," he warned, explaining that a 15 to 20 percent spike was common. "What you're going to see today might just be the most beautiful thing in the world."

I was skeptical. A smile froze on my face, but I nodded.

Brenda handed a tumbler to Keith, keeping the last one for herself.

I sniffed the concoction. It smelled and looked vaguely like Hershey's chocolate milk, but paler, thinner, grainier. *Really nothing like Hershey's at all*, I thought, wishing it were more familiar.

"Cheers!" Keith said. The three of us tapped the rims of our Tupperware cups against each other's; then I took a sip. It tasted somewhat like Hershey's chocolate with a cayenne kick. My daughter loves chocolate milk. Actually, she loves anything chocolate. I visualized Lindsey wrapping two trembling hands around a child-size plastic cup and lifting the liquid to her lips. A couple tastes later, she'd grin. A milk mustache would be decorating her twenty-nine-year-old upper lip. Lindsey. My special girl. My forever child.

I dabbed at the area above my mouth, hoping I didn't have a liquid mustache myself. "So, how does this work?" I asked, concentrating my gaze on Keith, trying to redirect my attention to the present. I was here to improve my writing, not dwell on things I didn't have control over, things I didn't have the power to change. *Like my daughter.* I drank the last swell of chocolate in one gulp and set the tumbler on the tile floor.

Keith tilted his head to one side. "How do you want it to work?"

Beyond the tapestries, a bird trilled.

"Is anyone else coming?"

"Doesn't look like it. Guess you were meant to have a private session."

I didn't know how I felt about that. Alone with a chocolate shaman in Guatemala. *Well*, I reminded myself, *his assistant is here, too.*

Keith closed his eyes and said nothing more. I waited, unsure how to proceed. With no guidance from the shaman, the silence felt uncomfortable. I hugged the silk pillow more tightly.

"Should I talk?"

"If you'd like to."

I paused for a moment. Then words tumbled out of my mouth, one after the other.

"I wanted a daughter. But not the one I got." My hand went to my chest. *How could I say that? To this strange man. The shaman of chocolate.* He wouldn't understand. Besides, I wanted to talk about writing. My mouth, my head, my heart must've had a different mission. "It wasn't always that way," I clarified. "I'd ordered a perfect girl. And for a while, she was exactly that. Perfect."

Water stung my eyes. A stream of tears rolled toward my chin. Although my heart didn't feel like it had increased its beats, my mouth released words at an unexpected velocity. I babbled that Lindsey had a grand mal seizure at sixteen months and that afterward, she developed essential tremors that made her head, arms, and hands shake like a Parkinson's patient, although Parkinson's was never her diagnosis.

I told the chocolate shaman how I'd searched for answers, for cures, for years. Yet it wasn't until Lindsey was six that an Oregon Health Science University doctor told me, "Your daughter is mildly mentally retarded." Immediately I was back in that moment, and I felt my body stiffen from the news. I preferred *intellectually disabled* or *mentally challenged* or *developmentally delayed*, even *special needs*. Anything was better than *that* word. Back then, though, *retarded* was the term they used. The sound of it still stung my ears, hurt my heart, made my stomach queasy.

I told Keith that the doctor said her syndrome was from an unidentified source, that she had a short in her neurological system, that she'd never process information the same way her peers did. As I spoke, I could hear the doctor's words. I could see my first-grader dressed in lavender corduroy overalls and a matching floral top, two blond ringlets bobbing on either side of her head.

She looked like Cindy Brady from *The Brady Bunch*. I thought she could have modeled for Macy's.

"And that doctor said"—my voice quavered—"when she's an adult, she will likely live in a group home." I still couldn't figure out how a doctor could predict such a thing when Lindsey was only six. "As far as I was concerned," I told the shaman, "a group home was the worst possible prediction." I wiped my nose. "Back then I couldn't picture my girl ever living in such a place."

Although all that had happened twenty-some years earlier, the pain still felt fresh. I slumped against the chocolate shaman's sofa.

"Your heart's been hurt," Keith finally said. "Badly. And you've protected it."

I opened my eyes and studied the shaman. He was looking at his eyelids. *How did he know that?*

At first I grieved not having gotten the daughter I planned for. The perfect one. But then Lindsey struggled in school. She had little interest in developing friendships. She still followed me around the house like a child. She chattered about her barrettes, the neighbor girl's barrettes. Over and over. I thought I might go insane and began imagining that wall around my heart. Sometimes Lindsey yelled hateful words. She hit; she bit. I added more layers to my wall. But I couldn't tell the shaman all that.

Instead I said, "When my daughter turned nineteen, she became sexually active and decided to have a tubal ligation." I lowered my head, and my tears dripped straight to the floor. "I miss all my potential grandbabies so much. My arms ache to hold them, to love them, to smell their baby-powdered bodies," I said. "My daughter made the right decision, but that doesn't mean I don't feel the loss." I gulped for air. "*Intensely.*"

That wasn't the worst of it, though.

"At twenty, Lindsey ran away with a man more than twice

her age." An anguished sob escaped my throat. "A predator, we called him, and for four plus years he isolated her in a house with tinfoil taped over the windows. Our daughter refused to come home. Law enforcement wouldn't help us. The police said she was of legal age and it wasn't a crime to pick a bad partner."

The wall around my heart grew taller, thicker, heavier. Ivy, weeds forced their roots into the mortar and strangled the bricks. Not only did my girl's bad choices complicate her life, they complicated ours, too, but we kept trying to save her. When we couldn't, the wall thickened. The mortar hardened.

"On the afternoon I learned my daughter and this man were homeless, I didn't think I could handle another ounce of sorrow." By then, the bricks had turned into a fortress. My heart felt completely shut off. I no longer felt anything.

"Can you really see my wall?" I finally asked.

Keith's eyes didn't open. "I feel it." He leaned back against his rattan chair, looking peaceful. "There's so much darkness. So much pain."

I copied the shaman and closed my eyes again. Long pauses seemed to be a part of the ceremony, and the patio turned silent. Another bird warbled. A hot breeze tousled a silk wall hanging near my head.

He was right. My heart felt black. Like a dark hole.

"Eventually, we rescued Lindsey." I was unsure whether I was supposed to keep talking, but my damn mouth wouldn't shut up. "When she came back to us, she wasn't the innocent young woman who'd left. She was angry. Hard. Hateful."

Keith didn't say anything. He sat in his chair, gently rocking back and forth. The silence lasted for so long, I wondered if he was bored, if he was confused by my sporadic ramblings, if he'd fallen asleep. I inhaled the sweet scent of a flower I didn't recognize. *Is the ceremony over? Should I go?*

Keith finally opened his mouth. "There's good news," he said. "You built the wall with bricks."

My eyes flew open. *I didn't say "bricks" out loud. Did I?*

"Not from steel or a solid slab of concrete. You built it piece by piece. So, if you want, you could take out a few bricks. Are you open to that?" The chocolate shaman's wire rims slid forward, but he didn't touch them, and he never opened his eyes.

I thought about his suggestion, then nodded slowly. "Yes."

"Would you consider putting a window in the opening?" Keith said.

A window in my heart sounded nice. Really nice. "Okay."

"What kind of window would you add?"

"It'd be white," I said, remembering the cute little two-story cottage we'd created for Lindsey. "With white grids," I added.

"Well, then." Keith's voice filled with glee. "Let's take out a few bricks and add one exactly like that."

My eyelids shut tight. One at a time, I removed three bricks. *Whoooooosh!*

Bright light hurled through the opening like a comet.

"Whoa!" Keith said. "Did you feel that?"

I did. I couldn't speak. The darkness behind the fortress filled with light, with heat, as if a roaring campfire had been turned on in a cave. An image of my girl standing in her cottage, wearing bright pink shorts and her favorite pink Hello Kitty T-shirt, filled my mind.

I wanted more light, more warmth. *More love.*

"Let's remove a few more bricks. For a bigger window."

"Okay," I said, keeping my eyes tightly shut. I removed a dozen clay rectangles. Radiance flooded my heart. My daughter's face came into view. A hot-pink headband pulled her dark hair away from her eyes. When she flashed me a quirky smile, her irises sparkled like bright stars. She stuck a tremoring arm through the strap of her Hello Kitty backpack and waved at me.

"Wow," Keith said. "Cool."

I watched as my white window with the white grids slid perfectly into the sunny opening.

"How does it feel?" he said.

"Wonderful," I said. My daughter flashed her movie-star eyelashes. My brain couldn't figure out how Keith was seeing what was in my heart, in my head, but he seemed to be doing just that.

"Would it be okay if this window opened and closed?" he said. "That way, you can open it wider on good days."

A huge grin spread across my face. "I'll make it a single-hung window. With a latch. So I can lock it on the bad ones."

"Brilliant idea," the guru said.

27

⤳ ⤴

The first Sunday in April, John and I drove the mile to FoxCreek Village to pick up Lindsey on our way to Easter at my sister's house in Newberg. She waited on the sidewalk, gripping two new European walking sticks as if they were two best friends. She'd worn off the tips of her first pair, so I'd replaced them with a superior model from REI. My girl was dressed in a knee-length, teal plaid skirt and matching top, white tights, white sandals, and an ivory down jacket with fake fur on the hood. Her dark locks were combed and pulled into a ponytail. She would have looked like any other fashionable young adult waiting for a ride had she not moved. Lindsey positioned one walking stick in front of the other, rocking from side to side, and slowly made her way to the car. John opened the rear passenger door, and she slid in, laying her two new best friends across her lap.

"I quit my job," I told Lindsey, explaining it was a planned termination on my part. The summer before, while working in Wichita, Kansas, I'd witnessed a tragedy. A young contractor fell from a two-story roof and died in front of me. After that, I lost the necessary drive to continue doing catastrophe work.

"Mom, you won't have money to travel. You won't be able to go anywhere. You'll be poor."

"Don't worry," I said. For a moment, I wondered if her concern could be due to her time with Emmett. Had living in a van, moving from place to place, traumatized my daughter? Maybe, but I didn't think so. Lindsey had always seemed to understand my obsession with exploring the world. *She's empathizing!* I thought, grinning. The window in my heart slid open an inch. "Dad and I have been saving for this new phase of our lives. We'll be fine."

But Lindsey wasn't giving up. "You know, Mom, in this e-con-me, you shouldn't of quit."

I grinned, peering in the rearview mirror, meeting my daughter's troubled gaze. "Dad and I have discussed this. If we run out of money, we'll sell the house and move in with you." I hoped my daughter detected the humor in my voice.

Lindsey's eyes grew wide. She shook her head. "No, Mom. I put my foot down." Her voice was firm. Her arms moved about wildly in the backseat of our car. "We get along like oil and vinegar. We fight like cats and dogs. You can't live with me."

I didn't correct Lindsey's ditty. She had her own way of saying things, but that didn't mean I could stop myself from toying with her. "We'd only move in for nineteen years," I said, reminding her that was the length of time she'd lived with us. "Turnabout is fair play, isn't it? Shouldn't we get to stay with you for at least as long as you did with us?"

"You can't," she said, pointing out that her apartment had only one bedroom. "Where would you sleep?"

John joined in on the fun. "We've already figured that out. We'll sleep in your room. You can have the sofa."

"Dad," she said, straight-faced, "Gabe and I have talked about this." Her face twitched; her eyes darted right, then left. She shook her head and crossed her arms. "We're putting you and Mom in a home."

John and I glanced at each other, raised our eyebrows, and cracked up. "Lindsey, we're teasing," I said.

"We don't plan to live with you," John added.

When we walked through Beth and Rob's front door, whiffs of honey-baked ham and cloves and yeasty dinner rolls baking in the oven greeted our nostrils. Mouths watered as twelve bodies gathered around an oblong dining room table. Hands linked together while Rob said grace. We passed the platter of ham, basket of rolls, bowl of mashed potatoes, gravy, my broccoli salad, Mom's cranberry salad, corn, and tossed greens with herb dressing, telling everyone John and I no longer had to worry about our future.

"Yep." I passed the butter dish. "We just learned Lindsey and Gabe plan to put us in a home!"

Beth brought us up to date on her daughter's upcoming wedding and how they'd shopped for a wedding gown that hugged Karley in all the right places; how they had tasted every kind of cake within a two-hour radius; and how they had finally agreed upon a country venue of painted white stables, wooden fences, and rolling green pastures. I envisioned my niece walking down the aisle on her dad's arm, quarter horses watching from a distance, whinnying at the bride.

We talked about the friend who'd recently welcomed a new grandchild into the world. Upon holding her, my friend had proclaimed, "She's absolutely perfect!"

I listened to these stories, tingles running from my toes to my head, happy for my sister's and my friend's joy. Yet a stab of envy fissured my heart. I'd never have the same relationship with my daughter that Beth or my other friends did with theirs. My gaze lowered. I stared at my hands for a moment, then rejoined the conversation.

During the forty-five-minute drive home, Lindsey and John both fell asleep. I passed a Farmers Insurance billboard and remembered a day not so long ago. One morning, Farmers assigned me sixty weather-related claims, every one of which needed immediate attention. Lindsey appeared in the doorway of my home office as I slammed the phone into the cradle, grumbling about the workload.

"Mom," Lindsey said, "you can choose happy or you can choose mad." For that moment, I was choosing mad. But the way Lindsey had tossed the same words I'd used on her right back in my face amused me and lightened my mood.

I glanced in the rearview mirror at my sleeping girl. The bond we shared continued to evolve. Our connection often felt like a roller coaster ride, with some pretty high highs and some pretty low lows. The lowest, of course, had been her time with Emmett. But that was over, I reminded myself again. All my life, I wanted perfect children. I believed I deserved them. *But why?* I didn't know. I hadn't been a perfect mother. I'd failed my daughter many times. Perfect was an impossible goal.

I drove the back roads between Newberg and Silverton, wondering why doctors had never been able to identify the cause of my daughter's mental challenges. I stared out the windshield and tapped the steering wheel. As aggravating as the unidentified/unknown part was, I thought, *It is what it is.* I can't change my daughter's diagnosis. *But I do have choices.* I could *choose* to accept and celebrate or I could choose frustration and anger. My internal travels had been many, but I'd finally chosen acceptance. Some days it was reluctant acceptance, but it was acceptance nonetheless. I smiled, suddenly realizing that if I had gotten everything I wanted in life, if every expectation had gone exactly as I planned, I would not have become the person I was now. And I certainly wouldn't have Lindsey stories to tell.

Once, my daughter had said, "Mom, I don't want the same things out of life as you do. I just want to be loved." I had told her, "I love you and Dad loves you and Michael loves you and Grandma and all your aunts and uncles and . . ."

But as I pulled into Silverton and turned right on Oak Street, I found myself thinking about this statement. It was sweet, innocent. And isn't love what people want most? Even though Lindsey made this statement when she was living with Emmett, I still thought it was wise. My hope now was that she'd learned that not all love was equal. Some love, like Emmett's, wasn't really love at all. I hoped Lindsey had finally discovered that she deserved not only love, but also respect. And whether she remained with Gabe or decided to go on and meet someone else, I hoped my daughter's partner cared as much about her as she did about him. I hoped Lindsey would find quality love.

～

The day after Easter, I lifted the calendar page and saw the Hello Kitty sticker I'd stuck on May 10 at the beginning of the year. In thirty-one days, my daughter would turn thirty. *I'm not old enough to be the mother of a thirty-year-old!* I smoothed my hair and thought about my baby, my toddler, my teen, and now my full-grown, adult daughter. I remembered her bouncy pigtails, her sassy personality. I recalled the many times Lindsey displayed bouts of resilience: she'd proven herself to be a dedicated employee; she'd successfully lived in her own apartment for several years now; she'd taken great care of Cuddles and Sally; she'd experienced a healthier boyfriend-girlfriend relationship; and she'd continued to pay twelve dollars per month toward her sponsor child with Children International. The window in my heart opened wide, and a waterfall of brilliant light poured in. I was so proud of my girl, I thought my glass panes just might burst.

Lindsey had reached this point in her life because of the support and kindness of many people. I didn't think John or I could have made this journey alone, and I believed her thirtieth birthday should be honored in a big way. Lindsey might never reach the many milestones other kids (including her brother) would: driving, college, a wedding (I was still hopeful), babies, or baby showers. But she could have a grand birthday celebration, at which we would recognize not only Lindsey but also all the people who had made a huge difference in her life (and ours).

"I don't want to stress her out," I told John, knowing such an event could ignite a major meltdown. "So I want her to be on board."

I explained the idea to Lindsey. "We'll include relatives, friends, businesspeople in our community, past teachers, and your coworkers."

To my amazement, she agreed to a party. "I want one of those pictures people sign." She used her hands to help describe the oversize mat with a photo in the middle that was marketed to brides and grooms. She had watched guests write messages on one during a backyard wedding reception we'd hosted for Michael and his bride a couple years before. Now, Lindsey wanted the same thing as her brother. I nodded in agreement. That was an easy wish to grant.

The invite read:

> Sometimes it takes a village to raise a child . . .
>   You have received this invitation because you've touched
>   Lindsey Atwell's life in some special way.
>   We thank you for that.
>   Please join us in celebrating her 30th birthday at an open house.
>   Enjoy food, beverages, and birthday cake.
>   No gifts, please.

May weather in the northwest is always iffy. I planned for stormy and cold, but May 10 warmed like a late-August afternoon. John and I erected a tan-colored canopy in the backyard. Vases filled with roses and peonies and tulips, every blooming flower from our garden decorated the den, the kitchen, and the cake table. Photo collages of Lindsey's life had been tacked to black posterboards.

Lindsey pointed to the ones she remembered. "It's fun seeing all these pictures," she said. She helped float one hundred purple and white helium balloons throughout the party area. When she saw the matching crepe-paper streamers dangling in the doorways, her face beamed. "I love twisty paper."

For the oversize mat, I set out several photos taken of Lindsey at different ages. Her hands shook when she picked up each snapshot. Her eyes examined the facial expressions.

"I like this one," she said, selecting an image of her three-year-old self in a taupe dress with tiny maroon flowers and matching silk ribbon stitched to the bodice. I had tied her golden-blond, wispy curls into a topknot with a maroon bow. Her chubby hands were folded in her lap. "I look happy," she added, leaving me to finish up.

I smiled. Lindsey did look happy; a genuine grin graced her lips. And those movie-star lashes! The photographer captured a mischievous gleam in my daughter's baby blues. My fingers touched the photo, and I studied Lindsey's image for several seconds, trying to find any indication that she had suffered some sort of birth defect. My eyes watered. I shook my head, mounted the photo on the mat, and laid it flat on a table so guests could pen their birthday wishes.

The menu had all of Lindsey's favorites: shrimp, cream cheese, and cocktail sauce dip, submarine sandwiches, potato salad, chips with wiggles, onion dip, and a frosted half chocolate–half white birthday cake with no fruit filling between the layers.

Michael's wife flew in from Texas. Michael called from Afghanistan, where he was working under contract. Grandma and cousins and aunts and uncles, Gabe and his parents, middle-school teachers, Norma Jean from the Silverton Flower Shop, and two Challenger softball coaches comprised some of the sixty-plus family members and friends who dropped by throughout the afternoon, each penning a special message for the guest of honor on the white mat.

As John and I lit the candles, Lindsey stood over the oblong confection, looking more like a child than a young woman in her sleeveless red sundress and cropped white cotton jacket. Her hair had grown out and now touched her shoulders. It was washed and brushed and hung in waves around her face. A red headband kept loose locks out of her eyes. I wished my dad could have been there to share this birthday with his special girl.

We all sang "Happy Birthday" loudly enough for the neighbors to hear. Lindsey's face glowed like the thirty lit candles on her cake. She gulped air and blew. After three tries, every candle was extinguished.

After the party, I drove Lindsey to her place. "I'm glad most people printed," she said. Her finger pointed to one of the penned messages. "I can't read cursive so well." She helped me place the mat with the childhood photo in the sleek black frame it came with, and we hung it on her apartment wall. We stood back, locked hands, and took turns reading the comments aloud.

When we finished, Lindsey grinned and nodded. "You're the best mom ever."

Her high praise caught me by surprise. I turned toward my daughter and noted her creamy complexion, her petite pink mouth, her innocent gaze.

"I love you," she said. Sparkles danced in her eyes like glitter.

I thought Lindsey was the most beautiful girl in the whole world. My lips curved into a smile that grew bigger and bigger.

"I wouldn't want any other mom," she said. "No one takes care of me like you. When I was little, you made me mind so I grew up good." She squeezed my hand and giggled. "And now I get to live on my own. You helped me be in-de-pen-dent. I'm so lucky you're my mom."

A gigantic beam of sunshine danced through the white-gridded panes in my heart, and my window opened wider. I swallowed hard, blinking, trying to dislodge the lump stuck in my throat. My *beautiful girl*.

A counselor once asked me if I'd learned more from the easy times in my life or from the difficult ones. I sat in his office, silent for a moment, and realized there was only one right answer. "The more difficult," I said, but at the time of the question, I had no idea I'd have to live four and a half years without my daughter. *But she's home now. She's safe. And she's doing great.*

My window opened even wider.

"I love you more, Linds," I said, squeezing my girl's hand and hugging her tight.

Acknowledgments

❧ ❧

M y heart is filled with gratitude. Ever since my early drafts (and oh, how rough those initial drafts were!), many friends and family have supported my writing. Yet, in spite of the incredibly raw materials I'd begged you to read, each one of you offered invaluable input, which encouraged me to continue.

Thank you, thank you to the following: Nancy Henderson, Jill Brueckner, Crystal LeBoeuf, Char Stahel, Carole Christensen, Diana Furman, Wendy Stec, Beth Molzahn, Kandi Savage, Betty Aldridge, Lyn Robbert, Sharon Cochrane, Annette Roth, Crystal Weber Moss, Nancy Pike Houston, Karen Swoboda, Tom Barton, Kristi Rieger Campbell, Marlena Fiol, and Christine Autrand Mitchell.

Although some of the individuals above read more than one entire manuscript, no one read as many as my friend, Diana Dolan Mattick. As a special education instructor, you generously gave of your time as I asked for clarifications and advice. The words "thank you" seem insignificant compared to your contribution to this project. I hope you know that I am forever grateful for your time and friendship.

James Annen, thirty-some years ago, you snapped an adorable photo our daughter. When you presented us with a copy, we immediately found a frame; it has been proudly displayed in our home ever since. I am thrilled that this is the image the editors selected for the cover of *Loving Lindsey*. Thank you for allowing us to use your gift in this way, but more importantly, thank you for being a lifetime friend.

Dear Cruise Group, you had to listen to stories while we were going through them. Then you listened and laughed over and over again. It is nice to have friends who act like this is the first time they've ever heard a tale. Thank you.

Ali Shaw, editor at Indigo Editing, provided my biggest ah-ha moment. When you uttered that my one long manuscript should actually be two separate books, immediately everything made sense. Thank you for that insight.

Thanks to Brooke Warner at She Writes Press for selecting my manuscript for publication. To Annie Tucker, thanks for all your fine edits and suggestions. And to Caitlyn Levin—you are the best project manager ever. Thank you for keeping me informed and on schedule.

For some reason, my nephew, Todd Fox at Foxwell Creative, believed in this story enough to want me to have a decent website. So he created one. Then he thought I needed an upgrade and created a new one that was even better. If it were not for you, Todd, I'd still be thinking about writing a special needs blog instead of irregularly writing posts. There are no adequate words to express how much I appreciate all you've done for me. Thanks for all the time, energy, and passion you dedicated to my online presence. You have been a joy to work with.

My family—immediate and extended—have lived through many of Lindsey's (and mine, too!) shenanigans. To my son, Michael, my dad, the late Evert F. Aldridge, Sr., my mom, Betty Aldridge, my sisters, Beth Molzahn and Kandi Savage, my brother, Evert Aldridge, Jr., (and all their families) as well as John's brothers, Tom and Bob Atwell, and his sisters, Karen Swoboda and Mary Gunstinson (and their families, too)— thanks for being heroes in Lindsey's life. Our story is proof that it truly takes a village to raise a child; I'm so glad you are part of our village.

When my husband finished reading one of the first drafts, he said, "We sure went through hell, didn't we?" Apparently, John had forgotten many of the stories until the manuscript nudged his memory. I realize we all have our own preservation techniques, and suppressing was one of his. I could not have raised Lindsey or started a business or written a book (let alone two) without John's support.

So John, you've always encouraged me to do what makes me happy. As corny as this sounds, you have been the wind beneath my wings, and I want to thank you for making all my dreams come true. "If I don't," my sweet husband tells me, "they will turn into nightmares." But that, dear folks, is really beside the point.

And finally, Miss Lindsey—although, your dad and I prefer merry-go-rounds, you have taken us on a rollercoaster ride with tons of loop de loops. If it weren't for you, I would have fewer stories to tell. Every single day, your tenacity can equally aggravate and inspire us. Despite your unique challenges, you've come a long way, baby! We are so proud of you.